POLITICS,
MEDICINE, AND
CHRISTIAN
ETHICS

OTHER BOOKS BY CHARLES E. CURRAN

Christian Morality Today

A New Look at Christian Morality

Contemporary Problems in Moral Theology

Catholic Moral Theology in Dialogue

The Crisis in Priestly Ministry

Absolutes in Moral Theology? (editor)

Contraception: Authority and Dissent (editor)

Dissent In and For the Church (with others)

The Responsibility of Dissent: the Church and Academic Freedom (with others)

CHARLES
E.
CURRAN

POLITICS, MEDICINE, AND CHRISTIAN ETHICS

A Dialogue with Paul Ramsey

FORTRESS PRESS   PHILADELPHIA

AUGUSTANA LIBRARY
UNIVERSITY OF ALBERTA

The author acknowledges with gratitude that the preparation of this manuscript was undertaken as one of a number of projects supported in whole or in part by the interdisciplinary program of the Joseph and Rose Kennedy Institute for the Study of Human Reproduction and Bioethics of Georgetown University, Washington, D.C. The Institute seeks to bring together scholars in ethics, biology, medicine, sociology, demography, and law to carry out methodological, historical, and applied studies in areas of individual and common concern to these disciplines and to society as a whole.

COPYRIGHT © 1973 BY FORTRESS PRESS

All rights reserved. No part of this publication may be reproduced, stored in a retrieval system, or transmitted in any form or by any means, electronic, mechanical, photocopying, recording, or otherwise, without the prior permission of the copyright owner.

Library of Congress Catalog Card Number
ISBN *0–8006–0500–4*

3504C73   Printed in U.S.A.   *1–500*

CAMROSE LUTHERAN COLLEGE LIBRARY

BR
115
P7
C83

/18,910

AUGUSTANA LIBRARY
UNIVERSITY OF ALBERTA

To my father
on his seventy-fifth birthday

ACKNOWLEDGEMENTS

A most pleasant duty is to acknowledge the assistance and interest of those who have helped me in this project. The School of Theology of the Catholic University of America granted me a sabbatical leave to work on this volume. The American Association of Theological Schools awarded me a faculty fellowship so that I could devote the time to this research. Above all, I am grateful to the Joseph and Rose Kennedy Institute for the Study of Human Reproduction and Bioethics at Georgetown University for my appointment as a Senior Research Scholar so that I might pursue the research and writing of this book. In this connection, I want publicly to acknowledge my personal indebtedness to the Joseph P. Kennedy, Jr. Foundation and to Sargent and Eunice Kennedy Shriver, and to express gratitude to them for their interest in and support of research in medical ethics. André Hellegers, the director of the Institute at Georgetown, graciously invited me to the Institute and created a climate in which this research could be carried on in dialogue with others interested in the field. The staff of the Institute has been most attentive in providing whatever was needed.

William H. Lazareth, Dean of the Lutheran Theological Seminary at Philadelphia, first invited me to write this book, encouraged me in the course of the work, and even served as an editor of the final manuscript. He graciously decided, together, with the editorial staff of Fortress Press, to publish this as a separate monograph and not as a volume in the "Confrontation Books" series of which he is the general editor.

My intellectual debts are many — in addition to those persons already mentioned. Graduate students in seminars at the Catholic University of America helped stimulate and shape my thinking. My colleagues at the Center for Bioethics — Francisco Abel, John Connery, Richard McCormick, Gene Outka, Warren Reich, and especially LeRoy Walters, the director of the Center, read my manuscript and throughout the year engaged me in fruitful discussions on these issues. But my greatest debt is to Paul Ramsey who spent many hours in conversation and in criticizing earlier drafts of the manuscript. The following pages express some disagreements with his thought, but I trust that the reader will also perceive my respect and affection for the man who signs his many letters to me with "Your friend, Paul Ramsey."

CHARLES E. CURRAN

Washington, D.C.
March 1973

TABLE OF CONTENTS

INTRODUCTION

Politics and medicine are two areas of human existence in which men must make decisions of great import. Political unrest and heated discussions about domestic and international politics have focused much attention on the ethical aspects of politics. Important questions such as nuclear war, guerilla war, revolution, nuclear deterrence, selective conscientious objection, and civil disobedience not only call for responses, but also require a deeper analysis of the meaning and function of politics and statecraft. Christian ethicists and churchmen have become more deeply involved in these questions in the last few years, and this involvement makes even more crucial the proper understanding of these questions and of the role of churches.

Medicine has perennially raised moral questions, but contemporary man is faced with startling new technological possibilities in this area. The furor over heart transplants remains a vivid memory, but it is only symbolic of the questions that modern medicine and biology will raise in the coming years. Man now has or will acquire great technological abilities in the area of medicine so that he can more readily interfere with the processes of his own living and dying. Man may even have the ability to direct the evolution and improvement of the human species itself. Scientists, themselves, are somewhat anxious about these questions and have recently attempted to inform the general public about the possibilities that might lay ahead. The fate of nuclear power, which science developed, and contemporary ecological problems remind us of the need for rational control of powers that science and technology will give to man.

This book will consider questions of political and medical ethics in dialogue with the writings of Paul Ramsey, Harrington Spear Paine Professor of Christian ethics at Princeton University. The content and methodological discussions will center on Ramsey's many considerations of these questions, but in the dialogue my own approach both to the methodology of Christian ethics and to the particular problems under discussion will emerge.

Why Paul Ramsey? The choice of Paul Ramsey seems obvious to anyone who has read and studied the area of Christian ethics. No one has written more than Ramsey in the two areas under consideration, so that the sheer quantity of his work would justify the dialogue with him. In addition, Ramsey has been the first Christian ethicist to devote himself in great detail to such questions as civil disobedience and the genetic manipulation of man.

However, the volume of his writings and the fact that he was the first Christian ethicist to treat these questions are not the only reasons for choosing Ramsey. In his discussions of these questions, Ramsey frequently cites the need for proper ethical discourse and theological methodology. This naturally raises the question of the adequacy and consistency of his particular approach to Christian ethics, and Ramsey's importance as a theoretician calls for such a critical dialogue with him.

Paul Ramsey's discussion of political and medical questions has not been casual. His writings indicate the way in which he has immersed himself in dialogue with political theorists and medical scientists. He appears to be equally at home with military strategists and biologists discussing the complexities of the human gene. His own thoroughness in acquainting himself with the data in these areas serves as a model for Christian ethical endeavor.

Ramsey's importance in the field of Christian ethics also comes from the fact that he, more than any other contemporary Protestant theologian, has exhibited in his writings a knowledge of and appreciation for some aspects of the Roman Catholic ethical tradition. This is all the more reason for a Roman Catholic theologian such as myself to enter into dialogue with Ramsey. In this way perhaps the ecumenical dialogue in this important area will be furthered.

One significant aspect of this dialogue can easily be overlooked. During the past decade truly startling developments have taken place in Roman Catholic ethical thinking. Roman Catholic ethics should no longer be considered as a monolithic system or methodology. There exists now within Roman Catholicism a growing pluralism both on the level of methodology and on the level of solutions to particular problems. In my opinion, this pluralism will grow so that it will be impossible to speak about *the* Roman Catholic ethical methodology or *the* Roman Catholic solution to a specific moral question as if there could be no possible disagreement on the question within Roman Catholicism. In the future, it will be increasingly difficult to draw a strict dichotomy between Roman Catholic and Protestant ethics. However, there are some divergent emphases in the different approaches which will become evident in my dialogue with Ramsey for I do theologize within the Roman Catholic ethical tradition even though such a tradition will be recognized in the future as increasingly pluralistic.

Ramsey's willingness to question some of the easy assumptions of the day makes him a most interesting figure. His discussions are calculated to make the reader ponder anew and more deeply the particular issues at stake. He has entered into critical dialogue with many of those who propose opposite opinions. One reviewer was so impressed with Ramsey's critical ability in dissecting and attacking the position of others that he breathed a public sigh of relief that Ramsey had never engaged in discussion with him.[1]

I also find four difficulties in a dialogue with Ramsey on these issues. First, there has been development in Ramsey's own thinking as his active and creative mind has grappled with these issues and with the methodological questions of Christian ethics. Perhaps the most fundamental question in Christian ethics concerns the sources of wisdom and knowledge for Christian ethics. Ramsey has espoused an approach which he describes as Christ transform-

1. John L. McKenzie, "Deeds and Rules in Christian Ethics," *Commonweal,* LXXXVI (August 25, 1967), p. 525.

ing natural law or love transforming justice;[2] but this approach, at the very least, was not explicitly present in his *Basic Christian Ethics*, which is not only the first book he published in Christian ethics but also his only attempt at a systematic approach to Christian ethics.

Basic Christian Ethics expounded a Christian ethics centered on *agape* which Ramsey understands as covenant faithfulness.[3] *Nine Modern Moralists,* published in 1962, propounds in detail a new element in Ramsey's thinking—a place for reason and natural law in Christian ethics. Ramsey objects to the excessive rationalism and deductive approach of some forms of natural law but is quite sympathetic to the revision of natural law proposed by Jacques Maritain with its insistence on man's inclination to or sense of justice.[4] Ramsey also opposes the "republication" of natural law by the authoritative teaching office of the Roman Catholic church which has introduced unnecessary inflexibility into Catholic natural law teaching.[5]

Ramsey does not want to affirm the sufficiency of reason alone. Catholic natural-law theory too easily forgets the reality of sin, but good and evil tendencies coexist in every moral decision and action. Love must also enter to reshape, enlarge, sensitize, and direct our apprehensions based on reason alone. Christ transforming natural law or love transforming justice adequately describes the position enunciated in *Nine Modern Moralists*. Ramsey himself insists that this development does not really contradict but only fills out the earlier approach. *Basic Christian Ethics* explained what was primary and distinctive in Christian ethics—*agape*. Coalition ethics, i.e., the union of *agape* with any other type of philoso-

2. Paul Ramsey, *Nine Modern Moralists* (Englewood Cliffs, N.J: Prentice-Hall, Inc., 1962). Hereafter cited as *NMM*. This book, some of whose chapters appeared earlier as articles in various scholarly journals, develops the theme of love transforming justice in greatest detail. The same concept is also present in *Christian Ethics and the Sit-In* (New York: Association Press, 1961) and occasionally mentioned without in–depth development in *War and the Christian Conscience: How Shall Modern War be Conducted Justly?* (Durham, N.C.: Duke University Press, 1961). Hereafter cited as *Sit-In* and *WCC.*
3. Paul Ramsey, *Basic Christian Ethics* (New York: Charles Scribner's Sons, 1950). Hereafter cited as *BCE.*
4. *NMM,* pp. 209–256.
5. *NMM,* p. 227; Paul Ramsey, "The New Papal Encyclical II," *The Christian Century,* LXXVIII (1961), p. 1079.

phical ethics, was denied in the sense that anything other than *agape* could be primary and distinctive in Christian ethics or stand on the ground floor of Christian ethics. The contribution of reason can, however, be secondary and supplementary as in the concept of Christ transforming natural law.[6]

In the following pages there will be some doubts expressed about Ramsey's consistency in his understanding and application of Christ transforming natural law in the questions of political and medical ethics. At this basic methodological level I think there exists a greater discontinuity in his development than Ramsey is willing to admit. The theological presuppositions of *Basic Christian Ethics* are such that they appear to exclude the possibility of affirming any goodness about human reason and the natural law. The contrast between *agape* and reason or natural law seems to exclude even secondary acceptance of reason and natural law, even though in the latter part of *Basic Christian Ethics* Ramsey makes some appeals to reason and to natural justice provided that love remains the senior and controlling partner.

In Christian ethics, there are three closely related questions: the relation of *agape* and human love; the eschatological question of the relationship between this world and the next; and the question of the relationship between human ethical wisdom and revealed ethical wisdom (natural law and Christ). In *Nine Modern Moralists* Ramsey asserts some continuity between natural law and Christ and at the same time affirms some discontinuity, but in the form of a transformationist motif. Such an approach should logically accept more continuity in the first two relationships of human love and divine love and of this world and the next. The later emphasis in *Nine Modern Moralists* seems to call for a recasting of some of the theological presuppositions of *Basic Christian Ethics,* which emphasize discontinuity in all these relationships. This is the major question of consistency which I would pose to Ramsey, but anyone dealing with this thought must appreciate the fact that his most systematic study of Christian ethics remains his first work which cannot adequately explain any later developments in his thinking.

In the area of the role of norms and rules in Christian ethics, a

6. *NMM,* pp. 1–8; Paul Ramsey, *Deeds and Rules in Christian Ethics* (New York: Charles Scribner's Sons, 1967), p. 122, n.41. Hereafter cited as *DRCE.*

very crucial area of debate in Christian ethics, others have detected a great development in Ramsey's thought.[7] *Basic Christian Ethics* contains a chapter on "Christian Liberty: An Ethic Without Rules" which strenuously argues against rules in Christian ethics.[8] Ramsey concedes that *agape* itself was so analyzed in *Basic Christian Ethics* as to leave standing the assumption that *agape* could come to expression in acts only and not in rules.[9] The entire thrust of *Deeds and Rules in Christian Ethics* was to show the existence of rules in Christian ethics both as derived from *agape* and as rules of practice in society.[10]

In my judgment, however, there is not as much discontinuity on this question as first meets the eye, even though there is obviously some development. Ramsey in his earlier work seems to be captivated by the rhetoric of a love ethic which is above and beyond laws and norms, but the concept of *agape* which he describes is the same concept of *agape* which serves as the basis for rules derived from love in his later works. There has been no real discontinuity in his concept of *agape* itself. *Agape* is derived from the righteousness of God and is described in terms of covenant faithfulness. *Agape* binds men to others not on the basis of merit or worth but of faithfulness. Ramsey's love ethic even in its first exposition is cut from God and not from man, so that it will have room for less relativity and change than other possible love ethics which begin with man. He insists that if *agape* is not a separate type of ethics it is closer to deontology than teleology, because *agape* does not depend on the good that can be derived from our actions but rather centers on faithful obedience.[11] Such a concept of love very logically does lead to the realization that there are rules and norms based on love, even though Ramsey does not explicitly admit this in his first treatment and seems to employ a rhetoric which would even deny it.

There are important questions of development in the considera-

---

7. James Sellers, *Public Ethics: American Morals and Manners* (New York: Harper & Row, 1970), pp. 195–205; Dewey J. Hoitenga, Jr., "Development of Paul Ramsey's Ethics," *Gordon Review*, XI (1970), pp. 282–290.

8. *BCE,* pp. 46–91.

9. *DRCE,* p. 122.

10. *DRCE,* pp. 1–10.

11. All these descriptions of *agape* are contained in *BCE,* but the explicit assertion that if *agape* is not a separate type of ethics it is closer to deontology than teleology appears in *DRCE,* p. 108.

tion of Ramsey or any other important thinker. The fact of development or change should not be interpreted pejoratively, for such development indicates the fact that an author is in dialogue with others and constantly rethinking his own positions in the light of the on–going discussion. In fact, one would be appalled at an intellectual position which from the beginning would not admit the possibility of development. However, the question of development does raise problems for the interpreter of another person's thinking and also for the consistency and coherency of the theory that a person might have enunciated earlier. In the specific questions of political and medical ethics there are some areas in which Ramsey has changed his thinking, and these will be pointed out at the appropriate time. The friendly critic must be willing to indicate that development in one area might call for a change or revision either in the more theoretical understanding or in other particular content questions.

There are other problems and difficulties in trying to present fairly and criticize adequately the political and medical ethics of Paul Ramsey. His writings on these questions are never truly systematic. Even his book *War and the Christian Conscience*, which is a somewhat systematic study, is, in itself, quite limited as indicated by the subtitle: "How Shall Modern War be Conducted Justly?". *The Patient as Person* does not constitute a systematic treatment of medical ethics but rather a discussion of certain topics and questions, and even these considerations do not always claim to be complete or systematic as is evident in the considerations of consent and of transplantation.[12] *The Just War* and *Fabricated Man* are collections of essays on different aspects of the questions of political and biomedical ethics.[13]

One cannot legitimately object to the serial form that these writings take. The very fact that Ramsey has been the first Christian ethicist to discuss some of these issues makes it impossible to expect a truly systematic treatment. However, the occasional nature of most of these writings does cause problems for the inter-

---

12. Paul Ramsey, *The Patient as Person* (New Haven: Yale University Press, 1970). Hereafter cited as *PP*.

13. Paul Ramsey, *The Just War: Force and Political Responsibility* (New York: Charles Scribner's Sons, 1968). Hereafter cited as *JW*. Paul Ramsey, *Fabricated Man: The Ethics of Genetic Control* (New Haven: Yale University Press, 1970). Hereafter cited as *FM*.

preter. Some of the theological and methodological presuppositions, e.g., his theory of the state, are not totally spelled out as he
comes to grips with the more particular problems of war, civil
disobedience or selective conscientious objection. Occasional
writings stress only those aspects which enter into the particular
question under discussion, but the interpreter must decide if some
elements are not mentioned because they do not fit into such a
discussion or because they have truly been neglected by the author.

Ramsey's writings are not only occasional but often polemical—
a fact that is interesting but that causes additional problems for the
proper evaluation and interpretation of his thoughts. He is often
arguing for or against a particular viewpoint. For example, he
wants to show that the Christian teaching on a just war is not only
the patrimony of the Catholic church and based on natural law but
belongs to the whole Christian church and is derived from *agape*.
Or he argues strenuously against those who have accepted a liberal theology with its understanding that resort to force by states
indicates a failure in statecraft. As a good polemicist, he will mar-
shal all the arguments he can for his particular position and even
seems to relish the role of attacking generally accepted positions.
Such an approach can easily lead to exaggeration and over–
emphasis. From the following pages it will be clear that on occasion I believe that Ramsey rightly stresses an aspect which is too
often forgotten in contemporary debates, but sometimes he over–
emphasizes or absolutizes such an aspect at the expense of other
important aspects.

There is another difficulty with Ramsey's writings—his prose
style. He has been criticized for his long, complicated sentences,
his purple passages, and his rhetoric which seems to get in the way
of his meaning. There is no doubt that reading Ramsey is more of
a chore than reading many other writers in the field of ethics.[14]
It would be a shame if his style prevented some people from
struggling with his thought. Sometimes it is the complexity of the
argument itself which requires careful scrutiny, but Ramsey does
add to the problems by the opaqueness of his prose.

14. E.g., Richard A. McCormick, S.J., "Genetic Medicine: Notes on the Moral Literature," *Theological Studies,* XXXIII (1972), p. 537.

There is another aspect to his prose, for occasionally his creativity and sense of humor bring smiles to the reader. Who else but Paul Ramsey would put the following entry in the index of a book as the sole entry under the letter "Y"—"Yeureka, the Author's Solemn Exclamation Upon Approaching the End of This Index."[15] In the light of the frequently repeated criticisms of his prose style, I think Ramsey takes great delight in the compliment paid him by John Fry. Fry devotes an appendix of his book to the prose of Paul Ramsey, but his judgment is highly laudatory. The marvelously shocking prose of Paul Ramsey makes the writings of other Christian ethicists drab and colorless by comparison.[16] In my judgment there is this element in Ramsey's prose, but it does not entirely compensate for the negative aspects of his style. Unfortunately at times the style seems to make comprehension more difficult.

In the light of my exposition and criticism of Ramsey's positions, I will develop my own approach to these particular questions. Naturally it will be impossible to develop fully my position on all these issues, but the major points of my approach will be clear. References will be given to places where I have developed my own thought at greater length.

A study of politics and medicine in the light of Christian ethics is not merely a substantive consideration of the various questions in these two important areas, but also a methodological inquiry about Christian ethics itself. Different approaches to Christian ethics can be criticized and evaluated by their ability to deal critically and adequately with these issues.

This book has the two-fold aim of studying political and medical ethics and of evaluating the Christian ethics of Paul Ramsey in these areas. The following pages can introduce the serious student to the subject matter of both these aims, but those more deeply immersed in the field can hopefully find here material for their own critical appraisal of these important areas of concern and of an important figure in contemporary Christian ethics.

15. *WCC*, p. 331.
16. John R. Fry, *The Immobilized Christian: A Study of His Pre-Ethical Situation* (Philadelphia: Westminster Press, 1963), pp. 149–163.

	Politics,
CHAPTER I	Christian Ethics,
	and the Church

POLITICAL ETHICS

Paul Ramsey has never developed a theology of the state as such, but his underlying theology of politics and statecraft serves as the context and basis for his discussion of current ethical questions in the realm of politics. He has published many articles on specific issues in political ethics. A somewhat systematic study of just war, *War and the Christian Conscience*, was published in 1961, whereas twenty–four of Ramsey's subsequent essays were published in *The Just War: Force and Political Responsibility*, in 1968.[1] Also in 1961 he published *Christian Ethics and the Sit-In* which deals with the question of civil disobedience.[2] Now in the 1970's Ramsey is again publishing lengthy articles on the question of politics and statecraft.[3] Since most of Ramsey's writings are in the form of essays on particular problems, there is no real systematic development of his theology of statecraft.

1. Paul Ramsey, *War and the Christian Conscience: How Shall Modern War Be Conducted Justly?* (Durham, N.C.: Duke University Press, 1961), and *The Just War: Force and Political Responsibility* (New York: Charles Scribner's Sons, 1968).
2. Paul Ramsey, *Christian Ethics and the Sit-In* (New York: Association Press, 1961).
3. Paul Ramsey, "Force and Political Responsibility," *Ethics and World Politics: Four Perspectives*, Ernest W. Lefever, ed. (Baltimore: The Johns Hopkins University Press, 1972), pp. 43–73; Paul Ramsey, "Does the Church Have Any Political Wisdom for the 70's?," *The Perkins School of Theology Journal*, XXVI (Fall 1972), pp. 29–40; Paul Ramsey, "A Political Ethics Context for Strategic Thinking," *Strategic Thinking and Its Moral Implications*, Morton A. Kaplan, ed. (Chicago: University of Chicago Press, 1973). My citations to this last article will be to the manuscript submitted by Ramsey to the publisher.

Ramsey writes out of the theological context of a Christian realism and often disagrees with both theological liberalism and the contemporary American ethos. Theological liberalism accepts the basic goodness of man and fails to realize his sinfulness. Liberalism's social teaching forgets the need of force and the role of order in society. There is an over–spiritualization of politics which places unlimited trust in negotiation and goodwill so that the need to resort to force really signifies the failure of politics. Christian realism argues against forgetting that we belong to two cities, and the City of God is not here. Meanwhile, men who share both a bright side and the darker side of sin must always appreciate the need for force and the importance of order in statecraft and politics.[4]

Theological Affirmations about Politics and the State

Christian theology tries to understand the purpose and function of the state in terms of its relationship to the work and plan of God. Roman Catholic theology in the past has understood the state in terms of its natural-law approach. The nature of men calls for them to form political communities so that they can accomplish as a group what individuals alone cannot accomplish. Man is by nature social and communitarian so that he is called upon to work cooperatively with other men to achieve the common good, but the common good of society rebounds to the good of the individual. The state thus has an essentially positive function of achieving the common good.[5]

The more traditional Protestant theory of the state with its heavy dependence on Lutheran concepts sees the origin of the state not in human nature but in human sinfulness. The state is an order of preservation which a gracious God has established so that the chaos and disorder of sin are prevented from spreading in the world. The state in this conception has the more negative function of preserving order, which is constantly threatened by the sinfulness of men.[6]

The theological understanding of the state coheres with one's

4. *Sit-In*, p. 48; *JW*, pp. xv, xvi, 479–488.
5. Heinrich A. Rommen, *The State in Catholic Thought* (St. Louis: B. Herder Book Co., 1945).
6. John C. Bennett, *Christians and the State* (New York: Charles Scribner's Sons, 1958), pp. 36–48. Bennett later develops his own constructive statement.

theological understanding of anthropology and of eschatology. A more positive anthropology logically calls for a more positive view of the state, whereas a more negative anthropology emphasizes the role of sin in relationship to the state. A Christian eschatology which sees a closer relationship between this world and the next gives a more positive role to the state. An eschatology stressing the discontinuity between this world and the next more readily embraces the view of the state as an order of preservation preventing the chaos of sin until God in his good time brings in the new world at the end of human history.

Throughout his writings, Ramsey has insisted on the state as an order of preservation brought about by a gracious God as the result of man's sinfulness, but at times he has also mentioned a more positive aspect to the role of the state. The positive aspect of the state in terms of its relationship to justice and at times even to love appears more often in his earlier writings and in some of his more theoretical and abstract statements. The later writings and the specific considerations of particular questions emphasize the state as an order of preservation because of the sinfulness of man.

His first book, *Basic Christian Ethics,* explains the nature of social institutions and justifies their existence, first of all and in large part, in terms of a restraint and remedy against sin.[7] There is also a more positive although seemingly secondary aspect of the state based on man's capacity for justice and his regard for the common good. In this connection, Ramsey accepts the famous dictum of Reinhold Niebuhr that man's capacity for justice makes democracy possible, but man's inclination to injustice makes democracy necessary.[8]

It was in his chapter on Tillich and Brunner in *Nine Modern Moralists* that Ramsey developed his understanding of Christ transforming natural law. Notice that the terms are expressed in their more ethical meaning, but these terms point to the actions of God. Ramsey wants to affirm a place for reason and justice especially as understood in terms of a sense of justice or injustice

7. *BCE,* p. 322.
8. *Ibid.,* p. 337.

which is too often denied in Protestant ethics with its radical doctrines of sin and grace. Love should convert, transform, redirect, extend, and reinvigorate justice and reason.[9]

Ramsey tries to correct Brunner in the light of Brunner's own assertion that every ethical consideration must be connected with the whole idea of God; that is, creation, preservation, and redemption. Ramsey argues that Brunner's later consideration of the relationship between love and justice is more dualistic and not conversionist or transformationist as it was in *The Divine Imperative.* Brunner speaks of the orders of creation which are the spheres of life—economic, political, and social—in which Christians and all men live their lives. Although Brunner uses the word orders of creation, his more general description sees them too much in terms of sinfulness and restraint. However, Ramsey asserts that in his specific discussion of the orders, Brunner does give the orders a more positive purpose indicated by the word creation in its more unambiguous sense. Thus there is the dual good of restraint against sin and some quest of justice which is accomplished by the orders.[10]

Brunner had spoken of two duties of the Christian with regard to the orders. The first duty is to maintain the orders, whereas the second duty is to try to transform or improve the orders. Ramsey wants to avoid the two extremes of either a dualism which allows no transforming power of love (so that love only gives the Christian the motive for doing his official duties within the order) or of a gradualism which optimistically hopes for a gradual penetration of the world by the kingdom. Ramsey claims that the proper interpretation can be found by relating our ethical actions to the whole idea and work of God which involves preservation, creation, and redemption. In this light Ramsey also wants to refrain from calling either one or another of these tasks (justice or love) man's first or second duty.[11]

It is interesting to note that the actions of God are mentioned as three-fold while Brunner speaks of two duties and Ramsey speaks of the work of justice and of love. In both cases, there is the

9. *NMM*, pp. 181-183.
10. *Ibid.*, pp. 202–207.
11. *Ibid.*, p. 208.

possibility of problems arising from reducing the action of God to
two ethical terms rather than to three. For Ramsey the Christian
must ensure a just, endurable, and just endurable order for the
preservation of human life and also search for ways for making the
secular orders not only more just but more humane and more full
of the spirit of love without unfitting them for the purpose for
which they exist as orders.[12] Note that even here the orders are
primarily orders of preservation which must then be improved
and somewhat transformed.

Christian Ethics and the Sit–In understands politics, the state
and the tactic of sit–ins in terms of the whole action of God as
Creator, as Ruler and Preserver of the fallen world and as Redeemer.[13] In considering the question of the law about property
rights destined to provide service to the general public (e.g., ho-
tels, restaurants), Ramsey first discusses the state and its law as an
ordinance of creation with the positive purpose of insuring justice.
The implications of creation in terms of justice and its openness
to being transformed by love constitute the first part of his treatment.[14] There is also a negative or restraining purpose of God in
the state and law which is derived from the darker side of our
human existence. Ramsey, in describing the preserving and restraining action of God, does not explicitly refer to the Noachic
Covenant, but he does speak of God's restraining grace by which
he preserves a tolerable fellow humanity against the ravages of sin.
The symbol of the garments of skin also refers to the preserving
act of God in the state and human society.[15]

As early as an essay written in 1962, Ramsey concentrates, in the
context of explaining just war, on the negative aspect of the state
and political life as God's merciful work of preservation in response to the sin of men. The political life of man in this world goes
on under the sign of Babel and nothing this triumphalistic secular
age can do will undo that verdict. Jesus Christ has come into the
world and sent his Spirit upon us, but political activity goes on
much as before under its own sign. The Christian does not have

12. *Ibid.*
13. *Sit–In*, p. 126; also pp. 25, 30.
14. *Ibid.*, pp. 17–39.
15. *Ibid.*, pp. 48, 49 and throughout the entire second chapter.

any hope in a cyclical appearance of paradise in this world or in a progressively better future that man will bring about in this world by his efforts. We live in two cities and not in the one city of man under construction. The political life of mankind will always be a realm of patient endurance until the end of time when God and not man will bring about the peace and unity of the kingdom or the City of God.[16] There are no balancing remarks about a more positive role of the state.

The collection of essays published in 1968 under the title *The Just War*, which also includes the previously mentioned essay, at times admits both the positive and the negative aspects of the state. However, more often only the fact that the state is an order of preservation and its negative aspects are mentioned. "It means that in the time of God's patience our political offices must serve to preserve the world against the destructiveness to which otherwise we all would be driven. The state is ordained of God as a 'garment of skin' (Genesis 3:21) in which human nakedness may be clothed, and in which men may together find a tolerably secure dwelling place."[17]

The emphasis on sin and its role in the political life of man is illustrated by the whimsical, one page parable, entitled "A Fable" which appears at the beginning of the essays collected in *The Just War*. "A Fable" pictures Eve as looking forward to the great future of the human race based on technological progress and social responsibility. Adam is portrayed as silent and downcast as Eve unfolds this vision of the future. "Adam looked with downcast eyes at the shadow upon their pathway cast from behind them by the angel's two flaming swords. He knew better than she the shape of the advancing generations. Yet his mind had no relish for this knowledge, and he too wishes that this new age might be launched from some other platform than the No-Returning."[18]

Since the publication of *The Just War*, Ramsey's writings place more and more emphasis on the state as an order of preservation based on man's sin without any explicit, substantial development of the more positive aspects of the state even though the more

16. *JW*, pp. 178–180.
17. *Ibid.*, p. 530.
18. *Ibid.*, p. xxi.

positive aspect is occasionally mentioned in passing. He proposes a mythopoetic view of politics and the state based primarily on the opening chapters of Genesis.[19] These myths of Genesis, all referring to man's sin and God's reaction to it in terms of preservation, constitute one of the best commentaries on government.[20]

One recent essay proposes the following understanding of the state and politics. Political life and government must be seen in the light of sin and the covenant of preservation which God made with Noah. By this means, God keeps men from self–destruction. Government and politics came into existence east of Eden under the shadow cast by the angels standing at the gates of paradise. In this tradition, Augustine remarks that Cain the first murderer founded the earthly city. The relative justice of all kingdoms, empires, and nations has in it some fratricide. Occasional references of this type in the midst of the longer biblical explanation mentioning only the first chapters of Genesis are the only positive aspects about his explanation. The Bible even uses the image of justifiable killing to symbolize the role of government in using evil to prevent further evil as part of the Noachic Covenant by which God through the state holds the world back from destruction. The mandate of government is to set a limit to the self–destructiveness that otherwise would break out. Evil is used to hold evil at bay so that within that context good can still be achieved, a commonweal be preserved, and politically creative action be put forth with the hope of success somewhat enduring. A more positive aspect of what takes place within the context of government is just mentioned and never developed in terms of its theological presuppositions of creation and redemption.[21]

Both the thought and the terminology are reminiscent of dualistic theories such as those versions of the Lutheran "two-realm" theory which see the state and the social life of man as a realm of sin under the covenant of preservation, which is a merciful work of the left hand of God. Ramsey himself speaks about the "alien work" of mercy.[22] In addition, it is interesting to note that his

19. "A Political Ethics Context for Strategic Thinking," p. 1.
20. "Force and Political Responsibility," p. 47.
21. "Does the Church Have Any Political Wisdom for the 70's?," pp. 29–34.
22. *Ibid.*, p. 30.

latest three essays on politics and the state all contain approving references to the theological ethics of Helmut Thielicke who explicitly adopts a "two-realm" approach to the question of politics.[23]

"Force and Political Responsibility," published in 1972, develops the mythopoetic view of politics. "I ask you to think *as if* you with all men are to be present at political creation, at the Fall, at Babel, and with Noah after the evil propensities of men's hearts in that generation deservedly ended in the first destruction—and the end of that end was government. What then would government mean?"[24] Such an approach might furnish Ramsey an opportunity to expound the aspect of creation in terms of justice and the political order. Ramsey does devote the first section of this article to developing the aspect of creation, but only to show that political creation involves the art of doing and not making. Political creation shows that statecraft is not a conclusion to be drawn from the calculations of builders or makers, but rather a question of doing, which means creating a new situation out of nothing.[25] Nothing is said in this context about justice. Then in the next section he develops at length the aspect of Fall, the Noachic Covenant and Babel.[26]

Ramsey's later writings on politics and the state at the very minimum emphasize and give primary importance to the state as an order of preservation based on God's gracious response in the light of man's sinfulness. The later Ramsey definitely leans in the direction of a dualist and not a transformationist understanding of the state and fails to relate the political life of man to the whole of God's action—creation, preservation, and redemption. There seem to be real differences between his later writings and the more abstract and methodological discussion of *Nine Modern Moralists*, as well as the earlier consideration of *Christian Ethics and the Sit–In*.

23. "Force and Political Responsibility," p. 56; "Does the Church Have Any Political Wisdom for the 70's?", p. 31; "A Political Context for Strategic Thinking," pp. 5ff.
24. "Force and Political Responsibility," p. 46.
25. *Ibid.*, pp. 47–52.
26. *Ibid.*, pp. 52–63.

Ethical Considerations of the State

Paul Ramsey as a theological ethicist often derives his ethical considerations from his theological affirmations. Frequently, he will move back and forth between theological affirmations and ethical considerations. Corresponding to the theological affirmations of God as creator, preserver, and redeemer are the ethical realities of justice, order, and love. Again, Ramsey's more theoretical and earlier discussions adopt a transformationist motif in relating order, justice, and love in society and the state and try to develop equally all of these aspects. His more practical considerations and his later writings emphasize the reality of order based on sin and seem to lose much of the positive content and the transforming aspect of justice and love.

The discussion in *Nine Modern Moralists* affirms the place of all these three ethical realities in general and in the considerations of the state, although the state as such is not the primary subject matter of this book. Most of the book develops the theological model of love transforming justice as an adequate understanding of the proper approach of Christian ethics. Ramsey affirms a content to natural law and justice based on a sense of justice and injustice and not derived deductively from the general to the particular.[27] He criticizes Tillich for not admitting a greater content to justice.[28] Love transforms this natural justice both by making it dynamic and creative. In his discussion with Brunner, Ramsey takes up the meaning and the function of the orders of creation proposed in the early Brunner. Ramsey argues for the role of order, of justice with its content, as well as the role of love transforming justice. The Christian realizes that the orders are related to the three-fold activity of God so that one must uphold the orders which serve as a dyke against sin. At the same time, the Christian works to make them more just, more humane and more full of the spirit of love without unfitting them for their purpose as orders.[29]

Christian Ethics and the Sit–In tries to develop a Christian understanding of the state in light of the questions raised by the sit–ins at public lunchcounters which occurred in the struggle for

27. *NMM*, pp. 195; 213–227.
28. *Ibid.*, p. 194.
29. *Ibid.*, pp. 196–208.

racial justice in the late 1950's. The theoretical discussion upholds the importance of all three elements—justice, order, and love in man's life in the political area—and there is a definite transforming function of love on justice and a transforming function of both love and justice on order. Ramsey develops the relationship between justice and love in terms of creation as the external basis and the possibility of covenant, while covenant is the internal basis and the meaning or purpose of creation.[30]

Ramsey proposes an understanding of justice which is not based on the rights of the individual person as such but on the fact that the individual is destined for life in fellow humanity with and for fellow man. Creation is the external basis of covenant so that justice must ensure man's life *with* fellow humanity so that he can be *for* his fellow man, which is the meaning of love. Property rights are established in the light of this understanding. Even private property is based not on the claim of man's human nature or his person or his labor, but because fellow humanity is precarious in him. Justice ensures the possibility of life with fellow man. Charity then stretches, converts, or elevates natural justice. Love transforms justice even in the community among men by proportioning justice in terms of distributing to people according to their needs. Charity, especially, makes itself felt in the order of justice through equity. Thus even in the life of man in community love tries to transform justice.[31]

Justice and charity are not the only ethical aspects in a consideration of the state. The legitimacy of order must be stressed alongside the claim for justice. Order and the observance of law are fundamental along with justice.[32] In the particular case of the sit-in, Ramsey argues for the "inn keeper's law" based on justice. Problems arise if the law does not recognize the inn keeper's law. One cannot merely appeal to the fact that the law is unjust and disobey it. Order as brought about by legal order remains an important function of the state because the state partakes of the preserving act of God restraining the sinfulness of men. A simple appeal to injustice does not suffice to justify disobedience or revo-

30. *Sit-In*, pp. 22, 124–128.
31. *Sit–In*, pp. 24–30.
32. *Ibid.*, pp. 47, 75.

lutionary change. Order remains a basic and independent factor in the ethical evaluation of the state and its functions, even though the existing order always partakes of the sin and injustice it tries to restrain. Without order there could be neither justice nor charity. American Protestant Christianity (to which I am sure Ramsey would now add much of Roman Catholicism in this country) often has too sentimental a view of advancing the cause of justice and too little concern to probe deeply into the meaning and theological justification of legality and order. Order is a value as fundamental for the state as justice, but justice and love do try to transform the existing order. We are obliged to preserve this world and not some other and to preserve an orderly even if unjust social or legal system while we engage in the struggle for justice within it.[33]

The practical considerations in *Christian Ethics and the Sit–In* seem to attribute very great weight to order and not much meaning to the transforming aspect of justice and charity. He considers, for example, the efforts of the New York City School Board of Education (in 1961) to bring about integration by allowing busing of black children to predominantly white schools. Ramsey objects to this concept of abstract justice which forgets about the order and fabric of community brought about by neighborhood schools.[34] Even in the matter of the church, Ramsey is not too sure that the churches should and can immediately become the vehicle for bringing about integration of the races. There must first be decisive changes in the black church, the white church, the state and white man's society before integration could take place.[35] Ramsey's practical applications lean heavily toward accepting the *status quo* in the name of order.

In subsequent writings on force and political responsibility, Ramsey, at the very least, modifies his emphasis. Perhaps the nature of his essays as discussions primarily with those who pay too little attention to sin and the need for order influences his heavy concentration on order. In his later writings in this area, justice does not really transform order and is often left undeveloped. Both justice and order are terminal values, but order is developed

33. *Ibid.*, pp. 49–51, 75–77.
34. *Ibid.*, pp. 51–55.
35. *Ibid.*, pp. 56–65.

in greater detail. The discussion of statecraft in the context of international relations characterizes the good of politics as embracing three terms: *lex* or the legal order; *ordo* or the order of power; and *iustitia* which he refers to as humanitarianism.[36] In the context of international politics he now introduces the third concept of the order of power.

Statesmen must take into account all three of these aspects so that the absolutizing of any one aspect is erroneous. Ramsey criticizes those who place all the emphasis on legal aspects and forget both the realities of power and of justice. Ironically, some Americans absolutize the legal element in foreign affairs by insisting on the observation of all treaties and national boundaries, while on the domestic scene they give little or no importance to the legal aspect or the conscience of the laws.[37]

What is the relationship among *lex, ordo,* and *iustitia?* There is an area of coincidence and overlap but not total convergence. Later he compares this relationship with the three interrelating circles which form the symbol for Ballantine beer.[38] A just and prudent politics will strive to increase the area of convergence in the middle. Ramsey's Christian realism prevents him from seeing a great transforming aspect to justice, but the three aspects which appear to be of about equal importance in politics and statecraft will perdure. He explicitly says that order is not a higher value than justice, nor is justice a higher value than order.[39] Even his most recent writing on the subject refers to both as terminal values in politics. Both are conditional to each other. Both justice and order are necessary.[40]

Every man and every nation in the world does not share a common understanding of justice, but each has only a partial view of the universal and not a universal view. There will always be disagreement and discussion on these matters. The political life of mankind is perennially carried on under the sign of the Tower of Babel. The Spirit of God can bring men together, but political

36. *JW,* Chapters 1, 2, and 20 with many other occasional references.
37. *Ibid.,* pp. 31–33.
38. *Ibid.,* pp. 12, 504.
39. *Ibid.,* p. 11.
40. "Force and Political Responsibility," pp. 72, 73.

activity after the resurrection of Jesus and the coming of the Spriit goes on much as before under its own sign. Notice here the lack of any transforming aspect of charity or love on the political situation. Political life of mankind for those who take seriously the *Book of Revelation* is a realm of patient endurance, for we live in two cities and not in the one world of the city of man under construction. This view demythologizes politics and puts it in its proper place. The hope of a cyclical recurrence or the hope of a progressively better future are not our hopes. To the end of this earthly city of patient endurance there will be wars and the rumor of wars. This is the nature of politics.[41]

Ramsey thus argues for the importance of justice and order and the need for force in politics to bring about and ensure order and justice. Perhaps the context of his discussion hinders him from any sustained development of the positive aspect of justice as there was in *Christian Ethics and the Sit–In*. There are continued assertions that justice is one of the factors involved, but this is usually downplayed or undeveloped. He merely asserts, for example, that men come to know justice through the *ius gentium* animating the historical community into which we are born.[42] Occasionally in his writings on war there are also assertions of justice transforming order and even redemption transforming reality, but such assertions are rare and do not appear to be a controlling concept or have much bearing on his practical applications.[43] These occasional or introductory references do not overturn the judgment that for Ramsey justice is a terminal value together with *lex* and *ordo,* and that justice in his later writings remains undeveloped with the realization that men see only a view of justice and never the universal view of justice.

Although the role or even the mention of love does not appear in many of Ramsey's occasional essays on politics, Ramsey does not want to leave love out of his considerations. His whole development of just war shows that it is Christian love which both justifies and limits the use of force. But the fact remains that love is seldom mentioned in these essays so that it has little or no applicable content and little transforming activity.

41. *JW,* pp. 178–180; "Force and Political Responsibility," p. 54.
42. "Force and Political Responsibility," p. 52.
43. *JW,* pp. 389, 390.

An important ethical consideration somewhat connected with theological affirmations concerns the proper definition, description or understanding of the state. Ramsey devoted one chapter in *War and the Christian Conscience* to Augustine's understanding of the state and appears to be in agreement with that concept. There is a real difference between Augustine's and the classical conception of the state, and the difference is at the level of the actual justice present in the commonwealth. Cicero had defined the state *(res publica)* as an assemblage associated by a common acknowledgement of right and by a community of interests. This definition embraces the common assumption of Greco–Roman political theory that justice is the ethical substance of the commonwealth. Augustine understands the state differently. It is an assemblage of reasonable beings bound together by a common agreement as to the objects of their love, whatever it loves. The state is based not on justice but on an agreement of wills.[44]

Augustine has maintained that man's loves for any other good than the *bonum summum et commune* are of their very nature fractricidal. That is why Cain who killed his brother is the father of the earthly city. At times the rhetoric might imply that Ramsey sees only fratricidal love in the state which seems occasionally to be simply identified with the city of man, but there is a mingling of fratricidal love and brotherly love based on love of God in human history. Augustine gives a radical critique of such justice as characterizes, has characterized or ever will characterize the kingdoms of this world. Justice as a personal virtue or any other love are not truly virtuous unless they are redirected by the love of God above all things. Otherwise it is only the form of justice. So too with social justice in society which is not directed or transformed by charity or the love of God. There can be no true justice or giving man his due unless God is given his due. The Christian is called upon to preserve and enlarge the area of agreements of will and the scope of peaceful orders on earth. Thus Augustine does not see the state primarily in terms of justice and does not expect to find great justice in the state.[45]

In *War and the Christian Conscience* Ramsey exposes the

44. *WCC*, pp. 24–26.
45. *Ibid.*, pp. 15–28.

Augustinian understanding of the state and the role of justice in the state as background to his exposition of the just–war teaching. In a very significant passage Ramsey reveals his own acceptance of the secondary and comparatively minimal role that justice plays in the state. "In any case, all Augustine's language about the purpose that lies at the root of the state, and his severe castigation of the resulting justice which still must be what justifies warfare, brings us remarkably close to that remarkable statement in the best book about 'limited warfare' that has appeared in recent years, to the effect that 'nations might better renounce the use of war as an instrument of *anything but* national policy.' "[46]

In *Christian Ethics and the Sit–In*, where he is not discussing war as such, Ramsey seems to be more positive about the role of justice even though it is secondary in the meaning of the state. Here Ramsey points out a somewhat mistaken emphasis in Augustine's definition of the state as an assemblage of reasonable beings bound together by a common agreement as to the objects of their love, or as the combination of men's wills to attain the things which are helpful to this life. The mistaken emphasis is the assumption that people first agree on the object of their love or on any particular national purpose or goal and thus become a people. The state is constituted by the agreement of wills to be a people, a covenant community of life with and for man, and not with and for particular objectives. Justice and other things follow from this basic agreement of wills to be a people. However, justice remains important and fundamental even if it is not primary. Not only is justice a form of a people's will to be a people, but justice creates that love or agreement of wills which constitute a people and differentiates, according to Augustine, a nation from a multitude. Such an agreement of wills depends on justice shared by all to the exclusion of none. In 1961, Ramsey urged that this nation must move rapidly to achieve a far greater measure of justice in the common life and especially in race relations. Such justice is an absolute prerequisite to the preservation for long of the habit of law observance.[47]

46. *Ibid.*, p. 29.
47. *Sit–In*, pp. 73–76.

There is a great difference between the theoretical understanding of the state in *War and the Christian Conscience* and a brief reference to the Augustinian definition of the state in *Nine Modern Moralists*. In elaborating the need for Christian ethics to accept both love and justice or natural law and to understand the relation between them in terms of transformation, Ramsey argues against those methodologies which would exclusively consider only one of these elements. Humanistic ethics forgets the covenant, whereas some Protestant ethics forget any form of natural community which is based on the inherent principles of justice based on creation. St. Augustine, according to Ramsey, in his definition of political society comes close to this Protestant error because he omits any reference to man's knowledge of justice in his definition of the state.[48]

It seems fair to conclude that there are discrepancies in Ramsey's appreciation of the role of justice in politics and statecraft. In considering more theoretical questions of moral methodology and in considering the domestic aspect of the state, Ramsey insists on a proper place for justice even though it is not primary. But in his discussions of war and of international politics the role of justice both in theory and in practice is considerably reduced. Perhaps some of the discrepancy comes from his different optiques. In theory he argues against some Protestants for a greater role for justice which has been admitted by Catholics. In questions of the state and especially in international affairs, he argues against liberalism, both Protestant and Catholic, which gives too much place to justice and love in the state. I admit there are some differences between domestic and international political ethics, but these differences do not adequately explain the different emphases which appear in Ramsey. Perhaps again the problem lies in the occasional and somewhat polemical nature of his writings.

There are important practical ramifications of this theoretical position. If the basis of the state is the agreement of wills, agreement on a particular point cannot be easily challenged in the name of justice. In a democracy especially, one must give the benefit of doubt to the conscience of the laws. If the law is unjust,

48. *NMM*, p. 181.

there are ways of trying to challenge and change the laws. If more importance were given to justice rather than the agreement of wills, then the presumption in favor of existing laws and policies would not be so strong and overriding in every case. In accord with his teaching, Ramsey maintains that many people today erroneously question the presumption of legitimacy in the decision of the state to wage war by insisting that the presumption should be in favor of peace. Once the decision is made to go to war, the presumption for the citizen shifts in favor of the justice of the war because the decision was made by the established and legitimate political processes.[49] If there were not this emphasis on the conscience of the laws and the presumption in its favor, the door would be open to individualism and anarchy.

Power, Force, and the Multi–national System

Ramsey sees sin as the reason for the existence of power and even armed force in politics and statecraft. Armed force is apparently that form of power which uses physical violence. Throughout his writings there is no other more positive explanation of the role of power and force in political ethics. What power really means is never developed by Ramsey. There are only very brief references to physical, economic, and other forms of power which are not armed force.[50] The nation has a monopoly of superior force within its boundaries and should use it to deter violation of law and to sustain the adherence of its people to law. Beyond its boundaries no state has a monopoly of power. The nation–state system results from the verdict of Babel, and according to the Noachic Covenant, power can only be limited by further and countervailing power.[51]

However as mentioned above there is a relationship between *lex, ordo,* and *iustitia.* The nations of this world do not live in a trust system but in an opposed system governed by move and counter-move in which power can only be limited by further power. The religious man who has not been bemused by one or another of the utopianisms or gradualisms of the modern mental-

---

49. *JW*, pp. 102, 275.
50. *Ibid.*, p. 8.
51. "Force and Political Responsibility," pp. 65, 66.

ity will understand this to be God's secret way of preserving the world as a human dwelling place until the end of time.[52] This brief summary needs further explanation.

Ramsey develops in greatest detail his insistence that power and the order of power are constitutive elements of the state and statecraft. Power belongs to the *esse* of politics, the very act of being politics, so that you never have politics without the use of power, possibly armed force. Power even belongs to the *bene esse*, the proper act of politics, so that you never have good politics without the use of power, sometimes armed force.[53]

The role and importance of power in the state indicate the element of coercion which is in the political community and thus distinguishes it from other human communities. This arises from the realization of human sinfulness and is therefore denied to some extent by those who assert the basic goodness of man as being unaffected by sin or that the power of the redeeming Lord is now overcoming such sin even in the realm of politics. Today there is a newer group opposing the use of power because the modern weapons of war are such that never again should men resort to armed force. Ramsey laments the fact that the present liberal consensus in Protestant, and even to some extent in Catholic, ethics denies this need for power, and even armed force in politics.[54] He sadly notes that even Reinhold Niebuhr now writes in favor of the liberal consensus by seeing the problem today in terms of the need to curb the use of power.[55]

The peace and order of the world cannot be maintained without usable power and the actual use of it in some form.[56] The error of liberalism rests on the assumption that force should be excluded if possible from politics and the need to use force indicates in a sense the failure of statecraft. Liberals think that negotiation will always be able to bring about justice and peace, but Ramsey often asserts that you cannot win at the conference table anything it seems evident you cannot win on the battlefield. The use of force

---

52. "Does the Church Have Any Political Wisdom for the 70's?," pp. 31, 32.
53. *JW*, p. 5.
54. *Ibid.*, pp. 5–9.
55. *Ibid.*, p. 487.
56. *Ibid.*, p. 89.

or even the escalation of force is not necessarily evil or bad. As a nation today we have inherited enormous responsibilities, and we must use power and force to carry out our obligations.[57] The crucial flaw in the thinking of liberalism and the American ethos is the silent assumption that we understand peace and justice to be related and guaranteed to be linked by an unseen hand.[58] The liberal American ethos still enshrines the perfectionist goal of banishing force from human history, but force at times is and always will be necessary for the protection of order and justice.

Ramsey's political analysis points out a structural defect in the present nation–state system of the world. The way porcupines make love is a parable of nations in this multi–national world. They cannot get along with one another and they cannot get along without one another. They make love and make settlements or they make war when they cannot reach or postpone settlements, but all these things are done carefully.[59]

Ramsey has pointed out the natural-law optimism of *Pacem in Terris*, but he heartily endorses the papal realism in pointing out the insufficiency of modern states to ensure the universal common good. Such insufficiency is not grounded in any contingent reason but in the structural deficiency of the nation–state system itself. Ramsey does not totally agree with the papal analysis of this structural defect. The pope speaks about the social value of the universal common good and the fact that the existing nation–state system is not proportionate to the attainment of these social values. Ramsey objects that this is true of all communities which pursue a common good but is not a proper analysis of the political community. Pope John tended to spiritualize politics and forgot the specific difference which characterizes the political community as such—the exercise of a monopoly of power.[60]

A proper interpretation of the state begins not with an understanding of human communities as such but rather with an analysis of power or force which is the distinctive characteristic of the political community. There is required a world community and

57. *Ibid.*, p. 486; "Force and Political Responsibility," pp. 52–54.
58. *JW*, p. 67.
59. *Ibid.*, p. 141.
60. *Ibid.*, pp. 83–85.

public authority which then can exercise its monopoly of power and force in a just and effective manner. Only when there is a world political community with an effective use of force can the moral right of individual nations to use force be denied. In the meantime—which for Ramsey is throughout human existence in the earthly city and before the swords are turned into plough-shares—individual nations need force and at times armed force to ensure even the imperfect justice and order of the world in which we live.[61]

The nation–state system has many problems, but it is here to stay. We are both condemned and blessed by the verdict of Babel which means that there never can be a final political unification of mankind. We should try to build up the earthly city, but idealists who strive for world political unity are doomed because they forget that we do not live in one world of the city of man in the making.[62] Babel condemns us to govern mankind through an opposed international system in which power is restrained by further power. This rift coming from sin cannot be overcome by any "good works" in the institutional field.[63] But the verdict of Babel is also a blessing. Any government of a world community would take a vertical turn toward unbridled upward expansion, arrogance, and boundless tyranny. The blessing of Babel now makes this impossible.[64]

The political life of man does not go on in a trust system. Ramsey describes the nation–state system as an opposed system, and sometimes leaves the impression that this exhausts the entire meaning of the nation–state system. In other places he adds that there is an intermingling of trust and opposed systems in the reality of the nation–state system. However, he insists on calling the multi-national system an opposed system and asserts that it can never be replaced by a trust system. The kingdoms of this world can never become the kingdom of God.[65]

61. *Ibid.*, pp. 85–90.
62. "Force and Political Responsibility," pp. 52–54.
63. "Does the Church Have Any Political Wisdom for the 70's?," p. 31.
64. "Force and Political Responsibility," p. 59.
65. "Does the Church Have Any Political Wisdom for the 70's?," p. 33; "A Political Ethics Context for Strategic Thinking," pp. 17–19.

In the light of the theological context, Ramsey cannot accept the fact that the present United Nations is an effective instrument which can thus eliminate the right and duty of nations at times to use force to promote and secure a more just order. There are inherent defects in the United Nations precisely because its structure presupposes and is built upon the nation–state system of the present. The United Nations should be strengthened but in the meantime one does not jump up and down on a sprained ankle.[66] However, in his later writings, he does not hold out any hope of overcoming the multi–national system.

Obviously Ramsey's theory of politics with its affirmation that power and even armed force is of the very essence of politics and of good politics does not mean there are no moral constraints on the use of power. In fact, his whole theory of just war insists that Christian love both justifies and also limits the use of armed force through the principle of discrimination and the principle of proportion. There are evil effects connected with the use of armed force and sometimes proportionate reason indicates that the good to be obtained by the use of force is outweighed by the evil connected with its use. The dilemma arises precisely because justice and peace require the use of force when no other means are suitable. Without resort to force would mean that order, peace, and justice would be threatened in this world.[67]

Specific Characteristics of Political Ethics

An important consideration in Ramsey's analysis of the state and politics concerns the relationship between individual or personal actions and political actions. Obviously the two are related, but there are important distinctions between them which are too often forgotten by the contemporary ethos. Ramsey has already defined the state in terms of its specific difference of power, and this factor remains a most important difference between private and political morality. In his later writings, he seems to veer more and more explicitly toward accepting a "two-realm" ethical theory which sees the state as the left hand of God serving primarily as an order of preservation.[68]

66. *JW*, pp. 486, 487.
67. *Ibid.*, pp. 89, 90.
68. "Does the Church Have Any Political Wisdom for the 70's?," pp. 29–33.

Ethics should not be externally related to politics. Political ethics mean modalities of ethics appropriate to politics, specifically different in important ways while not generically different from general ethical principles. The task is to clarify political ethics in its specific nature. Ethical values are not related externally or imposed from the outside on politics. Political ethics must discuss the meaning of politics and its basis in a general theory of competitive equilibrium.[69] One does not begin with general ethical values apart from the political reality itself. The question of whether Western ethical values are compatible with the nation–state system and with security within that system is a false question. If these values are not compatible, they have become unearthly and can in no way be politically effective.[70] Political ethics deals with the political order as we Christians know it in our mythopoetic vision. Strategic thinking, contemplation of wars and continuous preparation for the possibility of war are important aspects of statecraft.

There are also other specific characteristics of political ethics. In his earlier discussions of war and nuclear deterrence Ramsey employed the concept of "deferred repentance," and called it the main difference between public and private morality.[71] Ramsey uses this concept to show that the statesman may continue to serve, even though his nation relies on an immoral deterrent, if he continues to try to change the policy of his government to a moral deterrent force. This is obviously an important aspect, but it seems to me that it is also present outside the realm of politics.[72] Likewise in the light of Ramsey's later development it can no longer be called the primary difference between private and political morality which is located in the use of force as the specific difference of the whole political enterprise.

Ramsey also sees a very important difference between private and political ethics arising from the subject of political action which is the nation–state. The nation–state has its responsibility defined by the national good and the universal or international common good. In reality these two do not always correspond so

69. "A Political Ethics Context for Strategic Thinking," pp. 39, 40.
70. "Force and Political Responsibility," p. 55.
71. *WCC,* p. 12.
72. *Ibid.,* pp. 12, 310–312.

that tensions and possible conflicts are inevitable. In the light of this background the statesmen must determine what he should do politically. A nation's responsibilities are located in an area of congruence between the national common good and the common good of others or the universal common good. A charitable concern for mankind pressures us to assist as many as possible when we are able to do so. This is the area of political prudence, but one can sin against political prudence both by omission and commission.[73]

The statesman ought not do all the humanitarian good that can be done; he ought not do all the political good that can be done. He must ask whether what ought to be done politically ought to be done by us in the light of the fact that there are many other political actors on the scene. He must decide if we have the power to do the political good that ought to be done by us. The very nature of this type of prudential decision of the statesman is such that no one else is in a better position than he to make the final decision which requires the weighing of so many different aspects. They should never be characterized as anything other than decisions of prudence (Ramsey is here criticizing those who would call such actions immoral and fault the conscience of the person who made them). Nor can anyone ever make absolute statements about what the prudent statesman should do in these matters. By no means must the statesman do all the humanitarian good that can be done but only the political good that can be done prudently by his nation.[74]

Ramsey employs both the Aristotelian concept of prudence and the biblical notion of creation to understand the act of politics as an exercise of practical reason which involves doing and not making. The exercise is truly a creation *ex nihilo,* for the statesman brings into being things that are not. The statesman takes the risk of launching into the unknown by actualizing one of a number of choices, each of which has some plausibility before the event.[75] This is the realm of practical reason with so many contingencies. History reminds us how some statesmen have succeeded because

73. *JW*, p. 459.
74. *Ibid.*, pp. 9–19, 449–459.
75. "Force and Political Responsibility," pp. 46–52.

of subsequent events which neither they nor others could forsee. Political decisions are risks often taken in the face of impenetrable uncertainty. The very nature of such political acts and statecraft means that others cannot brand such actions immoral unless the action was foreknown to be predetermined to fail or to cost more than the end was worth. These conditions obviously are seldom present in the area of statecraft.[76]

His theory of political ethics and statecraft is worked out primarily in opposition to a theological liberalism which does not appreciate that the state is not the kingdom or the City of God and fails to understand the specific difference of political ethics. But Ramsey responds in some detail to the attack from the opposite flank, which espouses a realistic view of statecraft with no moral limits imposed on the state's use of power and force. Ramsey rejects the argument proposed by Richard Tucker that, even if the state is not the ultimate moral value, the state is at least a necessary condition to the higher values that it serves so that no other value can be more important in practice than the survival of the state. Ramsey responds that reasons of state are valid only so long as the state itself has reasons. The state can never contradict those very goals for which it is necessary and which alone justify its "reasons of state."[77]

Contemporary Factual Perceptions

A final political consideration is Ramsey's understanding of the political realities of the 1960's and especially the relationship between the so-called free world and communism. In the Introduction written specifically for the large collection of his essays in 1968, Ramsey urges the reader to pay attention to his exposition of the nature of politics, the political community, and the responsible use of force and not to dismiss the ethical and theological considerations by attributing to Ramsey an obsessive fear of communism. Ramsey's political ethics does not depend on the fact situation and his perception of it.[78]

Ramsey's warning is interesting and should be taken seriously

76. *JW*, pp. 455, 527.
77. *Ibid.*, pp. 417–424.
78. *Ibid.*, p. ix.

by the reader, but there is also another side to the picture. One of my criticisms of Ramsey's ethic in general and his political ethic specifically concerns his failure to pay enough attention to the contemporary factual situation. His formal ethic is often deontologically derived from Christian love. By cutting the ethical model from God and not from man, Ramsey opens the doors to the dangers of an ahistorical ethic. Historical reality might change many of Ramsey's presuppositions and values which must be considered in addition to his deontological principles. In addition it seems that one's perception of the present reality must influence his ethical judgments especially in terms of the priorities assigned and the relevant importance of the different values. Ramsey himself in one place admits that fact perceptions cannot be totally separated from ethical judgments.[79] I would contend that Ramsey's own analysis of the contemporary political events has influenced his ethics, but there is still some truth in his warning that his ethics deserves to be studied as a theoretical system apart from the political realities of the present and his perception of them.

Ramsey has expressed a very negative view of communism as a somewhat monolithic, undiversified, international movement. Ramsey makes the very obviously ethical statement on a number of different occasions that no Christian should willingly concur in the coming to power of a communist regime, nationalist or otherwise, and particularly not in a developing country.[80] There thus arises an obligation to assist others in resistance to communism, even of the more liberal variety, if there are no other alternatives. However, this political obligation must be seen in the light of political agency described above so that there is no practical obligation if it cannot be done or if it would produce greater evil than the evil prevented.

In assessing the political situation in Southeast Asia, he sees Vietnam as one instance of Communist expansion and thus a real threat to the freedom of the rest of Southeast Asia. Ramsey rejects the "domino theory" as inadequate, only because it is too rigid an

79. *Ibid.*, p. 398. One wonders if Ramsey in a different situation such as a South American country might not give less importance to order and more importance to justice. I think one can rightly ask him to lean against what would be the natural excess of people living in the most powerful nation of the world.

80. *Ibid.*, pp. 449, 492.

image to describe a situation which Ramsey compares with running a foot race in a car load of peas.[81]

At the same time Ramsey seems to have a very benevolent view of United States foreign policy. In the early stage of his writings, Ramsey did condemn as immoral a deterrence based on the possession of nuclear weapons. Ramsey continues to condemn a deterrent based on the intention to use counter–people warfare, but in the meantime he has accepted a moral use of nuclear weapons for deterrence purposes. Ramsey also criticizes as immoral the bombing of an iron and steel complex in North Vietnam on the basis of his understanding of the principle of discrimination, but he does accept the way in which, for the most part, the United States has conducted the war in Southeast Asia, obviously up to the time of his writing about it.[82] He argues in all these cases on strictly theological grounds, but one can wonder how much his theology is affected by his perception of political realities. In theory he sees the function of the United States to use its power in the service of an ordered justice and peace in this world.[83] In practice, Ramsey apparently understands our policies as part of the struggle for freedom and for stabilizing democratic forms of government in the world.[84]

Critique

The foregoing pages have tried to assemble in a somewhat systematic way the theory of political ethics and the understanding of the state operative in the many writings of Paul Ramsey. The following critique will indicate my differences with Ramsey pointing out, without any real systematic development, my understanding of political ethics and the state. Since this first section is somewhat introductory both for Ramsey and for the specific purposes of this book, more detailed criticisms will be reserved for the discussion of particular questions, especially the just war.

Theological affirmations about the state. Some developments and change of emphasis have been pointed out in Ramsey's discus-

81. *Ibid.*, p. 498.
82. *Ibid.*, p. 533.
83. *Ibid.*, p. xvi.
84. *Ibid.*, pp. 489–496.

sion. My general criticism of Ramsey is his failure in more recent writings to live up to his own criterion that political life, the state, and all of man's actions should be related to the whole activity of God as creator, ruler, preserver, and redeemer. In my opinion, Ramsey, especially in his later writings, gives too much importance to the preserving action of God in response to man's sinfulness and not enough importance to the action of God as creator and redeemer. This overemphasis serves as the principal theoretical reason for many of my more practical and concrete differences with Ramsey.

Ramsey has rightly pointed out that Roman Catholic political ethics has not given enough importance to sin because it saw political reality primarily in terms of the natural law which was associated with the divine action of creation. In the last hundred years especially, Roman Catholic theology has leaned even more in this direction. This is illustrated by the fact that papal encyclicals justified the right to private property on the basis of the rights of the human person, whereas Thomas Aquinas justified private property in the light of the sinfulness which affects men in this world. Contemporary Roman Catholic social thought, in its effort to overcome the separation between the natural and the supernatural which did characterize older Catholic social thinking, now tends to view all social morality in the light of grace and the supernatural. Even in the *Pastoral Constitution on the Church in the Modern World*, I do not believe that enough importance is given to the reality of sin and the realization that the fullness of redemption is not here and will occur only outside history. This document accepts too much of a realized eschatology. Thus some strands of contemporary Catholic political thought share much in common with Protestant liberalism.[85]

Perhaps one could try to make a case for Ramsey's internal consistency by pointing out the differences which are always present between the state and the other "orders of creation," to use Brunner's term. The state more than any other "order" is based on the preserving and restraining grace of God in the light of

85. For a fuller development on my criticism of Roman Catholic social ethics in this matter, see my *Catholic Moral Theology in Dialogue* (Notre Dame, Ind.: Fides Publishers, 1972), pp. 111–149.

man's sinfulness. Thus Ramsey's explicit discussion of the state should be different from his discussion of ethical methodology in general as it appears especially in *Nine Modern Moralists*. The fact still remains, however, that there is a great difference between his emphasis on sin in *Christian Ethics and the Sit-In* and in his later writings on politics and war. Nor can the distinction between domestic and foreign politics adequately account for this difference.

Even if Ramsey were entirely consistent in this question of the role and importance of sin, I would continue to disagree with what seems to be an exaggerated emphasis on the preserving act of God at the expense of his creating and redeeming actions. The preserving action of God must be seen alongside the creating and redeeming act of God. Sin does not destroy the work of creation, and the transforming power of redemption is always present even if the fullness of redemption will never come in history but only outside it. My view of the state presupposes an anthropology and an eschatology which are somewhat more positive than those proposed by Ramsey, but these aspects will be discussed later in greater detail.

Ethical considerations of the state. I would give a greater importance to the role of justice in the state than Ramsey does, especially in his later writings. This follows from the theological assessment which, in comparison with Ramsey, places less emphasis on the preserving action of God and more on the creating and redeeming acts of God.

My position, once again, would be somewhat closer to the position Ramsey elaborated in *Nine Modern Moralists* and *Christian Ethics and the Sit–In*, although in practice I would give more importance to justice than he does in his practical considerations of various problems such as limited busing or even integration of churches. In his later writings, Ramsey seems to give too much importance to order at the expense of justice. I would argue that justice is a more important value than order for the state even though at times the demands of order will mean that some injustice must be accepted. By giving a more positive interpretation to the state while still recognizing the negative aspects attributable to sin, one does not have to fear that a change in the *status quo* or a comparatively small disruption of order will bring about chaos and subvert the divine action of preservation. My practical disagreements with Ramsey stemming from the greater importance given to justice rather than order will emerge in the discussion of civil disobedience.

Not only do I see justice as a more important value than order in the state, but I also do not completely separate the two as Ramsey does, despite the fact that he admits some overlapping. The problem stems from Ramsey's laudable attempt to see the state in terms of the whole action of God as creator, preserver, and redeemer. Unfortunately, he generally relates order with only the preserving act of God and understands it in a negative sense as distinguished from justice and love. I see order itself in terms of the whole action of God so that order is not only the work of preservation but also of creation and redemption. Order in the state by its very nature calls for justice even though it will always fall short of perfect justice. Justice itself has an important ordering function in the life of the state.

Ramsey's concept of order also appears to be very static. The work of ordering should be a continual and dynamic process. My understanding of ordering is more open to accept the need for change and even some disruption in the very process of ordering itself.

Especially in the realm of international politics, Ramsey speaks not only of order and justice but also of power which is a conditional value in the service of order and justice. In theory and practice I would give more importance to justice in the trio of *lex, ordo,* and *iustitia.* One practical example illustrates Ramsey's tendency to give too much importance to the balance of power which is really a form of order at the expense of justice. In the situation involving Pakistan and what is now Bangladesh, Ramsey justifies the American tilt against India and in favor of Pakistan on the basis of his understanding of the balance of power in Asia which involves moving toward a three-power world and a five-power balance in Asia.[86] Ramsey analyzes the proper American response almost solely in terms of the balance of power, although he does

86. Does the Church Have Any Political Wisdom for the 70's?," pp. 36–40.

recognize that some might understand the balance of power as favoring our tilting toward India. In my analysis the primary consideration should be given not to considerations of the balance of power, even though these are important, but to considerations of justice. In this case the justice considerations argue that we should have tilted the other way.

Ramsey's analysis of this question brings up another important facet. He often argues that men will be ceaselessly debating about what justice involves in a particular situation because men have no universal views but only views of the universal. However, his own analysis indicates that the question of order, especially in terms of the balance of power in the international sphere, is likewise open to the same problem. Hence he is not justified in downplaying justice at the expense of order because there might be disagreement about what justice involves.

My position sees the need for order, but gives greater importance to justice. Perhaps one could describe this as a transformationist approach to political ethics. In his earlier writings, Ramsey explicitly called for a transformationist approach, even though I would argue that he did not give enough emphasis to the transforming aspect of justice on order. James Childress has described Ramsey's political ethics as Christ transforming natural law.[87] Especially in the light of Ramsey's later writings I do not find this transformationist model an apt description. Ramsey seems to come down so heavily on sin, the preserving act of God and order, that there is not enough importance given to justice and its transforming power, to say nothing of love or Christ. In his discussion of the justification and limitation of armed force in the just–war doctrine Ramsey does appeal to a transformationist motif, but most of the time there is little or no transformation about the actual political life of man in the order of preservation which is the state.

Ramsey also deemphasizes justice too much in his one–sided emphasis on a voluntaristic understanding of the state. Ramsey in his writings on war accepts this voluntaristic view of the state in the light of Augustine's definition of the state, even though else-

87. James F. Childress, *Civil Disobedience and Political Obligation* (New Haven: Yale University Press, 1971), pp. 87–100.

where he explicitly rejects such a definition because it does not give enough importance to justice. One does not have to adopt a rationalistic or classical understanding of the state to give more importance to justice than Ramsey does in his political ethics.

Power, force, and the multi–national system. My approach gives less importance to the role of power and even armed force and understands power in a broader perspective. Ramsey sees these realities in terms of sin and gives them great importance because of his emphasis on sin. I argue that power should be understood not only in the light of sin but in the light of the whole action of God. There are many different types and varieties of power—the power of love, of truth, of courage, of justice, of public opinion, of education, etc., as well as the power of violence and force. Ramsey too easily forgets about all these other types of power and their relationship to the whole action of God and not just to the restraining and preserving acts of God.

Power, especially in the form of armed force, should not have as important a role in the state and political life as Ramsey assigns even though it does have some role and importance. The cohesiveness of the state and the prevention of chaos relies on many things other than armed force, even though the state must have a monopoly of armed force in a domestic society. It will be pointed out later that the use of armed force in the just war tradition was always regarded as an *ultima ratio,* but Ramsey too easily accepts it as a normal occurrence. Thus there should be some modification in his assertion that power and armed force is of the *esse* and the *bene esse* of politics in accord with the tradition which saw armed force only as an *ultima ratio.* I would argue that it saw armed force only as an *ultima ratio* because its controlling vision of politics was not based so exclusively on sin.

Although there are statements to the contrary, Ramsey does assert that power is to be limited by further power, and arbitrary and unlimited power can only be limited by further power.[88] I do not see power, especially with the negative meaning Ramsey attaches to it, as the only way of limiting power. Justice, truth, humanitarian concerns, love, conscience, and public opinion are

88. "Does the Church Have Any Political Wisdom for the 70's?," p. 31; "Force and Political Responsibility," p. 60.

examples of many ways in which power is limited by something other than power or force. Ramsey's statements leave the impression that might makes right. Whoever has the most power will triumph. But obviously Ramsey himself would not carry the thesis to such a conclusion because he does admit limits on power even in terms of Christian love. These statements about power being limited only by power stand opposed to Ramsey's own analysis of force and power in his discussion of just war.

Also I differ with Ramsey's emphasis on the nation–state system as an opposed system. This element is definitely present in the nation–state system, but it should not be used as a completely adequate description of a system which Ramsey himself admits is intermingled with elements of a trust system. I would see a greater convergence especially in the modern world between the national common good and the international common good. There still remain differences and even apparent oppositions, but these do not justify the characterization of the multi–national system as an opposed system without any further qualification.

Contemporary Factual Perception. I also disagree with Ramsey's perception of the realities in the international political scene in the 1960's. Ramsey feared the threat to the so–called free world by a monolithic Communist power bloc—an approach which often characterized the cold war mentality in this country. Of course, my judgment today has the inestimable advantage of hindsight. Also it must be noted that Ramsey is far from an anti–Communist crusader. His references to communism are surprisingly few, but he did understand the situation in terms of a monolothic Communist challenge to the free-world.

This section has briefly criticized Ramsey's political theory and sketched my own approach. Despite some developments in Ramsey himself, his writings on politics and war, especially after 1961, show a remarkable theological and internal consistency. The central focus of this consistency is his recognition of a very important and even primary role of sin in his understanding of politics and the state. My disagreements with him very often stem from a disagreement about the importance and especially the apparent primacy which he gives to sin. The specific meaning of political ethics has not been developed in this critique, for this comes to the fore in the following section which considers the role of the church in politics.

CHURCH AND POLITICS

What is the role of the church in political affairs? What wisdom does the church have to give to the political aspect of human existence? How should the church and churchmen address the problems of modern political life? What can and should Christian ethics say to the magistrate? These questions obviously involve an understanding of the role and function of Christian social ethics.

Ramsey's Position

In this area again Ramsey is reacting negatively against the prevailing trends, especially as found in the statements of Churches and churchmen addressed to political questions. His book, *Who Speaks for the Church?*, severely critiques the way in which the Geneva Conference on Church and Society sponsored by the World Council of Churches in 1966 addressed itself to these questions.[89] Ramsey acknowledges that this conference arrived at conclusions with which he disagrees, but he contends not with the conclusions of Geneva but with their understanding that the church should give specific pronouncements of any type on political matters.[90]

His latest writings on the subject illustrate this same acknowledgement of the limitations of ethics and the church in matters of statecraft. He chooses with obvious relish the example of the Indian military action in Bangladesh in 1972 because it is a case of intervention not done primarily in terms of self–defense which the general American public, especially churchmen and academics, thought was justified. Ramsey points out that it will be difficult to determine if the action is just or not in terms of the use of the judgment of proportion based on counting the costs. If Bangladesh proves ungovernable, if it turns into another Vietnam for India, if it abets the secessionist movement in the Indian state of Bengal,

89. Paul Ramsey, *Who Speaks for the Church?* (Nashville: Abingdon Press, 1967).
90. *Ibid.*, pp. 17, 18.

then who can say it was just?[91] This somber and sober analysis shows that from the principle of proportion "no particular deed or political actuality can be deduced; that no church ethics or political ethics has any competence in this regard; that statecraft is fully responsible for political creation worth its costs."[92]

One who knew Ramsey's earlier writings was not surprised by the fact that the basic argument of *Who Speaks for the Church?* centers on the incompetency of the church to make specific, political judgments and pronouncements. From what Ramsey says in the book and elsewhere the reasons for this lack of competency can be developed.

The primary limit on the competency of the church stems from the fact that the church and Christian ethics must have specifically Christian warrants for its assertions.[93] The Christian church has the obligation of taking Christian love as far as it will go—but no further. It is a question of how far judgments are entailed in the shared affirmations of Christian ethics as such.[94] Church pronouncements, like Christian social ethics, are limited to the area of the specifically Christian as such.

Ramsey maintains that the specific solution of urgent problems is the work of political prudence and worldly wisdom. Here there is room for legitimate disagreement among Christians.[95] In his political ethical theory much of the work of the statesman and the magistrate is in the realm of the prudential. Occasionally, as in the case of just war, Christian love will point out the principle of discrimination calling for the immunity of non–combatants from direct deliberate attack. However, the subsumption of particular cases in this regard as well as the concrete application of the principle of proportion belongs to the realm of the magistrate and the citizen and lies beyond the competency of the church and of Christian ethics.[96]

"The principle of prudence (among a Christian's teachings) defi-

91. "Does the Church Have Any Political Wisdom for the 70's?," pp. 36, 37.
92. *JW*, pp. 455,456.
93. *Ibid.*, pp. 524, 525.
94. *Who Speaks*, pp. 52–55, 135, 136.
95. *Ibid.*, p. 19.
96. *JW*, pp. 455, 456, 510.

nitely refers the matter in question to the magistrate or to the political process for decision; and Christians as such can say no more than that this is the case."[97] The ultimate reason stems from the realization that there is no such thing as a Christian perception of facts or a Christian conjecture about consequences that might or might not occur.[98] One can call such actions immoral only if they are deliberately imprudent or uncharitable.[99] Thus with just these two limit cases the church and also Christian ethics have no competency to speak about matters of political prudence which encompass a vast amount of the realm of the political and include all specific policy decisions.

Ramsey argues for the need to preserve the difference and the separation between the church and the magistrate or the state.[100] In maximalist church statements, which try to give specific pronouncements on political affairs, the church blurs the important distinction between itself and all other groups in society and tries to assume for itself a role that it should not have.[101]

The church has no right or competence to take over the role of the state, the magistrate, or the citizen. The church does not have nor should it have a department of state. Ramsey ironically maintains that the older ecumenical movement (the Protestant) in its ethical teachings and the role it claims for the church affirms a closer identity between church and state, between Christian social ethics and the policy–making of the secular city, than did the medieval view of Christendom. There is today less recognition of the separation between church and state than there was in the Middle Ages, with the exception of Pope Boniface VIII's famous Bull, *Unam Sanctam*, issued in 1302. Meanwhile church pronouncements continue to indicate a poor and inadequate understanding of the boundaries and limitations of the church in the realm of the political.[102] Even Roman Catholic bishops have unfortunately begun to make such specific political pronouncements especially about the war in Southeast Asia.[103]

97. *Who Speaks*, p. 136.
98. *JW*, p. 484.
99. *Ibid.*, p. 524; *Who Speaks*, p. 136.
100. *JW*, p. 522.
101. *Who Speaks*, pp. 18, 19.
102. *Ibid.*, p. 31.
103. "Does the Church Have Any Political Wisdom for the 70's?," p. 35.

The motivating force behind maximalist church statements is a triumphalistic view of the church which tries to find a new position of leadership for the church—this time in terms of being the immediate conscience of political life. There is also mingled with this triumphalism a desire for relevance which requires these very specific statements and not just general principles. The church must be more disciplined in its approach and accept the limits of its competency in terms of the specifically Christian aspects so that it does not try to take over the function of other offices and roles in society.[104]

Ramsey sees here the reality of heresy in the true Pauline sense of the term. If the church adopts particular actions or positions for which there are no specific Christian warrants, it introduces divisions into the life of the church. Some Christians might legitimately hold other specific positions, but for reasons which are not specifically Christian. We cannot put the engine of the Christian religion behind these positions which do not have specifically Christian bases. Different opinions about the war in Vietnam, for example, arise because of different interpretations people have about the domino theory. However, there is nothing the church as such can and should say about the domino theory precisely because such a judgment lies outside its competency. Ramsey thus assumes there is a specifically Christian ethical consideration upon which all Christians agree and which is the only area of competency for the church in speaking to the problems of statecraft.[105]

Church pronouncements on politics must speak for the whole church and not just for one part of it. Ramsey insists that Protestants too easily get around this by the device of having conferences and groups which speak to the church and not for the church. But, in reality, they often do speak for the church and try to obtain a maximum of publicity for their specific pronouncements on political events.[106]

The Second Vatican Council of the younger (Catholic) ecumenical movement, to its great credit, did not, for example, forget the Christian who serves in the armed forces of his country.[107] Ramsey

104. *Who Speaks*, pp. 26–57.
105. *JW*, pp. 456, 520 ff; *Who Speaks*, pp. 55–57.
106. *Ibid.*, pp. 456–458; *Who Speaks*, pp. 32, 33, 124, 125.
107. *Who Speaks*, pp. 132, 133.

urges the tactical device that anyone who attends meetings and conferences which presume to speak for the church should mentally bring with him to the meeting a fellow Christian who disagrees with him on specific economic, political, or social conclusions. As the Christian church we cannot pronounce against this man and his conclusions.[108] Church pronouncements must speak for the whole church on the basis of the specifically Christian aspect and not on the basis of political, economic, psychological, or sociological theory.

There are other theological factors which influence Ramsey's understanding of the role of the church in political questions. Both the substance of specific church pronouncements and the form of recent church conferences or meetings which issue them presuppose a certain type of theology and theologizing which Ramsey cannot accept. Ramsey refers to the predominate theology of the Geneva conference as a "truncated Barthianism." This can best be summarized in terms of the fact that the Christian tries to discern what God is doing in the world to make and keep human life more human. There is a penchant here for thinking of God as acting always in particular ways and that Christians are able to discover with some certitude precisely what God is doing in our world. Ramsey refers to this approach as a truncated Barthianism because it wants to see all reality under the second article of the Creed (Jesus and his Lordship) and fails to see that Christian life and politics also come under the first and third articles of the Creed. Thus such a theology forgets creation and reduces the future to the present action of Jesus in the world, which, in reality seems to leave no room for sin, for criticisms of the present and for the realization that the City of God exists in the future and outside history.[109]

Note the triumphalism inherent in such a theology with its collapsed eschaton, its failure to appreciate that sin is also working in our world and its claim to be able to know with certitude what God is doing in this complex and difficult world in which we live. Ramsey constantly recalls the two cities of Augustine so that one

108. *Ibid.*, pp. 56, 57.
109. *Ibid.*, pp. 76–78.

can never identify Christian social ethics with the different social, political, and economic policies that will always exist in this world. There can be and are a legitimate number of versions of what God is doing in this world and as Christians and the church we should not fault the consciences of others who differ with us not on specifically Christian grounds but on political or economic theory.[110]

Such a theory has contributed to an emphasis on the prophetic element as an important aspect of the church's teaching function in the world. Ramsey naturally has difficulty accepting such a prophetic role for the church and church pronouncements precisely because of the specificity and certitude that accompany such an understanding of prophetism as well as the too easy identification of the present political situation with the kingdom. It is very difficult for us to discern what God is doing in the world. Ramsey insists that politics is science and not prophecy.[111] He maintains that despite the prophecy of Isaias, King Ahaz was right in repairing the water works to bring about the protection of Jerusalem.[112] Contemporary Protestantism has joined prophetic, momentary response to God's action with concrete political decision–making to the utter confusion of what can and cannot be said in Christ's name.[113] The churches must accept the discipline of the self–denying ordinance which properly limits their competence.

This type of theology adopts a very inductive approach as it strives to ascertain what God is doing in the world to make and keep human life more human. Study conferences such as those at Geneva are structured in accord with this theology. Laymen and professional scientists outnumber theologians. The structure is geared to bring about a fruitful dialogue so that the church can speak competently on the problems facing our society. Ramsey finds it incredible that 400 people from all over the world could in two weeks draw up approximately 118 paragraphs of conclusions concerning church, society, and government amid the technical and social revolutions of our times. Ramsey is opposed to this

110. *Ibid.*, p. 21.
111. Paul Ramsey, "Politics as Science not Prophesy," *Worldview*, XI (1968), pp. 18–21.
112. "Does the Church Have Any Political Wisdom for the 70's?," pp. 19–21.
113. *Who Speaks*, p. 128.

format and procedure precisely because the Christian church and Christian theology have no warrant to become this specific. Christian social ethics does not come about through theologians and scientists dialoging together about specific political policies.[114]

Ramsey also bolsters his theological argument by showing that the apparently very relevant and particular pronouncements made by church bodies actually remain quite general and irrelevant. Note that again Ramsey is not content to argue merely from his somewhat *a priori* theological grounds, but he goes into a detailed analysis of many of these statements by the Geneva Conference and other church bodies to show that as a matter of fact they are not truly relevant and specific. Some statements, for example, balance a particular piece of advice to one party with a piece of particular advice to another party, but the result is a generality such as let there be no war.[115]

When the church does speak in the area of social ethics, it must avoid the extremes of irrelevant generalities and relevant particularities which go beyond the competency of the church as such. In theory he distinguishes between direction of the action and a directive for the action, between decision–oriented or action–related economic, social, and political analyses following from Christian themes and specific policy formation that cannot be formulated on this basis. He criticizes the statements made at Geneva on both Vietnam and nuclear war as being too specific and beyond the competency of the church as such.[116]

One of the better models he proposes to Protestants is the model of the Second Vatican Council and the encyclicals of the later popes. Ramsey praises especially the in–principled statement of the Vatican Council about the indiscriminate use of weapons in war which spoke on the basis of Christian principle and did not overstep its competency by trying to make specific judgments about particular weapons through what is for the church an illegitimate subsumption of cases. *The Pastoral Constitution on the Church in the Modern World* expressly calls attention to the limitations of the church speaking in the area of political ethics and

114. *Ibid.*, pp. 60–75.
115. *Ibid.*, pp. 29–45.
116. *Ibid.*, pp. 75–118.

thus follows in the tradition of Pope John, who in *Pacem in Terris* expressly states that some problems can be solved only by the virtue of prudence.[117]

Ramsey has frequently praised the restraint with which Pope John proposed his famous "opening to the left," which called for greater dialogue and detente with the Communists. John cautiously and properly said that it can at times happen that meetings are helpful. There was here none of that blind faith in the power of negotiations which too easily seems to affect the American ethos.[118] Likewise the plea for peace by Pope Paul at the United Nations did not go beyond the competency of the church itself by proposing any specific peace plans or formulas. The pope made the prayerful suggestion that the Vietnam conflict be taken to the United Nations, while carefully noting that judgment of political questions was outside the competency of a religious leader as such.[119]

Thus Ramsey believes that church statements on political matters should be minimalistic and go as far as Christian love can go —but no further. This would be the church, as church, teaching and give direction to statesmen without taking on the function of the magistrate and the citizen which is beyond its competence. The church, for example, should not demand unilateral withdrawal from Vietnam or condemn every escalation of the fighting, since these are matters pertaining to political prudence.

Critique

I have three major criticisms of Ramsey's approach, because of which differences I would not restrict as much as Ramsey the role of the church and the teaching function of the church in the area of politics. First, Ramsey unduly restricts the role of Christian ethics and the church to specifically Christian warrants as such. Theologizing out of the Roman Catholic tradition, I am at home with a different perspective. The Catholic church has often insisted that its teaching on moral and social questions was based not only on the gospel and revelation but also on reason and the

117. *Ibid.*, pp. 125–135.
118. *JW,* pp. 483; 505.
119. *Ibid.,* p. 505; *Who Speaks,* p. 53.

natural law. On the basis of the natural law which is imprinted on the hearts of all men and which Christians share with others, Pope John proposed the teaching contained in his encyclical *Pacem in Terris*.[120] There are some problems and difficulties with such an approach, but the basic insight that Christian ethics and the teaching of the Christian church do not rest only on specifically Christian warrants remains in my judgment most valid.[121]

The Christian vision and teaching must include all the truly human. The ultimate theological justification for this position rests on the doctrine of creation integrated into the whole of God's action. Christian ethics and the church can and should speak in the light of the whole of God's action and not just a particular aspect of it, to use the same argument which Ramsey employed against Brunner. The Christian can and should understand creation in the light of the total action of God and the full Christian perspective, but on the basis of creation he will share much ethical wisdom and knowledge with all mankind. Nothing truly human is outside the pale of the Christian.

My second major difference with Ramsey concerns the exact meaning of the Christian and the moral judgment. This follows somewhat from his restriction of the Christian judgment to specifically Christian warrants, but there are two other important proposals with which I would disagree: the relationship of the Christian moral judgment with particular political judgments, and the relationship of the Christian to the prudential judgment.

Despite some overlap, Ramsey asserts it is necessary to make a vital distinction between "Christian moral judgments on the one hand and particular political, legal, and military judgments on the other. . . ."[122] Our author maintains that not every decision is a moral decision and not every moral decision is a Christian decision.[123] I would distinguish between human or Christian decisions and purely technical or scientific decisions. Technical decisions such as the mathematical judgment that two plus two equals four

120. Pope John XXIII, *Pacem in Terris*, n.5 *Acta Apostolicae Sedis*, LV (1963), p. 258.
121. For a more detailed elaboration of my thought on the development of Catholic social ethics, see my *Catholic Moral Theology in Dialogue*, pp. 111–149.
122. *Who Speaks*, p. 53.
123. *Ibid.*, p. 135.

rest wholly on technical data and do not bring into play the truly human perspective. Human decisions must take into account all the more particular perspectives such as the sociological, the political, the pedagogical, the military, the eugenic and every other aspect that might have some bearing on a particular moral question. The crisis of human culture today seems to arise precisely because we must make human decisions in the midst of such complexity when we cannot expect to have all the requisite knowledge.

No one of these partial perspectives can ever substitute for the truly human perspective. Every particular perspective is narrower than the human and runs the danger of absolutizing what should only be a partial perspective. Our culture realizes this in practice, for even the United States has civilians and not military personnel running the defense department. Teachers alone should not make up boards of education. Hospital boards should contain more than just doctors. We have suffered too much from the narrowness of the expert, who does not have a truly human perspective for making human judgments. There are very few technical judgments which are just military, political, or economic. Most of the judgments Ramsey is talking about are truly human judgments, but they do require technical data as well as factual perceptions. These decisions require the total human perspective to judge and to relativize the essentially limited perspectives of any one science. Truly human decisions of this type cannot be merely political or economic decisions but are truly moral and Christian.

The other aspect of my disagreement about the meaning of Christian moral judgments or decisions centers on the proper understanding of the prudential judgment. I believe that prudence obviously does involve much factual perception and much risk taking about possible future consequences, but it also involves the importance and understanding of the moral values brought to bear on decision–making. Moral values are also a part of the prudential decision even though this also involves fact perceptions and calculated risks. Precisely because moral values are involved, the Christian ethicist and the Christian church do have something to say in this area. Our prudential judgments are affected by our moral values and the relative importance placed upon them. Ramsey gives the impression that these are judgments involving just facts or calculated risks involving the consequences of my actions but unaffected by Christian concerns and moral values.

Ramsey himself has statements which indicate that in some places both in theory and in practice he does not admit that great gulf between the prudential or factual on the one hand and the moral on the other. Prudence or practical wisdom in actual exercise is always at the service of justice and charity and finds fit embodiment for man's sense of justice, as well as fit embodiment for charity.[124] Why can't Christian ethics or the Christian church maintain that some particular action does not seem to be a fit embodiment for justice or for charity?

In practice, Ramsey's own prudential judgments are affected by his Christian perspective and charity. One of the recurring questions in the area of abortion concerns the judgment about the beginning of human life. It seems to me that this is a type of prudential judgment. Ramsey not only insists on the need for Christian ethics and the church to make such a judgment; he also argues that his Christian understanding of the sacredness of human life and the fact that ours is an alien dignity brings him to choose the moment of conception as the beginning of human life, even though the fertilized ovum is no more than a blob of tissue in the uterus or no greater in size than the period at the end of this sentence.[125]

I would argue that prudential judgments are truly moral judgments because they do involve moral values. Since they involve also much technical data, fact perception, and estimation of possible consequences, it is true that one cannot exclude the possibility that his judgment is wrong. Likewise the church cannot exclude the possibility that its particular teaching or judgment is wrong, but this still remains an area of moral and Christian decision-making.

My third general criticism of Ramsey concerns his understanding of church and its moral teaching. He assumes that the church

124. *NMM*, p. 5.
125. Paul Ramsey, "The Morality of Abortion," *Life or Death: Ethics and Options,* Edward Shils, et al. (Seattle: University of Washington Press, 1968), pp. 72–73.

has competency only within the realm of the specifically Christian and there is agreement on this so that divisions should not be brought into the life of the church. Again, I theologize within a different context, for Roman Catholicism has recently gone through the painful experience of realizing that there can be dissent within the church on moral questions, and this is not heresy. Ramsey himself must recognize that on many moral issues he is at variance with his fellow churchmen which is particularly true in some of his positions on questions of medical ethics. Others would not accept Ramsey's teaching on the principle of discrimination in warfare, which he claims is deontologically derived from Christian love. Even on specifically Christian warrants, disagreements exist within the church or within any particular church. There is no reason why there cannot be such possible differences within the church on moral questions. My objection would be to the claim that such specific judgments are proposed as the only possible Christian or church position.

My criticisms center on the fact that Ramsey's understanding of the teaching office of the church and the area of competency of Christian ethics is too restrictive. He wants to restrict the church just to the specifically Christian warrants which he generally interprets in terms of *agape*. In practice he is even more restrictive because he wants to restrict *agape* just to the deontological aspect. Ramsey does admit that there are also teleological concerns in Christian ethics, but in practice he now effectively eliminates them from the purview of the church. As will be mentioned in the discussion of war, he also unduly restricts Christian ethics in the same way. Another aspect of this same restriction is the reduction of church statements just to the principles which can be enunciated on specifically Christian warrants. But Christian ethics embraces much more than just principles. At the very least one must also consider the subject and his dispositions, goals and ideals in the Christian life, moral values, and the decision–making process itself. My understanding of the Christian and Christian love would see these realities as somehow or other also including the human and all its aspects. Christian love embraces or at least is mediated and made incarnate in and through the human. Ramsey seems to propose almost a disincarnate notion of the Christian and of Christian love which always remains above and separated from the human.

Although I disagree with Ramsey's approach, I also have some disagreements with the mentality that he is opposing. Specifically, I too oppose a theological actualism which infers that God is acting in specific actions in such a way that Christians and the church can immediately hone in with certitude on the specific actions of God. Likewise I agree that a contemporary desire for relevance, together with a triumphalism of the church, fails to recognize the legitimate relative autonomy and competency of many other institutions in society including the state. The church cannot possibly have the expertise to speak out on all the complex moral and social problems facing society.

My own solution is based on the realization that good moral discourse should carefully distinguish between the general and the particular, with the realization that the competency of Christian ethics and of the church teaching can include all truly human decisions, but in different ways. In the area of the more general the church can speak with a high degree of certitude. Above all the church should concentrate on this aspect of its teaching mission by entering into the area of what John Coleman Bennett has described as "middle axioms"—somewhere between vague generalities and specific statements on particular issues.[126]

The church must try to clarify and enunciate these intermediate goals, values, and attitudes, which should be present in the situation. For example, the church can and should say that people should examine their consciences to make sure they are not opposed to busing because of some racial prejudice or that powerful nations such as the United States must be ever watchful lest power is used selfishly for our own prestige and aggrandizement at the expense of others. In the matter of welfare reform, the church should enunciate the Christian teaching that the goods of creation are destined for all mankind, and this must influence our legislation. In season and out of season, the church must proclaim the Christian bias in favor of the poor. Ramsey himself would probably not object to statements of this type, but at times the church must go further.

126. John Coleman Bennett, *Foreign Policy in Christian Perspective* (New York: Charles Scribner's Sons, 1966), pp. 144–160.

On occasions, the church should speak out even on specific issues, but it must exercise caution. Obviously the church cannot and should not speak out on every moral and social question facing society. Even though I maintain there is a legitimate Christian and human dimension to these questions, there are many other institutions and organizations interested in these questions with their particular competency and expertise. Through a discerning process, the church must try to identify the more important questions facing our society. Then all the necessary technical data and factual perceptions must be studied so that the information necessary for a competent judgment is at hand. When, finally, the church speaks out on such issues, it must speak with the realization that because of the complexity and particularity of such specific questions the church cannot exclude the fact that other Christians might dissent from such a proposed solution.

If possible, the teaching should be proposed in such a way that the important values present in such a decision are discussed and then the situation interpreted in the light of these values. In the realm of the more specific, the possibility of dissent or the fact that there might be other Christian approaches cannot be forgotten. The church in this way provides some moral guidance, but at the same time recognizes its limitations. Such an approach gives due regard to both the teaching function of the church and to the complexity of specific political and social questions with the recognition that other competencies are also involved in these matters.[127]

---

127. My approach is developed at greater length in my *The Crisis in Priestly Ministry* (Notre Dame: Fides Publishers, 1972), pp. 103–146. Other considerations of the same question which enter into dialogue with Ramsey's position include: R. Bruce Douglass, "Ramsey in Review: Who Speaks for the Church?" and Ralph Potter, "Silence or Babel: The Churches and Peace," *Moral Issues and Christian Response,* Paul T. Jersild and Dale A. Johnson, eds. (New York: Holt, Rinehart and Winston, 1971), pp. 55–71; Roger L. Shinn, "Paul Ramsey's Challenge to Ecumenical Ethics," *Christianity and Crisis,* XXVII (1967–68), pp. 243–247.

| CHAPTER II | The Just War and Other Specific Questions |

Having discussed the more theoretical questions of the ethics of statecraft and politics as well as the role of the church and ethics in politics, our inquiry now turns to the more specific questions in political ethics. Ramsey has written about almost all the major problems facing our contemporary society, and at times he has considered these questions in greater depth than other contemporary Christian ethicists. No Christian ethicist today can discuss these questions without coming to grips with Ramsey's presentations. This chapter will begin with the important question of just war which rightly merits the first and longest consideration. Then the following topics will be treated: justifiable revolution, nuclear war and deterrence, selective conscientious objection, and civil disobedience.

JUST WAR

The just war has been the central issue in Ramsey's own writings on statecraft. This question of just war has served for him as the prism in which his understanding of politics has been applied to this particular question. The just-war theory is precisely a theory of statecraft.[1] No contemporary Christian theologian has written more about the Christian ethics of war than Ramsey. In many ways, war is the most central specific question in political ethics

1. *JW*, p. 260.

because it brings together all the aspects of political ethics and it has been the most important issue in our society for the last four decades. History also testifies to the importance and centrality of this question for Christian ethics and for human life in this world.

The Context

The political and historical contexts in which Ramsey develops his theory on war center on the questions of nuclear war, deterrence, and insurgency warfare. These are the issues that have faced the world community in the last two decades. Ramsey's thought is evident from the subtitles of his two books on the subject. The earlier book, *War and the Christian Conscience,* published in 1961, bears the subtitle: "How Shall Modern War be Conducted Justly?" The collection of his essays published in 1968, *The Just War,* is subtitled: "Force and Political Responsibility."

The intellectual context also helps to situate Ramsey's own approach. Ramsey locates himself between the bellicists and those who tend to reject the use of force, especially nuclear force, or who at least too greatly reduce the use of force in the modern world. Ramsey's teaching on just war sees Christian love as both justifying the use of force and limiting this use. The bellicists fail to see any limits to be placed on the use of force and accept the use of force, provided that the end is good and there is some proportion between the good we accomplish and the evil we bring about. On the other hand, there are many today who, especially in the light of the possibly horrendous consequences of the use of nuclear weapons, would argue against any resort to force at this time or at least greatly curtail the recourse to the use of force.[2]

Contemporary Protestant ethical thinking shapes the theological context within which Ramsey wrote his earlier work. Although a more systematic presentation than his later collection of essays, this earlier work is not truly systematic for it does not study the whole question but concentrates only on some aspects. Ramsey wants to recall to Protestants that a theory of just war is a part of the whole Christian tradition and does not belong only to the patrimony of the Roman Catholic church. Ramsey insists that just war is based on *agape* and not on any alien natural-law theory. It

2. *Ibid.,* pp. x–xvii.

was *agape* which both justified Christian resort to arms and at the same time limited the use of force.[3]

According to Ramsey, Protestant ethics in the 1950's and 1960's has embraced a teleological ethics based on a future–facing *agape* so that present action is justified only in terms of the future good. This is the consequentialism in ethics which Ramsey is constantly attacking. Consequentialism leaves out a great portion of Christian ethics, which must concern itself not only with the end in view but also with the means. The morality of means cannot be determined only in terms of the end in view, but there is an independent evaluation of means so that certain means cannot be justified by any end no matter how much good results. In the specific question of war, too often Protestant ethicists use only a prudential calculus. Against this trend, Ramsey asserts his deontological ethics, for agape *proscribes* certain means no matter what the end.[4]

Ramsey also contends against what he calls the American ethos, which has helped spawn a peculiar concept of the aggressor–defender war. War is legitimate only as defense against unjust aggression, which Ramsey describes as the doctrine of the just occasion, as the criterion for determining the right of recourse to force. This aggressor–defender doctrine is often joined with a resolve to banish force entirely from the political arena, and this becomes the goal of political ethics. Connected with this spiritualization of politics is a voluntarism, which asserts before war it is possible to avoid the catastrophe of war, but once defensive war is necessary it places no moral limits on the defense needed to turn back the aggressor.[5]

Another interesting aspect arising from the American ethos is the technological approach that tries to make the resort to arms impossible. Ramsey asserts that technology alone can never accomplish the goal of banishing force from politics. Technology can never accomplish what man himself is unable to accomplish. This technology would still be based on a deterrent which Ramsey would find immoral, and it still would not accomplish its goal.

3. *WCC*, p. xix.
4. *Ibid.*, pp. 3–14.
5. *JW*, pp. 42–69.

There is no way for technology to develop the perfect deterrent which would assure that nations no longer resort to arms.[6]

Closely connected with this ethos is the liberal theological viewpoint that agrees with the basic thrust of trying to banish force from politics. Thus these people do not really appreciate the just-war doctrine. Many so–called nuclear pacifists share this goal of banishing force entirely from politics even though they pretend to use and accept the just-war theory as a way of indicating the immorality of nuclear weapons. James Douglass, a Catholic pacifist, tries to make perfectionism the ground floor of the Christian life. The result of this is to make the church reject the use of force and become a sect, so that it exists outisde the sphere of politics in this fallen world. Douglass transforms the cross of Christ into a political alternative, but you cannot simply elevate political agency in this way. In this fallen world, force cannot be displaced from any connection with justice and peace, for justice, peace, and concern for others might at times require the use of force.[7]

Ramsey engages in a dialogue with Robert W. Tucker, whom he interprets as upholding no moral limitations on war except the necessities of statecraft alone, even though Tucker does realize there is some immorality in war. The necessity of statecraft means precisely that there are times when evil must be done for the good of the state. But there are no moral limits on the use of force in such a defensive war.[8] Obviously Ramsey is also opposed to Christian pacificism although he does acknowledge it as one option for the Christian. He does not directly refute the religious pacifist position as wrong. Rather he wants to prove positively that Christian *agape* can and does justify as well as limit the use of force.[9] In the light of this background, Ramsey's own development of the teaching on the just war should be more understandable.

Justification and Explanation

The Christian understanding of *agape* shaped the teaching on the just war. Ramsey willingly admits the historical fact that the

6. *Ibid.*, pp. 168–177; *WCC*, pp. 231–272.
7. *JW*, pp. 259–278.
8. *Ibid.*, pp. 391–424.
9. *Ibid.*, p. 501.

early Christians were pacifists and that the first Christians known to have been soldiers were recruits under Marcus Aurelius fighting in the extremities of the empire in A.D. 177. The change-over to just war was not a fall from the original purity of Christian ethics, even though it did apparently reverse the earlier position. It was merely a change of tactics, for the basic strategy of Christian love remained the same. Just war came into being because of the demand of love and service for the neighbor who was being attacked. Thus, love could be and was a motive for early pacifism as well as for just war.[10]

In many different places, Ramsey explains that the concerns of neighbor–regarding love justify the resort to arms as necessary to protect innocent neighbors. Frequently, he illustrates his thesis by developing the parable of the Good Samaritan. Ramsey wonders what Jesus would have the Samaritan do if he came upon the person while the robbers were in the process of attacking him. The obvious implication is the fact that in a world in which there are many neighbors and in which the fullness of redemption and reconciliation are not yet here, there will always be some neighbors who strike, attack, and oppress other innocent neighbors. The Christian can see the work of Christian love and mercy in terms of protecting the innocent neighbor from tyranny and oppression. This presents a decisive fork in the road for Christian conscience. Some will opt for focusing their attention in Christian love on the neighbor in need in the person of the enemy and adopt a pacifist stance. Others will focus their attention on the neighbor who is the victim of the oppression and try to repel the hostile force.[11]

Ramsey argues not only that Christian love logically leads to the use of force to protect the innocent neighbor, but also that, historically, this was the origin of the just-war theory. Augustine evolved this theory on the basis of his understanding of Christian *agape* and not on some natural law or rationalistic basis. The Sermon on the Mount urges the Christian to turn the other cheek. The central significance of *agape* is a concern for the neighbor and not for oneself. Thus it seems that Christian love would never allow one

10. *WCC*, pp. xv–xviii.
11. *JW*, pp. 142, 143, 150, 151, 501.

to kill an aggressor merely on the basis of self–defense. For this precise reason, Augustine would not allow the Christian to kill his aggressor in self–defense. Augustine did not develop his theory of just war by building on the concept that nations have a right to defend themselves against aggression in the same way that individuals have this right.[12]

One of the developments in ensuing Catholic natural-law theory was the shift to a greater emphasis on reason and natural law than was present in Augustine. Even in Thomas Aquinas there are still vestiges of the controlling power of love. Thomas did allow the individual the right to kill in self–defense, but he affirmed that the person could not intend to kill his assailant. Love, which would never allow one to kill another for his own good, was still at work in a somewhat abbreviated way, even in Aquinas.[13]

The just-war theory came into existence as an expression of neighbor–regarding Christian *agape* trying to fulfill its political responsibilities. The fact that all political activity in the life of the earthly city is carried on under the sign of the Tower of Babel and under the covenant of preservation obviously influences the way in which love must make decisions and carry them out to protect certain neighbors.[14]

This development of the Christian just-war theory differs considerably from the aggressor–defender concept of limited war, which is so much the product of our contemporary ethos. Christians did not originally develop the just-war theory in terms of defense of self against unjust aggression. Ramsey does permit military intervention even when it is not done primarily in terms of defense against unjust aggression. One, at times, can and should use force first and also use it legitimately in these circumstances. In this world of *lex, ordo,* and *iustitia,* it may happen that injustice has the power, and/or it may be legal. At times, in the name of justice, it might be necessary to intervene beyond the legal boundaries. Justice, at times, is better achieved if nations have the prudence to use their power and force early. War can be initiated legitimately for the sake of justice even though no military aggres-

12. *WCC,* pp. 15–39; *JW,* pp. 150–152.
13. *WCC,* pp. 39–46.
14. *JW,* pp. 178–180.

sion has occurred.[15] The most the aggressor–defender concept will allow is a preemptive attack which assumes that the enemy has already taken the initiative.[16] At times, political prudence will dictate the first use of force in trying to bring about greater peace and justice in this world as truly the work of Christian love and service in this world.

Ramsey pursues this same type of dialogue with the more recent statements of the Roman Catholic hierarchical magisterium on the question of war. The traditional just-war theory in Catholic theology admitted three reasons for recourse to war: *ad vindicandas offensiones* (to gain vindication against an offense); *ad repetendas res* (to retake something); and *ad repellendas iniurias* (to repel injuries or aggression). Pope Pius XII, in the 1940's, had taken into account the extraordinary destructiveness of modern war and concluded that offensive war is a sin, an outrage, and an offense. War can be justified only in terms of self–defense. Pius XII thus took away the other two traditional reasons justifying the resort to armed force in the just-war tradition.[17]

Pope John XXIII, in *Pacem in Terris,* seemed at first to take away even the resort to arms in terms of defense, but this opinion arose in the light of an erroneous English translation of the encyclical. Even in the light of the "official" but inaccurate translation which affirmed that "it is hardly possible to imagine that in the atomic era war could be used as an instrument of justice," Ramsey uses all his powers of persuasion and argumentation to indicate that the pope did not totally withdraw the right to war.[18]

Ramsey obviously does not want to believe that the pope thus made the Roman Catholic church a sect and withdrew the church entirely from the political community and the military establishments of all nations. John XXIII, in Ramsey's interpretation, which is so typical of his power to analyze in such a way that he can read statements in accord with his own position, stated the framework

15. *Ibid.*, pp. 19–41.
16. *Ibid.*, p. 68.
17. *Ibid.*, pp. 77ff., 191ff., 308.
18. The better translation reads: "Thus in this age which boasts of its atomic power, it no longer makes sense to maintain that war is a fit instrument with which to repair the violation of justice." This is generally interpreted to be in accord with the earlier teaching of Pius XII which still permits defensive war.

for the discussion and not the conclusion. His statement was a challenge to theologians and politicians to find out if, in this atomic age, war could ever be an instrument of justice. The pope's judgment in this case was based on his assessment of the principle of proportion, but there might be other possible assessments.[19] Ramsey also wants to interpret even the correct translation to say that perhaps John did not mean to withdraw morally the right to war or its threat to remove wrongs in cases other than armed aggression. In this way again he points out the inadequacy of reducing the just-war doctrine to self–defense against aggression.[20]

Conditions or Limits of the Just War

Ramsey insists that the same *agape* which justifies the resort to force also limits war and its conduct. The just-war tradition generally speaks of the limits of war in terms of the right to wage war *(ius ad bellum)* and the limits on the conduct of war *(ius in bello),* which are governed by the principle of proportion and the principle of discrimination. Ramsey emphasizes the limits on the conduct of war and specifically develops in great detail the limitation entailed in the principle of discrimination. Christian love inspired the Christian to go to war to protect and safeguard the innocent neighbor against an enemy whose deed was objectively causing harm and injustice. War to refrain the harming neighbor could never be extended to justify direct attacks on those who were not the bearers of the injustice. *Agape* thus developed the principle of the moral immunity of non–combatants from direct attack in time of war.[21] Ramsey insists that this is the primary way in which war is limited; that is in terms of its conduct. "Since at least everyone seeks peace and desires justice, the ends for which war may be fought are not nearly so important in the theory of the just war as is the moral and political wisdom contained in its reflection upon the conduct or means of war."[22]

Augustine did not emphasize the justice of the cause permitting the resort to arms but only the principle of discrimination which

19. *JW*, pp. 192–210.
20. *Ibid.*, pp. 208–210.
21. *Ibid.*, pp. 143–144; 151–153.
22. *Ibid.*, p. 152.

was derived from *agape.* Ramsey points out that for Augustine justice was not the foundation stone for the state. In speaking about justice in war Ramsey quotes only from Book XIX of the *City of God* and downplays the role and positive function of justice. "It is a lively sense of man's common plight in wrong doing and of the judgment of God that overarches the justified war, and not, except perhaps in an incidental implication of what Augustine says—a sense of or clarity about the universal ethical standards that are to be applied."[23]

Ramsey goes on to maintain that if Augustine did assert that there is always only one side that can be regarded as fighting justly in wars, he should not have believed this.[24] Augustine's downplaying of justice in the reality of the state and his insistence on the fratridcidal nature of the loves that form the earthly city influenced his not insisting on the justice of the cause. "The just-war theory cannot have meant for him the presence of justice (i.e., the temporary order and form of these divided loves) on one side; its absence on the other."[25]

In keeping with his downplaying of the role of justice and of the *ius ad bellum,* Ramsey rejects the tribunal model of war and accepts in its stead the model of war as an arbitrament of arms. According to the tribunal model, the injustice of the cause is known and the aggrieved nation thus carries out the punishment of the guilty nation. Ramsey rejects such a model because he despairs of arriving at objective certitude as to the overall justice of the cause. In this world there is constantly much disagreement about justice precisely because our apprehensions of justice are always less than the universal view of justice presupposed by the tribunal model.[26]

In practice, our author seldom gives any consideration to the criteria of the just war that refer to the *ius ad bellum.* In discussing selective conscientious objection, he does mention these conditions—that war must be for a just cause; that it must be officially declared by proper authority; that war must be the last reasonable

23. *WCC,* p. 28.
24. *Ibid.*
25. *Ibid.,* p. 31.
26. *JW,* pp. 131–132.

resort; that not every just cause is worth the fires of war. Ramsey refers to these tests as the teleological tests for the just war, which refer the matter in question to political prudence.[27] However, he has restricted the competency of Christian ethics in the area of political prudence so that there is very little that Christian ethics can say about the criteria of the *ius ad bellum*. The fact that Ramsey does emphasize the deontological aspect of Christian love especially in the question of means in war is another reason explaining his passing over any real consideration of the right to wage war.

These reasons—the downplaying of the role of justice; the emphasis on the deontological aspect of Christian ethics; the fact that prudential decisions belong to the competency of the magistrate —contribute to the fact that Ramsey as a matter of fact does not develop the limiting conditions of the *ius ad bellum*.

What about the *ius in bello* or the just conduct in war? Ramsey admits there are two principles employed in this area: the principle of discrimination, and the principle of proportionality. However, the main emphasis in all his writings centers on developing the principle of discrimination. In *War and the Christian Conscience* he traces the genesis and history of the principle. Ramsey finds this *agape*-derived principle of discrimination in Augustine and the *agape* aspect of it still somewhat present in Thomas Aquinas. Aquinas, by not allowing the victim to intend to kill his assailant, continues to prohibit what love prohibits: the direct killing of any man as an end in itself or as a means of preserving the life that a Christian should love far less than he loves God and his neighbor who might now stand before him in the guise of a murderer or robber.[28]

War and the Christian Conscience then traces the development of the rule of double effect and its use especially in Catholic moral theology. After Aquinas, the rule of the double effect was applied to conflict situations involved with killing the innocent and not the case of the unjust aggressor. This rule tried to sort out the many different effects that our actions have. The death of another can

27. *Ibid.*, pp. 129–130.
28. *WCC*, pp. 34–45.

never be a direct effect of my action, but death as an indirect effect can be justified for a proportionate reason. Thomas, in his discussion of the unjust aggressor, stressed the subjective aspect of intentionality. One could not directly intend to kill the assailant. In the historical development after Thomas, the objective aspect of direct and indirect was developed. A means which is objectively wrong may never be used to accomplish an end, no matter how good it is. The agent must have the right intention. In addition, it must be objectively determined that the action is good or indifferent in itself and the evil effect is not the means to the good effect; but both are associated effects of the action as logically (not necessarily temporally) prior cause.[29]

In the light of this historical development Ramsey states the principle of discrimination in warfare which he derives deontologically from *agape*—one cannot directly intend or directly do the death of non–combatants. The moral immunity of non–combatants from deliberate, direct attack includes two important concepts: the meaning of deliberate, direct attack, and the meaning of non–combatants.

Deliberate, direct attack involves both the subjective intention and the objective act. One can never intend directly to kill innocent people—in this case non–combatants. The act of warfare itself must be directed at military targets and not at non–combatants. The Christian can never use innocent civilians as a means of getting at enemy troops or installations. Human acts often have many different effects. The immunity of non–combatants from deliberate, direct attack never said that non–combatants cannot be killed in war. Often innocent people are tragically killed while one is directly attacking legitimate military targets, but the direct killing of innocent people is always murder whether it is done in war or outside war. Unfortunately, we as a nation too often forget the difference between murder and indirect killing so that in the end we seem unable to distinguish between murder and the tragic, although necessary, indirect killing that always takes place in war.[30]

29. *Ibid.*, pp. 45–59.
30. *Ibid.*, pp. 135–153; *JW*, pp. 397–403; "A Political Ethics Context for Strategic Thinking," pp. 55–56.

A deliberate, direct attack is an act, which in the words of Vatican II cited approvingly by Ramsey, is aimed indiscriminately at the destruction of entire cities or of extensive areas along with their populations. This is a more popular and readily understandable formulation of the concept of deliberate, direct attack.[31] The difference between direct or indirect is not primarily a question of quantity or numbers, but the intent and objective nature of an act aimed indiscriminately at combatants. This understanding is true no matter what kind of weapons are employed and remains an invariable moral principle.[32]

Ramsey does admit that the distinction between combatant and non–combatant is somewhat relative and the function of military technology at any given period of time. Combatancy depends upon the closeness of the person to the function of bearing arms. Ramsey insists that it is not necessary in war to be able to distinguish at all times who is a combatant and who is not. It suffices to know there are non–combatants present, not who they are or where they are. Ramsey strenuously denies that war has become total today so that there are no longer any non–combatants. A non–combatant does not necessarily mean a harmless person but one who does not participate directly or with immediate cooperation in the violent and destructive action of war itself.[33]

In the light of his understanding, Ramsey condemned some of the allied bombing in World War II, especially the bombing of Dresden, as well as the dropping of the atomic bombs on Hiroshima and Nagasaki. These bombs were not aimed at particular military installations but rather were aimed at entire cities with the intention of trying to bring the enemy to admit its defeat. Even if such bombings ultimately shortened the war and saved lives in the long run, they were still morally wrong. Ramsey staunchly maintains that counter-people or counter-city warfare is always immoral and can never be justified. War can never be total, but Christian love requires the limitation of war especially in terms of this principle of discrimination.[34]

31. *JW*, p. 372.
32. *Ibid.*, p. 355.
33. *WCC*, pp. 67ff; *JW*, pp. 153ff.
34. *JW*, pp. 353–355, 534.

The American ethos tries to avoid war and banish the use of force, but once war begins there seem to be no limits. War did not become immorally total primarily because of the technological discoveries of atomic and nuclear weapons, but because in the minds of men the distinction was erased between combatants and non–combatants, and men forgot the moral immunity of non–combatants from deliberate, direct attack.[35] It is immoral to engage in counter–city warfare. It is likewise immoral to deter the enemy with the intended threat that we will attack his cities and population even if it is only a reprisal for what he has first done to us. Indiscriminate attacks on enemy cities or population centers or the intention to do so remains immoral and cannot be justified for the Christian.[36]

Weapons of mass destruction which are not tactical and limited are immoral. The moralist and also the church must constantly proclaim that counter–city or counter–population warfare is always wrong; warfare must be limited to counter–forces warfare. The ultimate decision about particular weapons and their moral use lies outside the competency of the Christian ethicist or the church as such. Earlier Ramsey expressed a personal hesitation about the use and possession of any multi-megaton bombs, but he later admits that there can be tactical nuclear weapons.[37]

The principle of discrimination thus limits warfare, but it does not condemn as immoral all killing of non–combatants during war. Ramsey illustrates the proper understanding of the principle of discrimination with two important examples in contemporary discussions. Ramsey willingly admits that the nuclear bases and military installations at Omaha, Neb., and Colorado Springs, Colo., are legitimate military targets even though in the process of destroying these military targets great destruction will be done to these cities and their civilian populations. The fault is ours for placing these installations so close to populated areas. The onus of wickedness cannot be shifted to discriminate acts of war aimed at the military targets which will unfortunately have the side effect of causing much civilian damage.[38]

35. *Ibid.*, pp. 59ff.
36. *WCC*, pp. 218ff; "A Political Ethics Context for Strategic Thinking," pp. 59–76.
37. *WCC*, pp. 153–170, 283–295; *JW*, pp. 211–358, 342–347, 358–366.
38. *JW*, pp. 213, 438, 481, 509.

A similar question arises in the conduct of insurgency warfare. Guerilla warfare is, in many ways, the modern form of warfare. According to Ramsey guerilla warfare is morally wrong because it strikes the civilian population while attacking as few military targets as possible. The immoral means of such warfare make it immoral no matter how much good might come from it.[39] For the same reason, Ramsey opposed the indiscriminate use of a national boycott against a company which had one independent store in a particular locality which was involved in segregationist practices.[40]

What about counter-insurgency warfare? Ramsey frequently uses the analogy that the guerilla lives among the people like a fish in water. He realistically asserts that insurgents can finally be overcome only by social, economic, and political reform, but military force might be needed in the meantime. If the guerilla chooses to fight between, behind, and over peasants, women, and children, it is he who has enlarged the target area so as to bring unavoidable death and destruction upon a large number of innocent people.[41] Counter–insurgency warfare can be just from the viewpoint of the principle of discrimination so that it is mainly the principle of proportion which is of determinative significance in this case.[42] A large number of the adult population may be combatants and not immune from direct attack. The remainder of the people in the area can be brought within the range of legitimate collateral damage, i.e., they are not directly attacked, but they unfortunately are the indirect victims of the attack aimed at combatants. Realize that for Ramsey the principle of proportion can rule out such indirect killing as being disporportionate.

Writing in 1966, Ramsey believes that the bombing against North Vietnam had been discriminate, although he later objected to some indiscriminate bombing aimed at iron and steel works. Ramsey also believes that a correct assessment of the bombing of the central highlands and other areas of South Vietnam under the control of the Viet Cong is discriminate. The problem is to determine if it is proportionate. Too many people have erroneously

---

39. *Ibid.*, pp. 480, 481.
40. *Sit–In*, p. 107.
41. *JW*, pp. 434–439, 480–481, 507–509.
42. *Ibid.*, pp. 435, 436.

condemned this bombing as indiscriminate.[43] The fact that these weapons may be disproportionate also urges us to take the time, effort, and money to produce weapons of war that cause less damage. Ramsey is willing to accept the use of tear gas and to develop other forms of less disproportionate weapons even though he does recognize some risk of uncontrollable escalation.[44]

In addition to the principle of discrimination, the principle of proportion also governs the morality of the conduct of war *(ius in bello)*. Ramsey has often asserted, both in his writings on nuclear warfare and on counter-insurgency warfare, that military action becomes disproportionate long before it is indiscriminate.[45] Warfare is disproportionate when it no longer has the capacity to effectuate political purposes that are worth it in terms of a cost/effect analysis of all the factors involved. Proportionality serves as a very important limit on the conduct of warfare, and a limit that applies even sooner than discrimination.[46] Since Ramsey, at times, considers things just from the perspective of discrimination and finds that they are moral, it does not follow that such actions would also be proportionate. In this matter it is easy to receive a false impression of what Ramsey is really trying to say. Remember that part of the context is his dissatisfaction with the way in which many people talk about indiscriminate killing when in reality it is not indiscriminate although it might be disproportionate.

But Ramsey does strongly maintain that the judgment of proportionality lies outside the competency of the ethicist as such and of the church as such. "And no perspective upon politics more definitely refers the matter to be decided to the statesman and to the public forum than the principle of proportion."[47] The ethicist, churchmen or ihe church, as such, cannot determine that the collateral civilian destruction necessary to defeat the enemy cannot be a lesser evil than an enemy victory. Ramsey very succinctly

43. *Ibid.*, pp. 441–445; 533–534. One wonders if these judgments do not involve a subsumption of cases which Ramsey elsewhere claims are beyond the competency of the ethicist as such.
44. *Ibid.*, pp. 465–478.
45. Ibid., pp. 294, 435, 436.
46. "Does the Church Have Any Political Wisdom for the 70's?," p. 56; *Ibid.*, pp. 403–406, 444–449; "A Political Ethics Context for Strategic Thinking," pp. 57–58.
47. *JW*, p. 455.

summarizes his own thoughts on this question: "Since the amount of combatant destruction and the amount and quality of the collateral civil damage is governed by political prudence, this is the crux of the decision statesmen must make. Private individuals and groups of citizens of course should contribute to the democratic debate that in its measure forms public policy. Christians who engage in this debate do so out of the inspiration of their faith, no doubt; but they do not bring to it any particular instruction that foretells how the proportionately right national decision should be made, or that enables them in advance to attach the label 'immoral' to one and not possible to another of the alternatives."[48]

Ramsey maintains that Christian ethics could not justify or incriminate particular wars without the addition of certain presumptions about the fact situation. Fact-finding and fact-perception, however, do not belong to the area of ethics, or the church or conscience as such but to the realm of prudence. The ethicist and the church should be concerned about clarifying moral discourse and moral concepts.[49]

In this context, Ramsey wants to enter a clarification about his attitude to the American involvement in Southeast Asia in the last few years. He contends that as ethicist he neither endorsed nor condemned the American action in Vietnam. Ethics, in his view, proscribes or endorses sorts of actions, but should not enter the realm of political prudence by subsuming cases under principles of analysis. Indeed, Ramsey claims that editorial changes made in the titles of two of his essays may have contributed to the misconception that he was making particular conclusions about the justice of the Vietnam war. His title, "Dissent from Dissent," was changed to "Vietnam: Dissent from Dissent;" while his title, "How Shall the Vietnam War be Justified?" was changed to "Is Vietnam a Just War?" But these essays themselves refrain from particular judgments of proportionality and prudence about the justice of that war.[50]

48. *Ibid.*, p. 439.

49. The limits of Christian ethics in the area of prudence are often mentioned in Part Five: "Vietnam and Insurgency Warfare," which includes Chapters 18 to 24 of *JW.* Also recall the discussion in Chapter One.

50. "A Political Ethics Context for Strategic Thinking," pp. 60–61; "Does the Church Have Any Political Wisdom for the 70's?" pp. 35–36; *JW,* pp. 489–512. Ramsey in a private interview described the problem of the misleading titles.

Critique[51]

Historical analysis. Our author does not really present a full historical development of the just-war tradition. Ramsey's own pioneering work in this area, especially among Protestant ethicists, has occasioned many further historical studies. However, his historical approach is too sketchy and inadequate. One comes away with the impression that Ramsey has taken certain texts and in a brilliant way showed how they fit in with his interpretation of the just-war tradition. But it is obviously easier to criticize Ramsey today in the light of the voluminous literature which has appeared on the history of the just-war theory since Ramsey first wrote on the subject more than ten years ago.

Ramsey's treatment of Augustine is much too restricted and consequently erroneous in presenting his total approach to the question of war. The only texts Ramsey cites are from Book XIX of the *City of God,* but there are difficult hermeneutic problems about these texts. There are at least eight major texts outside the *City of God* in which Augustine treats the question of war, but Ramsey does not mention these texts.[52]

There is a need to study the just-war tradition not only in its intellectual history but also in terms of the political, social, and cultural circumstances of the time. Again one cannot criticize Ramsey for failing to do this, since his purpose was not to write

51. For a helpful bibliographical essay on Christian ethics and the question of war, see Ralph B. Potter, *War and Moral Discourse* (Richmond: John Knox Press, 1969), pp. 87–123. I have also been helped by reading the following unpublished dissertations: Ernest Ruede, O.F.M. Conv., "The Just War Theory and the Problem of Deterrence" (unpublished S.T.D. dissertation, Accademia Alfonsiana, Rome, 1969); Stephen Edward Lammers, "The Just War Tradition: An Examination of Some Modern Claims to That Tradition" (unpublished Ph.D. dissertation, Brown University, 1971); Frederick Hooker Russell, "The Medieval Theories of the Just War According to the Romanists and Canonists of the Twelfth and Thirteenth Centuries" (unpublished Ph.D. dissertation, The Johns Hopkins University, 1969). I must make special commendation of two excellent dissertations which were of immense help to me: D. Thomas O'Connor, "War in a Moral Perspective: A Critical Appraisal of the Views of Paul Ramsey" (unpublished Ph.D. dissertation, Claremont Graduate School, 1972); LeRoy Walters, "Five Classic Just War Theories: A Study in the Thought of Thomas Aquinas, Vitoria, Suarez, Gentili and Grotius" (unpublished Ph.D. dissertation, Yale University, 1971).

52. These other texts have been mentioned by a number of the commentators on Augustine's teaching, but for the following list I am indebted to LeRoy Walters, "Augustine and Calvin on War: A Study in Comparative Ethics," an unpublished paper. Augustine's discussions of war can be found in the following texts: *On Free Will,* pp. 1, 5, 11–12; *On the Lord's Sermon on the Mount,* pp. 1, 19, 20–56, 68; *Against Faustus,* pp. 5, 22, 70, 74–79; *Epistle 47 to Publicola,* p. 5; *Epistle 138 to Marcellinus,* pp. 2, 9–15; *Epistle 189 to Boniface,* pp. 4–8; *Questions on the Heptateuch,* pp. 6, 10; *Epistle 229 to Darius,* p. 2.

such a detailed history. But one can interestingly compare his treatment on pacifism in the early church with his discussion of just war. His intention is to show that acceptance of the justified war is not a fall from the purity of love as expressed in pacifism but rather is a demand of that same Christian love. He sees *agape* behind both, but he explains the reality of Christian pacifism not only in terms of *agape* but also in terms of a mixture of motives —danger of idolotry, anti–imperialism, unhealthy attitudes toward physical reality, apocalyptic expectation. He still maintains that a Christian pacifism was in the main a consistent deduction from the new foundation laid by Christ.[53] His treatment of the justification of war fails to mention any other considerations except *agape* although there obviously were other considerations impinging on the development of the just-war teaching. In fact some might argue that other considerations were more basic than *agape*.

Ramsey interprets Augustine as justifying the recourse to arms in the name of *agape*, but he furnishes little direct proof of this.[54] At the very least, Ramsey does not give enough importance to the reality of justice which is present in the thought of Augustine. Augustine did define the just war in the following terms. "Just wars are usually defined as those which avenge injuries, if a people or city, on which war is waged, has neglected either to punish what has been done wickedly by its own [citizens] or to give back what has been carried away."[55] Augustine also insists that war is not a matter of taking revenge on others but rather a means of punishment or correction.[56] There is also disagreement with Ramsey's assertion that Augustine maintained that both sides in a war could have justice on their side. Roland Bainton interprets Augustine as saying that only one side could be just; whereas Frederick Russell admits that for Augustine both sides could have a just cause, but one is more just.[57] At the very minimum one has to

53. *WCC,* pp. xv, xvi.
54. *Ibid.,* pp. 15–33.
55. *Questions of the Heptateuch,* 6, 10.
56. Herbert A. Deane, *The Political and Social Ideas of St. Augustine* (New York: Columbia University Press, 1963), pp. 160–163.
57. Roland H. Bainton, *Christian Attitudes Toward Peace and War* (Nashville: Abingdon Press, 1960), p. 99; Russell, "The Medieval Theories of the Just War According to the Romanists and Canonists of the Twelfth and Thirteenth Centuries," pp. 58–59.

conclude that Augustine does mention considerations of justice which serve as limiting factors or criteria concerning the *ius ad bellum*.

Even among those who tend to see Augustine's view of the state as more negative, there is still a greater appreciation of justice in the state and justice in the just-war theory than there is in Ramsey. Herbert A. Deane characterizes the state as the return of order upon disorder, but he develops the criteria by which according to Augustine war is just or not *(ius ad bellum)*. Deane also interprets Augustine as characterizing war as a legitimate punishment for a state that openly flaunts the standards of earthly right and justice.[58] Even if Augustine does justify the resort to war in terms of *agape*, justice still plays an important role in determining when a war is just.

Ramsey's interpretation of Aquinas as still employing *agape* as the primary consideration because he does not permit the defender to intend to kill the assailant also seems open to question. One could very well come to this conlcusion on the basis of natural law or human reason. Justice demands that I only intend to incapacitate my aggressor or stop his aggression and not kill him. Ramsey himself in a different context does accept such a "natural" and non–agapaic explanation of Aquinas.[59] Ramsey, without sufficient warrant, tries to interpret Aquinas in accord with Ramsey's own thesis.

There are also questions about the historical development of the principle of discrimination as proposed by Ramsey. There is no developed position in Augustine at all on the protection of innocents or non–combatants in times of war.[60] Ramsey does not explicitly claim to find such a developed theory in Augustine, but he definitely claims to base his understanding of the principle of discrimination on Augustine's teaching that the Christian cannot kill his own assailant. Since there is no explicit discussion in Augustine on non–combatant immunity, and since Ramsey himself

58. *The Political and Social Ideas of St. Augustine*, pp. 160ff.
59. Raul Ramsey, "The Morality of Abortion," *Life or Death: Ethics and Options*, Edward Shils, et al., pp. 84–86.
60. Richard Shelly Hartigan, "Noncombatant Immunity: Reflection on its Origins and Present Status," *Review of Politics*, XXIX (1967), p. 209.

recognizes that there is no parallel between killing in war and killing in self–defense, I would question Ramsey's interpretation. In fact, Augustine does not see killing (either of innocent or guilty) as the primary moral problem in war, but the real evils in war are love of violence, wrongful cruelty, fierce and implacable enmity, etc.[61] Richard S. Hartigan concludes his study of the particular question with the observation that Augustine indicates explicitly, often and in several contexts, that he is unconcerned with the fate of the innocent so far as the necessities of just war are concerned.[62]

As an historical fact, the moral immunity of non–combatants from deliberate, direct attack was not formulated until the time of Francis de Vitoria in the sixteenth century and apparently was not derived from *agape*. This is a later development in the tradition, greatly influenced by such limiting factors in war as the Peace and Truce of God, which then saw non–combatants as innocents who are immune from direct attack. The later tradition in its philosophical and especially legal aspects solidified and developed the position put forth by Vitoria.[63]

At the very least, this historical development argues against the fact that from the beginning the principle of discrimination formulated as the moral immunity of non–combatants from deliberate, direct attack was historically present as deontologically derived from *agape* and proposed by Augustine. The principle seems to have developed in the course of time in the light of the on–going Christian experience of the reality of war and efforts to limit war. Remember that the concept of direct and indirect, especially in terms of the objective act and not just the intention, is a comparatively late development in Roman Catholic moral theology which came well after Thomas Aquinas.

My position on the substantive question of just wars differs somewhat from Ramsey's. I do believe that war at times is a reluctant necessity, but I would take very seriously the notion of the last resort and always find a great reluctance about making the deci-

61. *Contra Faustum*, XXII, p. 74; Richard Shelly Hartigan, "Saint Augustine on War and Killing: The Problem of the Innocent," *Journal of the History of Ideas*, XXVII (April-June, 1966), p. 203.
62. Hartigan, in *Journal of the History of Ideas*, XXVII (1966), p. 203.
63. Hartigan, in *Review of Politics*, XXIX (1967), pp. 204–220.

sion that war is necessary. The limits of war, especially the *ius ad bellum* and the principle of proportion, should receive much greater emphasis than they do in Ramsey; and this serves then to limit war much more than Ramsey does. Likewise I maintain that this position—a very reluctant necessity to admit the justice of war because of the many evils that accompany it as well as the limits on the right to war and the conduct of war—does not depend on any specific Christian criteria but could be arrived at on the basis of human reason and our perception of justice.

War as ultima ratio. A very important criticism of Ramsey focuses on his too easy justification of war and his failure to more severely limit the resort to arms so that it is truly a last resort or *ultima ratio* as the tradition maintained. Augustine obviously agonized over the whole question of the resort to arms; Ramsey too easily justifies war in the name of *agape.* He does not seem to appreciate the great hesitance that should accompany such a decision, and then leaves no real way of limiting war in a moral way when it concerns the *ius ad bellum.* Why does Ramsey accept too readily the resort to arms?

First, the understanding of Christian love and its ramifications in this question. Ramsey has frequently pointed out that one cannot simply call non–violence the Christian approach to social ethics and social justice. Ramsey often speaks about Christian love as non–resisting love and as an ethic of preferential love for the neighbor. No Christian could kill to defend his own life, but when other persons are in need the Christian should resist the evil done to those persons.[64] Non–resisting love becomes a preferential ethic for the concern of the neighbor in need. Non–resisting love comes to acknowledge the single exception that force should be repelled and bearers and close cooperators in military force directly should be repulsed lest more harm be done to certain neighbors.[65] He maintains an infinite qualitative difference between resisting and non–resisting love; whereas the question of choosing violent or non–violent means is a question of economy in the effective use of force,[66]

---

64. *BCE,* pp. 166–184.
65. *Sit–In,* pp. 100–123.
66. *JW,* p. 502.

Between violent and non–violent means, I think there is more than just economy in the effective use of force. There does seem to be a qualitative difference between violent and non–violent means both in theory and in practice, even though it might not be as great a qualitative difference as between resisting and non-resisting love. By admitting in practice no qualitative difference between violent or non–violent means, Ramsey has no firebreaks to argue against the escalation toward violence. Both Christian and human considerations would tend to see a greater qualitative difference between violent and non–violent means. Think, for example, of the different effect on the one engaging in violence or non–violence. It appears that once Ramsey justifies resistance he is left with only the limits of the principle of discrimination and the principle of proportionality, whose application lies beyond the competence of the ethicist and the church as such. There is not enough tension in his thought between violence and non–violence.

Secondly, the same lack of tension appears in Ramsey's understanding of the relationship between pacifism and the acceptance of the justified war. The first and decisive fork in the road for Christian conscience in this matter is between pacifism and the acceptance of war, depending on whether Christians focus their loving gaze on the neighbor who is the enemy or on the neighbor who is the victim of hostile force.[67]

The problem here appears to be the either–or aspect of it, with the resulting danger that the whole picture is not kept in view. The analogy of the fork in the road indicates that each position then goes its own way and there is no influence of pacifism and its perspective on war. War is thus accepted in the name of *agape*, too easily, with no real limitation and with no sense of tragedy and reluctance—despite occasional mention of some reluctance. There should be a horror of going to war and a striving for peace on the part of all men that contributes to a real reluctance for any nation to embrace war. Once Ramsey puts the engine of Christian love behind the resort to force (to use an image he frequently employs against those who use Christianity to justify their pruden-

67. *JW*, p. 501.

tial, political decisions), he does not seem able to accept the "last resort" characteristic of war, the reluctance that must always accompany such a resort to arms, and the need to put strong moral limits on the recourse to war. The Christian attitudes to pacifism and resort to war are not exactly the same, even if on occasion love can reluctantly accept the use of force.

Underlying many of my particular disagreements with Ramsey's approach is the moral evaluation, as well as the horror and revulsion connected with war and killing. Ramsey properly insists on the important distinction between murder and killing, but he seems to give too little ethical significance to killing, be it the direct killing of combatants or the indirect killing of non–combatants. The disvalues involved in taking life are such that this can only be done with great reluctance, as a last resort, and with some truly overriding value to be obtained. Perhaps Ramsey remains unduly influenced by the Augustinian notion that death does not constitute the primary evil of war, because physical death is a reality that we will all experience at one time or another.

For the Christian and the believer the greatest gift received from God is the gift of the fullness of life in union with God, but the gift of physical life is the necessary condition and symbol of the gift of eternal life. The sacredness of human life remains the cornerstone of human existence in this world. The individual's right to life forms the most basic right to be preserved and enhanced in human society. War cannot help but affect our understanding of the value and importance of human life. Amid the realities of war, human life becomes very cheap and expendable.

In addition, war also generates so many of the other evils which Augustine himself described in terms of love of violence, insensitivity and hatred to neighbors, feelings of revenge and reprisal. War wreaks great hardship and suffering on peoples in terms of destruction of property, ways of living, the separation of families, the loss of homes, the constant fear of death. The excesses connected with war have been present throughout history, even, and maybe even especially, in our own day. Think, for example, of the demand during World War II for unconditional surrender, a demand which is certainly against the Christian understanding of the function and limitation of war. Amidst the reality of war there seems to be an escalating tendency away from the fundamental moral considerations.

At times, Ramsey's approach seems much too rationalistic in the bad sense of the term, as if he does not truly appreciate the horror which must be connected with war. Especially in the light of his downplaying the conditions and criteria for just war, Ramsey too readily accepts the reality of war. One can read all his writings on war without having any impression of the horrors involved in modern warfare. The distinction between murder and killing is of fundamental importance, but the taking of life, even reluctantly, should be very upsetting to the moral sensitivities of human beings who realize the precarious gift that is life. Ramsey appears to draw too strict a dichotomy between moral wrong and merely physical evils, such as killing and warfare.[68]

A third specific disagreement concerns the emphasis placed on sin by Ramsey and its application to the question of just war. Again he rightly calls to mind the fact that sin is a part of reality and must be taken into consideration, but he overemphasizes sin at the expense of other elements in the Christian perspective of man and the world—creation, incarnation, redemption, and resurrection destiny. Ramsey does not give anough importance to the positive value of creation still existing even after sin; nor does he pay sufficient attention to the transforming (albeit a limited transforming power) aspect of redemption and resurrection destiny on our human existence. This is an important theological difference between Ramsey and myself, and it does have significant practical ramifications. The predominate influence of sin too easily justifies recourse to coercive force.

However, Ramsey also appears to be somewhat selective in his understanding of the effects of sin. Although an acknowledged follower of Reinhold Niebuhr, he does not appreciate the fact that sin particularly affects the judgment of nations and communities, especially powerful nations tempted to abuse their power. *Moral Man and Immoral Society* tried to put man on guard against the effects of sin and of pride in the judgment and actions of nations.[69]

---

68. *BCE,* pp. 182–184; *JW,* pp. 431, 533–536.
69. Reinhold Niebuhr, *Moral Man and Immoral Society* (New York: Charles Scribner's Sons, 1932).

Any balanced Christian approach to the question of war should give some consideration to this viewpoint. There will always exist great dangers of self-deception, especially on the part of powerful nations which are most prone to self–assertiveness in the name of justice. Ramsey apparently disregards this aspect of the Christian teaching on sin as it applies to nations and war today. In a somewhat polemical way he insists on the fact that power in the modern world brings with it great responsibilities—a fact that cannot be denied; but power also brings with it great temptations. This aspect of human sinfulness serves as a constant reminder to check our own motives and purposes as a nation in the matter of war.

All these important theoretical differences point to the practical difference that I do not think Ramsey takes seriously enough the fact that war must be an *ultima ratio*. Ramsey obviously mentions the *ultima ratio* on many occasions, but he interprets it as a just barely reasonable form of human activity. This appears to be a generic judgment that puts war too easily into the category of reasonable human behavior, and does not forcefully point out that each time one must agonize with the reluctant decision of accepting war as the only possible solution.[70] Interestingly, Ramsey does occasionally stress the *ultima ratio* character of war which appears quite regularly in the context of revolution, but is often not mentioned in the context of war.[71] Perhaps other factors which are neither deontological nor specifically Christian have exerted some influence here.

Ius ad bellum. I also differ with Ramsey's approach to the moral limitations on war—a point which only accentuates his too ready acceptance of war in the name of Christian love. Specifically Ramsey downplays and even negates the role of justice in the matter of the just war, so that for all practical purposes he gives little or no attention to the *ius ad bellum.* He limits himself to considerations of the *ius in bello,* and then primarily to the principle of discrimination. There are occasional and seemingly peripheral references to the *ius ad bellum* and the matter of just cause, but Ramsey does not develop this very important aspect of the limitation of war.

70. "Force and Political Responsibility," pp. 57–60.
71. *JW*, pp. 460–528.

Perhaps natural-law thinkers in the past have too readily exalted the power of man's reason to arrive at truth and certitude in these matters, but Ramsey errs by maintaining that men cannot arrive at adequate judgments about the justice of the cause. By practically ignoring man's ability to arrive at a judgment about the just cause of war, Ramsey takes away what must be a very important limitation on the right to resort to force. The very fact that deception in this area is so possible, should make one all the more careful to stress the importance of this judgment despite the obstacles in the way of discovering the absolute and totally objective view of things.

The just-war tradition, in my view, does need some correction in terms of its model of war as a tribunal with the one nation punishing the fault and guilt of another nation. Obviously one cannot expect from nations involved in a dispute the impartiality of a judge; nor should a nation exercise this office toward another nation. But I cannot agree with Ramsey, who apparently jettisons considerations of justice and sees war under the model of an arbitrament of arms. He is correct in rejecting the test of wills as a model for war, but war is also more than an arbitrament of arms.[72] At the very least it is an arbitrament of arms in the service of a just and peaceful social order. Ramsey's selection of an arbitrament of arms as the model for war is consistent with his deemphasis on the role of justice in the state and especially in the just-war theory. Even though the older tribunal model is inadequae, a proper model of warfare must include in a primary place elements of justice and not just an arbitrament of arms.

Although one can indicate a general consistency in Ramsey's downplaying of the role of justice, there also appears to be some inconsistency involved, especially by his practical neglect of the considerations of justice. His own theories do not permit him to neglect completely the aspect of justice. His general ethical theory gives an important place to justice—a point he strongly affirms against some Protestant ethics. He admits a place for justice in his understanding of the state with the three concentric circles of *lex, ordo,* and *iustitia.* He justifies war to protect and help the innocent neighbor, but this certainly implies a judgment about the

72. *Ibid.,* p. 221.

justice in the situation. When talking about the possibility of arriving at a true judgment of justice in the matter of the right to war, he refers to the overall justice of the different regimes; but the judgment about the just cause in war does not and should not be that broad. In his first book, Ramsey does admit that the prince and the soldier can and should make a judgment about the relative justice in the conflict between one side or another.[73]

I grant there is difficulty in making such a decision when the person himself or his nation is involved, but this is all the more reason to insist on the need to make an honest decision in this matter and to point out the dangers of a narrowly selfish approach. Without this consideration, one effectively robs the just-war tradition of perhaps the most important limitation on the resort to armed conflict.

Ius in bello. In discussing the limitations on the conduct of war, Ramsey does mention both the principle of discrimination and the principle of proportion, but he severely limits the competency of ethics and of the church in the area of proportion. This, in my judgment, is an undue limitation which again has disastrous consequences in terms of real limitations on warfare. There are really two different reasons for these limitations. Ethics is limited because it deals with the questions of moral discourse and concepts, but has no specific competency in the area of prudence. The church is limited because it deals only with the specifically Christian aspects, and thus prudential decisions lie beyond its scope and competency. Ramsey does recognize the competency of the citizen as such in this area of political prudence.

Chapter One explained my disagreements with Ramsey's restrictions of the role of ethics and the church in the matter of political prudence and the realm of proportionality. These same reasons with special emphasis on the nature of the prudential judgment are likewise operative in his restriction of ethics as such, and not just the church, in the matter of proportionality. He apparently takes away from the competency of ethics as such a very great area of the prudential or the teleological. Ethics, for all practical purposes in the matter of war, is narrowed down to the

---

73. *BCE,* p. 173. He also occasionally mentions the need to make judgments about the relatively more just cause, e.g., *JW,* p. 385.

deontological aspect which surfaces in the principle of discrimination.[74] Ramsey almost reduces the role of ethics to the question of explicitly formulated, general principles which are deontologically derived from *agape*. I would maintain that ethics can and should say much more about the area of proportionality, even though on specific questions it cannot claim to have such certitude as to exclude all fear of error. Likewise ethics must consider virtues and dispositions of the subject, proximate goals and ideals, and the moral judgment itself.

Ramsey's in–principled love ethic, with its deontological basis and downplaying of the teleological and prudential, also leads to other problems because it does not and cannot give sufficient importance to historical, contingent reality. In summarizing Roman Catholic hierarchical statements on peace and war, Ramsey points out that the popes have recently restricted the right to war only to the case of defensive war, a judgment which is based on the horrendously destructive power of modern weapons of war.[75] Ramsey's deontological ethic which does not depend on the contemporary facts and which has little to say in the area of prudence cannot really be an adequate ethical approach in an era which calls for a more historically conscious approach. Ramsey really does not give sufficient attention, and by his method cannot give sufficient attention, to the terrible destructive power of modern weapons. At times, it seems that he recognizes this fact and does make some comments in the light of prudential judgments which his system would seem to exclude from his competency. Generally speaking, however, his method does prevent him from giving sufficient attention to changing circumstances such as the destructive power of modern war.

The same, somewhat limited, love deontology also prevents a just evaluation of all the elements that enter into the human decision in the matter of war. Ramsey, even in his first book, argued

---

74. Occasionally Ramsey himself seems to make some judgments based on prudence, but he might claim that he is here speaking as a citizen and not as an ethicist. Perhaps the best example of this is found in "Toward a Test-Ban Treaty," *Worldview*, VI (1963), pp. 4–10. Here he definitely gives prudential advice to the magistrate. Interestingly, this essay was not included in *The Just War*. This same tendency appears in much of his writing on deterrence.

75. *JW*, pp. 77–79, 307–310, 375–377.

that pacifists often see physical death as the greatest evil, whereas for the Christian perspective this is not so. Christian *agape* was able to justify the physical deaths which accompany war when this is necessary. However, once having justified the taking of physical life, Ramsey then passes over many of the other moral problems connected with war which should at least be mentioned and elaborated so that they may be weighed in the judgment of proportionality. Augustine, as Ramsey, did not see physical death as the worst evil in the world or even in the case of war, but Augustine did call attention to the other evils that war engenders such as violence, greed, hatred, and enmity. These are important factors which exert a deleterious effect on human society and cannot be neglected in any consideration of war.

I turn now to the principle of discrimination itself. I would deny that it is necessarily derived from *agape*. A better knowledge of the historical tradition as mentioned above would argue against Ramsey's contentions. Logically, justice, natural law, and human reason could arrive at the same conclusions. Historically, it seems that it was justice which shaped the principle as it finally emerged in the sixteenth century. Here, too, there seems to be some inconsistency in Ramsey's argument for the principle solely in terms of *agape*. In one place he acknowledges that the same principle could be derived from the Old Testament. He likewise admits other ways in which one can arrive at the same principle.[76]

Furthermore, in developing the principle of direct and indirect killing, he quite closely follows the Catholic teaching which claims to be based on reason and the natural law. He argues that *agape* would change the Catholic teaching on direct and indirect only in the case in which both child and mother would die unless some action is taken. Ramsey thus strenuously upholds *agape* as bringing about the principle of discrimination, but he uses Catholic natural-law theorizing to determine the precise meaning of this principle. In the specific details of the moral immunity of non–combatants from deliberate, direct attack, Ramsey admits there is no difference between what *agape* calls for and what reason calls

76. *Ibid.*, p. 145. His position on selective conscientious objection (*JW*, pp. 124–137) assumes that all men in a pluralistic society can accept this principle of discrimination.

for. I think Ramsey does not really prove any distinctive contribution of *agape* to the principle of discrimination.

A second question concerns the deontological character of the principle of discrimination. Ramsey in this and other questions argues strenuously that all of Christian ethics cannot be reduced to teleology or to consequentialist considerations. In the question of war, Joseph Allen has argued that one can arrive at the principle of discrimination from a consequentialist perspective provided that one takes into account the broadest perspective of consequences. The danger in teleological calculations, according to Allen, comes from trying to justify the means in terms of only one end and failing to consider all other consequences.[77]

In general, I think Ramsey does not give enough importance to the role of teleological considerations. In addition, in other places he does seem to exaggerate the deontological character of Christian ethics and *agape*. However, I would tend to agree that the principle of discrimination does rest on non–consequentialist grounds. I fear that in the name of consequences the protection of the innocent from direct attack is too easily jeopardized.

One other problem concerns the exact meaning of the principle of discrimination and its distinction from the principle of proportion. Ramsey wants to keep the two quite separate. The principle of discrimination corresponds to the intention of the act and the principle of proportion to the consequences of the act. The question of numbers does not determine if the killing is direct. Thus Ramsey conceives as a direct killing an act whose primary thrust is directed to the elimination of one very important combatant even though a thousand innocent persons may be killed. However, he does recognize that the immediate effects but not ultimate consequences are tied up with the intention of the act. He reluctantly admits that in extreme cases it will be proper to move from events in the objective order to intention.[78] I see no theoretical reason why Ramsey could not conceive of the killing of one most important combatant as direct even though a hundred thousand innocents might also be killed.

77. Joseph L. Allen, "The Relation of Strategy and Morality," *Ethics*, LXXIII (1962-1963), pp. 167–178.
78. *JW*, pp. 348–358, 397–402.

I would give more importance to the objective aspect of the intention as known from the immediate effects of the act itself. Ramsey seems to be able to stretch the principle of discrimination further than I would be inclined to do. In addition his assertion that the principle of proportion, which would be more restrictive in these cases, lies outside the competency of ethics as such means that Christian ethics does not limit warfare as much as it should. Thus I would argue against the morality of the American bombing in South Vietnam on the basis of the principle of proportion. In addition I am dissatisfied with Ramsey's assertion that such bombing is discriminate.

JUSTIFIABLE REVOLUTION

Ramsey has written comparatively little—not even one full essay—on the question of revolution; but he has raised the subject on a number of different occasions. He has tried to evaluate revolution in the context of his whole understanding of the use of force to achieve political purpcses. In some contemporary writing on revolution today there is a romanticization of revolution and a failure to appreciate the harsh realities involved in war. Ramsey acutely points out the dangers of this romanticization and attempts to impose the demands of logic upon the situation. He stresses the connection that must exist between the question of war and the question of revolution, since they both deal with the use of armed force to achieve political purposes.[79]

In *War and the Christian Conscience* Ramsey devotes a chapter to the question of justified revolution, but he really comes to grips with only one aspect of the question which at that time appeared to be the most important—the fact that just war called for the authorities officially to declare war. The just-war tradition made the magistrates responsible for declaring war; but who may resist and legitimately initiate the use of force against the government and magistrates? Does this forbid all possible revolutions? According to Ramsey, Luther was conservative on this point and denied the right to revolution, but Calvin did give this power to the lesser magistrates and opened the door to the interpretation that even

79. *JW*, pp. 427–464, 480–481, 508–509.

private citizens can at times act in a magisterial capacity.[80] Ramsey's historical development in this chapter is very sketchy and does not point out the arguments for revolution and tyrannicide which had been proposed before Luther.

This theory of constitutional or official revolution is of great significance. The lack of justice is not the only criterion to justify revolution. One must wait long past the point where simple justice began to be violated until there arises some one or some group capable of representing a better *pax–ordo* and capable of bringing this to pass without letting worse befall.[81] Notice the consistency here with Ramsey's general insistence on order as a terminal value together with justice and with his understanding of the state as based on a union of wills.

His later writings discuss only two important aspects of the question of revolution in our day. First he argues against a romantic theology of revolution which too often assumes an uncritical acceptance of all revolutionary movements. Ramsey here insists on the judgment of God on all human enterprises, as well as the need for some order to replace the older order. In keeping with his political theory he does propose a justified revolution theory, but he insists that war is a last resort and other means must be tried first.[82]

The second question which Ramsey addresses in the matter of revolution is the principle of discrimination. He logically applies to revolution the same approach he used for just war. The principle of discrimination applies in war, in revolution, and in domestic resistance. A just or good cause is not the only ethical consideration. Unfortunately, in the matter of revolution too little attention is given to the independent question of means. Ramsey maintains that the two forms of modern war—nuclear and guerilla—have both become indiscriminate. Ramsey, without any modification or qualification, condemns insurgency warfare because it deliberately strikes at the civilian population even though it might do this only selectively. The fact that it is selective terror does not redeem what is inherently wrong.[83]

80. *WCC,* pp. 114–133.
81. *Ibid.,* p. 124.
82. *JW,* pp. 460, 528.
83. *Ibid.,* p. 432.

In domestic resistance, the fact the something is non–violent does not make it necessarily right, for resistance can be non–violent and indiscriminate.[84] As noted earlier, Ramsey illustrates such a wrong method in the boycott of national companies because of the segregationist policies of a somewhat independent outlet in a particular case.[85]

In the question of revolution, Ramsey tries to apply the principles that govern the use of force and political responsibility. There is definitely a consistency in Ramsey's approach, but at the same time there are some divergent emphases which might come from his theological ethics but also from his own human instincts. In reality, Ramsey does restrict the *ius ad bellum* in the case of revolution much more so than he did in the case of the just war. Recall the insistence here on revolution as a last resort as well as the important role that the need for order would have in limiting the right to revolution. The impression received by the reader is that Ramsey the polemicist writes to uphold against others the fact that war can be justified, while he tries to dampen the easy acceptance of revolution on the part of many in our contemporary society. In the process it seems that, at the least, his different emphases are not always totally consistent.

When Ramsey discusses the just-war criterion of a reasonable expectation of success, he mentions that there can never be assurance on this point. The statesman always exists in a world in which there is action, interaction, and counteraction. In later writings, Ramsey indicates that this fits in with the ethical description of responsibility developed by H. Richard Niebuhr.[86] But in this context one obviously can never have assurance about what the outcome will be. Ramsey remarks that it was Hitler's stupid decision to open up a second front with Russia that rendered Churchill's decision to go to war a reasonable one.[87] In the matter of revolution, the rhetoric stresses a greater emphasis on the need for an assurance of a future structure and order in society.

Ramsey's understanding of insurgency or guerilla warfare is

84. *Ibid.*, p. 461.
85. *Sit–In*, pp. 106ff.
86. "A Political Ethics Context for Strategic Thinking," pp. 10–17.
87. *JW*, p. 526.

strange—for he defines it in such a way that it is always immoral since it involves direct strikes on the civilian population. At the least this indicates that he is very much influenced by what he perceives to be the fact situation in the insurgency warfare he refers to (especially Southeast Asia). Insurgency does not necessarily have to be carried on this way, and should at least be defined neutrally so that one can then judge just insurgency from unjust insurgency.

I would agree with Ramsey that the principle of discrimination is applicable in the case of revolution just as it is in war, but I would be more flexible in my interpretation than he. Ramsey defines the combatant as anyone who is an actual bearer of force.[88] In a revolutionary situation the bearers of the hostile force are truly those who are perpetrating the grave injustice. Again, in this case, one can apply Ramsey's understanding that non–combatancy is not a question of one's subjective innocence or guilt, but rather the function he has with regard to force or, in my opinion, also injustice. This would logically include a greater number of persons in the role of "combatants" than those who are actually wielding force and weapons of war in the defense against a revolution. Those who are functionally involved in perpetrating the grave injustices that justify revolution are also truly combatants. The revolutionary or guerilla is not morally restricted by the principle of discrimination to attacking directly only soldiers and military personnel.

I also agree with Ramsey's position that resistance is not Christian, or ethical, or right only because it is only non–violent, for non–violent means may also be indiscriminate. But again Ramsey does not give enough importance to the distinction between violent and non–violent means. There are degrees of being a bearer of injustice so that one cannot accept merely the absolute distinction between "combatants" and "non–combatants." So too there are important degrees of difference between violence and non–violence. There can be degrees of perpetrating injustice which would never justify killing but which might justify non–violent forms of resistance.

88. *Ibid.*, p. 435.

Ramsey correctly insists on having a logically consistent position on the use of force for political purposes, a stance too often forgotten by some contemporaries who romanticize revolution. Nevertheless, it does seem that he stresses more the limitations on revolution than he does on war. Likewise he fails to mention a significant difference between the two in the contemporary context. The danger of escalation both in countries involved and in weapons employed is much greater in the case of war. Nuclear weapons, for example, would not be used in a revolution.

One other significant factor escapes his attention—what may be called a Christian bias toward the poor and the powerless. I realize there are many problems in bringing this to bear on the political scene and that it is only one element out of many that must be considered. The Christian, however, can never forget the special claim of the poor and his need to tilt in their favor. The people seeking revolution are usually those who are poor and oppressed, a fact which cannot necessarily justify revolution or the means employed, but an important consideration nonetheless.

In general, I would be more flexible in the case of justified revolution than Ramsey, both in terms of the right to revolution and in the understanding of the principle of discrimination in the revolutionary situation. I still share his admonition against those who romanticize revolution and forget about the importance of some order and future structure for society, as well as the human costs in any resort to violence.

NUCLEAR WAR AND DETERRENCE

Modern war in the 1950's and 1960's came to mean insurgency warfare; but, even more, it meant of nuclear war and nuclear deterrence. Ramsey again outlines his own "just war" position as existing between the technological bellicists on the one hand and the nuclear pacifists on the other. Technological bellicists have some help from that ethos which tries to do away with war completely. As a result, they will be willing to threaten anything to prevent war, or once war has started they will place no limitations on defensive war. In this context, our country developed its notion of minimum nuclear deterrence based on the threat of massive retaliation on Soviet cities and population if they had first attacked us. This threat of nuclear annihilation or destruction serves as the umbrella protecting nations from ever going to war in these nuclear days.[89] On the other hand, nuclear pacifists are opposed to any use and possession of nuclear weapons, even for deterrence and propose unilateral disarmament.[90]

Ramsey argues on the basis of his interpretation of the just-war theory, but again giving primary importance to the principle of discrimination, for rational armament and rational disarmament. Our nation will always need armaments to fulfill its manifold responsibilities in the contemporary world, but we should never use or intend to use weapons which are counter-city or counter–people warfare. This calls for eliminating such weapons, but building up a weapons arsenal which is both moral and strong enough to deter. Such rational armament and disarmament will probably be more costly than the minimum deterrence which tries to get "more bang for the buck" but which is immoral in its dependence on counter–city warfare.[91]

Nuclear deterrence is one area in which Ramsey admits he has changed his mind over the years based on both a better knowledge of the facts and a better understanding of the moral principles.[92] The entire discussion on this issue, which consumed quite a bit of Ramsey's time and effort in the early 1960's, illustrates the wide-ranging intellectual interests of our author as well as his keen, analytic mind in dealing with the logical explanation of his position. Specifically, he was in dialogue with both military strategists and with theologians who were discussing in great detail the implications of the principle of the double effect in this area.

In *War and the Christian Conscience*, Ramsey accepts as a matter of principle deontologically derived from *agape* that a nation cannot employ or use weapons that are used for counter-people

89. *JW*, pp. 42–69.
90. *Ibid.*, pp. 215ff. Here Ramsey tries to show that these two opposed schools are really brothers under the skin who believe strongly in peace by disarmament.
91. *Ibid.*, pp. 211–258.
92. *Ibid.*, p. ix. On page 251, Ramsey claims that the change in his opinion is due to the fact situation, but the fact situation of whether having nuclear weapons involves an immoral intention to use them indiscriminately also involves some moral theory about the different kinds of having and also an extended moral analysis of the role of indirect effects.

or counter–city warfare rather than for counter–forces warfare. There is an interesting embellishment of this basic thesis. Ramsey tries to argue in one entire chapter that warfare is not feasible, deterrence is not feasible, and what is more, politics is no longer feasible unless this central war with its intrinsically unjust counter–people approach is abolished. He urges the leaders of the world to tell us that no human or political good can come from doing anything so essentially wrong or irrational.[93]

But Ramsey has often insisted that the principle of discrimination in war is deontologically derived and asserts what can never be done no matter what good can be accomplished. Here he definitely spends a long chapter trying to point out that this immoral approach is not feasible. Certainly there is nothing wrong in employing such an argument, but for Ramsey there is the problem that he has insisted on the non–teleological character of the principle of discrimination. At least in theory what is deontologically wrong might be feasible. In practice there is the danger that feasibility might become so strong a consideration that it erodes deontological concerns, so that military success overrides moral considerations. Earlier I called attention to the fear that Ramsey's interpretation of discrimination might be too broad. In deterrence he has later retracted a position which he once hesitatingly proposed. There is also another problem with Ramsey's employment of an argument based on feasibility. He admits that professionally as an ethicist he has no interest in proving a moral deterrent to be an effective one.[94]

What is rational, politically beneficial armament? In this section of his earlier book he explains in great detail the position of Thomas E. Murray with whom he generally agrees, except for some reservations on the question of the morality of multi–megaton weapons. Ramsey argues for cutting back our weapons system to rational armament which may and really does involve building up our overall weapons system at greater cost in intellectual effort, moral resolve, and financial backing. Ramsey here enters rather hesitatingly and reluctantly into the question of fact where he has

93. *WCC,* pp. 218–272.
94. *JW,* p. 336.

no competence as an ethicist or as a Christian as such. He believes against Murray there is greater consistency in pressing the argument for rational armament against the possession or use of any multi–megaton bombs at all.[95]

He does not see an *a priori* reason for a radical distinction between nuclear and chemical bombs, for the moral question really concerns just use in counter–forces warfare and clearly unjust use in counter–people warfare. Ramsey tends to think that rational nuclear armament must be confined to the lower ranges of kiloton and fractional kiloton weapons, which are close to the conventional weapons they replace.[96] With his typical rhetoric and flare for using the phrases of others in a different way he calls for unilateral, rational armament, and disarmament on political, military, and moral grounds.[97] Nations must make an essentially unilateral resolution to use only just and purposive means for legitimate and limited ends, although the reality of delayed repentance can enter into this question for the statesman who is a Christian and trying to bring about a moral deterrent.[98] Ramsey argues at length that moral values alone and not technology will bring about a proper moral limitation of war.

The change in Ramsey's thinking on deterrence emerged in 1963. Previously his moral judgment together with his fact perception (which he hesitatingly accepted as a layman and not as an ethicist) led him to condemn our nuclear deterrent which was based on counter–city reprisals and to argue somewhat hesitatingly against the use and the possession of multi–megaton bombs, for in both cases there seemed to be a true intention to do something morally wrong; i.e., to engage in counter–city warfare. Even in his later writings, Ramsey maintains that it will always be wrong to have such an intention. Ramsey's later writings phrase the crucial moral question in these terms: "whether possession of massive nuclear weapons is reducible to the crime of planning to use them over civilian targets."[99]

95. *WCC*, p. 280.
96. *Ibid.*, pp. 292–294.
97. *Ibid.*, p. 301.
98. *Ibid.*, p. 308.
99. *JW*, p. 252.

Ramsey responded in 1963 that the technical possibility of nuclear deterrence before and during war can now be indicated, as can its compatibility with the moral prohibition of both the use and the intention to use nuclear weapons or any kind of weapons in direct attack on centers of population.[100]

Earlier in this pivotal essay Ramsey had tentatively mentioned a series of policy decisions which seem imperative at this hour for the free-world's security. He developed here a graduated type of deterrence with firebreaks as an employment of arms which is moral, rational, and effective. To suspend morality from the threat of attacks on cities and population centers is both morally wrong and not effective in deterring lesser types of war. Rather than begin (and end) with the ultimate threat of counter–population warfare, Ramsey instead builds up a series of graduated policy strategies with firebreaks in between which thus are morally in accord with both the principle of discrimination and the principle of proportionality.[101]

The more important concern is how Ramsey now justifies a nuclear deterrent including the possession of "massive nuclear weapons."[102] Ramsey is now obviously convinced of the need for an effective deterrent for both guaranteeing security and preventing war. He develops in detail the type of deterrence that is morally permitted without becoming immoral through the intention to engage in counter-population or counter-city warfare. In this and subsequent articles, including a fascinating debate contained in a CRIA pamphlet, *Peace, the Churches and the Bomb,* Ramsey exposes and explains his concept of the legitimate deterrent use of nuclear weapons.[103] This interesting, but long and complicated debate cannot be adequately summarized in a few pages, but the patient reader will find it a good example of scholastic debate— with both the strengths and the weaknesses of such a debate.[104]

---

100. *Ibid.*
101. *Ibid.,* pp. 225–248.
102. *Ibid.,* p. 252.
103. *Ibid.,* pp. 211–258, 314–366.
104. *Peace, the Churches and the Bomb,* James Finn, ed. (New York: Council on Religion and International Affairs, 1965). Contributors include John J. Wright, Theodore R. Weber, Walter Stein, William V. O'Brien, Justus George Lawler, and Paul Ramsey. Ramsey responds to his critics in this symposium in an "Occasional

The first form of acceptable deterrence is that obtained from disproportionate combatant damage. This presupposes, as Ramsey does, that nuclear weapons may be used against legitimate military targets. It is not necessary to invent some possible military uses in such exceptional cases as a fleet at sea, for many military installations in the nuclear age are fifty or more miles in diameter.[105]

In 1972, Ramsey has considered again some of these questions about deterrence and military strategies, and he reports with obvious relish that some military planners and strategists are now accepting counter–combatant forms of deterrence and not making deterrence depend on counter–city warfare. The threat to attack armed forces only would be moral and effective because nations would regard the loss of whole armies a graver threat than the loss of a few cities. This situation would also make powerful nations vulnerable to challenges by conventional weapons on the part of third powers.[106] Ramsey is now willing to admit that a counter–combatant deterrent, if effective, may be required by the principle of proportion rather than the counter–forces deterrent he proposed earlier. The counter–forces deterrent suggests a threatening power concentrating on nuclear forces which would entail risk of greater destruction than counter–combatant warfare or deterrence. Ramsey as a moralist was trying to determine the morally accepted limits for deterrence, but the principle of proportion in the light of some contemporary strategic thinking might call for counter–combatant deterrence or warfare as the practically less destructive.[107]

The second step in Ramsey's graduated deterrence arises from the deterrence coming from the collateral civilian damage that is itself unavoidable and unintended. Collateral civilian damage is an indirect effect of war waged in accord with the principles of discrimination and proportionality, for in almost all cases direct at-

Paper" published in 1965 by the Council on Religion and International Affairs and reprinted as Chapter 15 in *The Just War*.
105. *JW*, pp. 251–253; "A Political Ethics Context for Strategic Thinking," pp. 62–67.
106. Paul Ramsey, "The MAD Nuclear Policy," *Worldview*, XV (1972), pp. 16–17.
107. "A Political Ethics Context for Strategic Thinking," pp. 67–69; "The MAD Nuclear Policy," pp. 17, 18.

tacks on military targets will also cause other civilian damage. Ramsey first referred to this deterrent effect as the "indirect effect of the foreseeable indirect effects of legitimate military conduct."[108] Walter Stein in the ensuing debate in *Peace, the Churches and the Bomb* accuses Ramsey of a radical abuse of double-effect categories which require the moral dissociation from the indirect effects. But I cannot dissociate myself from the indirect effects if I really want them in order to deter the enemy. The decisive flaw in Ramsey's position comes from the dependence of the deterrence on the collateral civil damage which is essential to the purpose of nuclear strategy, directly indispensable, radically wanted and yet to be sanctioned as a side–effect.[109]

Ramsey in the light of this dialogue modifies his description of the case without in any way changing the conclusion. Collateral deterrence is better described as a direct and wanted effect of the unwanted, indirect, collateral consequences of even a just use of nuclear weapons. There is no reason why we should not want the immediate and direct deterrent effects of the prospects of extensive collateral damage, which, although unavoidable, is radically unwanted in fighting a modern war. Deterrence is prospective, whereas Stein's argument presumes that deterrence is retrospective so that he argues backward from the actual deterrence to the here and now.[110]

Ramsey then offers three analogies to prove his proper use of the categories of direct and indirect effect. One analogy does in my opinion show an abuse of double-effect categories. John Rock obtained important biological and medical knowledge by gathering fertilized ova from the uteri of women who for medical reasons had to undergo hysterectomies. The doctors told the women to chart carefully the time of coitus so that the doctors could then determine how old the fertilized ova were when found in the excised uteri. Ramsey presupposes in this case that the fetus at this time is a human being. The killing in this case was unintended and indirect because there were legitimate medical reasons for doing a hysterectomy, and the act was directly intended and done as a

108. *JW*, p. 252.
109. *Peace, the Churches and the Bomb*, p. 81.
110. *JW*, pp. 318–321.

hysterectomy for medical reasons. The fact that Doctor Rock thus obtained fetuses for study was the direct and wanted effect of the unwanted, indirect, collateral consequences of a just hysterectomy.[111]

There is a fallacy in the argument here which comes from a failure to appreciate all the ramifications of non–intending, which means that one must try to prevent the indirect effects if this is possible. It would seem that the proper conclusion, based on Ramsey's presuppositions, was to tell the women not to have intercourse in the days immediately preceding their operation rather than encourage them to have intercourse at this time, because there is an obligation to prevent the indirect killing if this is possible.

In the case of the collateral civilian damage resulting from legitimate bombing there is also an obligation to use the means that will bring about the least collateral damage possible, all other things being equal. This could very well argue against the use of nuclear weapons in situations in which other bombs would suffice to destroy the military target and would not have such disastrous collateral damage. The use of nuclear weapons could be wrong on the basis of proportionality long before the principle of discrimination was violated. Ramsey willingly admits this in theory. However, his legitimacy of deterrence is based only on considerations of the principle of discrimination and the fact that this collateral damage would not be intended.

Ramsey's third form of graduated deterrence comes from the dual use that such weapons have by their objective nature. This nation should declare its intention never to engage in counter–city or counter–population warfare, but the fact that the weapons can be used in such a manner will have a deterrent effect. This is a powerful deterrent inherent in the weapons themselves that cannot be removed.[112] However, here again it seems there is an obligation to clearly renounce the intention to ever use them in this way, a fact which this nation has not done.

The fourth aspect of his proposed graduated deterrence has

111. *Ibid.*, pp. 321–325.
112. *JW*, pp. 253ff, 329ff.

always been more questionable in Ramsey's own mind, and lately he definitely rejects it. This deterrence arises from deliberately intended ambiguity to deter the opponent. Some might argue that the aspects of graduated deterrence mentioned in the first three steps are not effective enough to deter the action of the enemy so that it will be necessary to go one step further. Ramsey emphatically opposes any intention to engage in counter–city warfare, but at one time he hesitatingly proposed the possibility of deliberately encouraging some ambiguity about our intention. The appearance of a partial commitment or the appearance of a possible commitment may be enough of a commitment to deter the enemy. Ramsey thus acknowledges some value in what pejoratively has been called the argument from bluff. From the first time he hesitatingly proposed such deterrence, Ramsey has expressed reservations about it.[113]

The question is whether deterrent effects which flow from a specific type of studied ambiguity about our real intention can really not involve a wrong intention. How can such deterrence in the technical language be *praeter intentionem?* Deception in war is not necessarily wrong, but one might argue that in this case the truth is due to the enemy. In the light of this, Ramsey prefers not to appear to deceive in this case, but still if it is necessary to bring about deterrence and save life, he is willing to go along with it. There are also problems of implementing this in a democracy.[114] He never does respond to the objection that in such a situation of deception, some lower echelon people would necessarily have to have the intention of using the weapons in an immoral way even though the leading magistrates know they never would use them in this way. Someone, to make the deterrent believable, would have to have the intention to pull the switch to initiate counter–city warfare. Notice that in his latest writings Ramsey has rejected this approach because he does not see how an imput of ambiguity about the counter–people use of nuclear weapons is possible without morally intending it.[115]

Ramsey continues to argue against the morality of minimum

113. *Ibid.,* pp. 254–258, 299–302, 333–336.
114. *Ibid.*
115. "The MAD Nuclear Policy," p. 18.

deterrence based on the intention to engage in counter–city warfare. He did change in accepting the need for an effective deterrence with nuclear weapons and continues to argue for the need of a greater number of tactical nuclear weapons which are called for by a morally limited war and deterrence strategy.

In general, I disagree with Ramsey's position in terms of his acceptance of so much nuclear deterrence. On the basis of discrimination I would be more hesitant to admit the morality of multi–megaton weapons. On the basis of proportionality there seems to be no proportionate justification for such massive nuclear weapons with their tremendous destructive power. This argues not only against the massive nuclear weapons but especially against the great number of such stockpiled weapons. Here I can only indicate briefly what would be the first steps in my own approach.

Ramsey willingly admits that he is trying to be as maximalist as he can in the question of deterrence. He takes advantage of the fact that nuclear war becomes a disproportionate means to any political purposes long before it becomes indiscriminate. Graduated deterrence must threaten something disproportionate in order to be effective in deterring the other. But he quickly adds that not every threat of something disproportionate is necessarily a disproportionate threat. The political good to be obtained by deterrence is the prevention of all the evil effects of war or the escalation of war's destruction. Threats proportionate to such great goods can obviously go quite high. There can be disproportion involved when something is done but not necessarily disproportion when it is merely threatened, because the compensating goods are more important in the case of deterrence.[116]

Even accepting Ramsey's formal argument about the difference between a disproportionate threat and a disproportionate act in war, I would still insist that he does not limit proportionality enough. I apparently see greater evils connected with war and its threat than he does. Likewise by withdrawing both the competency of the church and the ethicist in this area he again loses an important source of limitation.

116. *JW*, pp. 269, 270, 302–307; "The MAD Nuclear Policy," p. 19.

One of my continuing differences with Ramsey is that the human act is broader than any of its particular aspects such as the military or the political science aspect. For this reason, I do see the competency of the ethicist and the church in the realm of the prudential precisely because Christian and human values are at stake here. In his third reply to the objection that graduated deterrence threatens something disproportionate Ramsey responds that there is an obligation never to mean to do and accept damage disproportionate to political goals, but he supposes no military commander would calculate on actually doing any such thing.[117] Perhaps Ramsey is emphasizing only the subjective intentionality of the commander, but as a matter of fact military commanders have, even by Ramsey's own admissions, done such things. The theoretical basis for such a possibility is the fact that the military aspect is only one limited part of the total human picture.

Another important contingent factor which does not receive enough importance in Ramsey's theory is the danger of escalation which would be present in any use or threatened use of nuclear weapons.[118] Historical reality in the last few decades reminds us that escalation has occurred very often as attested to by the bombings in World War II both with conventional weapons and with nuclear weapons. The wars and police actions following that have shown some restraint in this matter, but the danger of escalation remains great, especially as soon as one passes the nuclear threshold. Again, in theory Ramsey is not able to give enough importance to this very significant aspect which depends on considerations of prudence.

Ramsey's choice of an arbitrament of arms as the model for war, although better than the model of a test of wills, is conducive to a maximalist tendency in the matter of arms and deterrence. Obviously the side with the stronger arms will win. This seems to forget that there are always factors other than brute force involved in conflicts between nations. Granted that it is hard to

117. "The MAD Nuclear Policy," p. 19.
118. Ramsey occasionally mentions the danger of escalation (e.g., *WCC*, pp. 296, 297), but he does not develop this at length, nor does it really enter into his determination of the upper limits of deterrence.

weigh, but the elements of justice and right should have some effect on a nation and their resolve. It seems that lately in this country we have come to appreciate some of these other factors. This is a somewhat nebulous factor, but one cannot realistically assess the human situation of nations just in terms of armed force. There are many other types of power which are not based on sin or the need to constrain sin and which are operative even in relationships among nations.

SELECTIVE CONSCIENTIOUS OBJECTION

Ramsey's writings on just war have occasionally brought up the question of selective conscientious objection, but his major treatment comes in a long essay which appears in the *The Just War* and appeared in shorter form elsewhere in 1968.[119] His discussion is interesting both in terms of its consistency with his own position on just war and in terms of Ramsey's usual willingness to challenge what appears to be the accepted party line in contemporary church circles.

In part of a chapter in the earlier book, *War and the Christian Conscience*, Ramsey points out that not even conscientious objection to all wars is a right that the Constitution gives to all, but rather is an exception or privilege granted by Congress. No political society can continue to exist if as a matter of principle it accords absolute rights to possible errant individual consciences. Such an aggregate individualism would destroy the possibility of political community. Ramsey then held that the churches should appeal to Congress for the possibility of exemption on the ground of just war objection to particular wars. He does not necessarily advocate that Congress adopt such an approach because it may run counter to the very purposes of government and seriously impair its right to repel injury. Ramsey realizes that his moral acceptance of the just-war theory does not necessarily entail the legal recognition of such a theory as the basis for selective conscientious objection.[120]

119. *JW*, pp. 91–137; *Conflict of Loyalties: The Case of Selective Conscientious Objection*, James Finn, ed. (New York: Pegasus, 1968).
120. *WCC*, pp. 128–133.

The problem centers on the conditions necessary to make this a legal right and all the prerequisites for granting it legal status. Invoking his negative evaluation of recognition by the current American ethos of the necessity of a responsible use of armed force, Ramsey does not believe that SCO can become a legal reality until there has been an upgrading in our political discourse. Too many people think that war is always wrong and that the just-war theory is a means to discredit wars, one by one. Likewise, there is a rampant individualism which does not give enough importance to the conscience of the laws which calls for the benefit of the doubt about justice to be given to the authority who has made the decision to use force.[121]

Ramsey reviews the report of the National Advisory Commission on Selective Service, which was against SCO, as well as the minority report, which favored it. The acceptability of SCO depends on two things. First, there must be a moral ethos supporting a moral consensus about the proper use of force on which the individual can base his judgment about a particular war, for otherwise there would be only rampant individualism which is diametrically opposed to the very existence of political communities. Second, there must be criteria to determine the sincerity of the person and his beliefs about SCO. Political community cannot continue to exist without these two safeguards.[122]

In determining the moral grounds for one's decision, there must be such grounds apart from the political reasons on which the authority of the community has based its decision to go to war. Political community demands that a nation be able to dispose itself authoritatively in a particular way with the citizens acknowledging the authority of the disposition unless and until they can clearly say that it is unjust.[123] Recent Supreme Court decisions and legislative enactments have not helped because they have expanded the concept of religion so that it is even harder to distinguish the religious and the ethical from the political. However, as Christians with an understanding of the transcendence of the person we should try to find some way of expressing this transcen-

121. *JW*, pp. 95–99.
122. *Ibid.*, p. 100.
123. *Ibid.*, p. 123.

dence in terms of some form of exemption granted to conscientious objection to a particular war.[124]

Ramsey raises as a possibility that the sincerity test alone, especially in terms of some type of alternative services, might be all that is required with no judgment about the validity of the decision and the grounds on which the decision against the war was made. Ramsey is not willing to accept just a sincerity test because, as he proposes it, it is not based on the transcendent moral claim of the person but on the political claim that this will make for a better political community. But this political judgment can be rebutted if, as a matter of fact, it does frustrate the purposes of political community.[125]

Ramsey then proposes his own approach. The objective moral consensus to which appeal can be made and which is distinguished from merely political considerations involves two approaches. First, the international law because of which the individual could object to a particular war insofar as it is in violation of international conventions and the laws of war and in violation of agreements to which his nation is a party. Second, violations of the principle of discrimination in the just war. This would eliminate as a basis for SCO the teleological tests not because they are any the less moral but because they cannot be adequately distinguished from serious political opposition to a particular war.[126] Since Ramsey willingly admits that modern war becomes disproportionate long before becoming indiscriminate, he is adopting only a very restricted form of SCO.

Ramsey presents an interesting and forceful presentation of his position even though his one essay cannot be considered an exhaustive discussion of the question. However, there are some problems of consistency in his own approach. He wants to find some room for selective conscientious objection because the case for it is an intrinsic moral one while the obstacles are in the empirical order.[127] In reality, he proposes arguments against some forms

124. *Ibid.*, pp. 107–124.
125. *Ibid.*, p. 127.
126. *Ibid.*, p. 130. It is interesting to note that Ramsey admits here that opposition to the war on these grounds is not merely prudential but also moral. This appears to be inconsistent with some of his other statements.
127. *Ibid.*, p. 124.

of SCO which are not merely empirical obstacles which might be embedded in law or culture. He rejects the use of the teleological tests because of his understanding of politics and government and their relationships to morality.

Ramsey has insisted that the principle of discrimination is derived from Christian *agape,* but he now wants to make this the basis for selective conscientious objection in a pluralistic society. He at least implicitly admits that all citizens on the basis of moral reasoning can arrive at such a principle. On the other side of the coin, he fails to realize that in a pluralistic society not all citizens could agree on his understanding of the principle of discrimination. In reality, there is great dispute even among Christians themselves about this principle.

The teleological tests for the just war have been abandoned because these involve the area of political prudence which serves as the basis for the public policy decision so that moral objection to a particular war cannot be distinguished from serious political opposition. Even Ramsey's deontological test can bring about the same problem. Ramsey has acknowledged that the subsumption of cases or the judgment about the discriminating nature of a particular weapon or of a particular attack is also a matter of political prudence. In this case the judgment is not as morally pure and distinguished from the political judgment as our author seems to indicate.

Another problem, perhaps more in the form of a question to be answered, concerns whether an isolated instance or how many instances of indiscriminate attacks would be necessary before one could object to a particular war. Ramsey must come to grips with this question.[128]

My own position would be to favor a broader selective conscientious objection with the realization that a judgment about this is always open to change in the light of what happens in any political

128. For a discussion of Ramsey's position on SCO, see John A. Rohr, *Prophets Without Honor: Public Policy and the Selective Conscientious Objector* (Nashville: Abingdon Press, 1971), pp. 175–180; also, see Marvin M. Karpatkin's review of *A Conflict of Loyalties* in *New York Times Book Review* (November 2, 1969), pp. 10ff. A rejoinder by Professor Richard W. Day defending Ramsey and a further comment by Karpatkin appear in *New York Times Book Review* (November 30, 1969), p. 62. Ramsey himself responded in *New York Times Book Review* (February 1, 1970), p. 24.

community. I have problems with two aspects of Ramsey's thinking which appear throughout his political theory because of which
I would be more open to the possibility of SCO. First, I think he
wants to separate too easily the political and the moral judgment.
I argued that he too tightly restricts the competency of the ethicist
and the church because of this distinction. In this essay he admits
that there is a moral question involved but it must be separated
from the political question, for otherwise, political community
would be fractured. I do not think that such a separation is possible. As indicated above, even Ramsey's deontological principle of
discrimination involves political prudence in its specific applications. It is impossible to separate totally the moral from the political in this question.

Second, Ramsey has insisted on understanding the state in terms
of the agreement of wills of the people and overemphasizing order
at the expense of justice. I would give more room to justice, a
position which in theory more readily accepts disagreement on
particular, individual questions. The question can be asked if allowing an exception in this case might not lead to allowing exceptions in other cases and destroying the life of the political community. However, since this issue involves killing and one's very
immediate cooperation in the act of killing, this particular question can be distinguished from most other questions in the life of
the political community.

In practice it seems to me that the sincerity test alone could
serve as the basis for the judgment made by the state in particular
cases. There will always remain the problem of agreed-upon moral
standards in a political community. I do not think that the granting
of SCO on such a broader basis would jeopardize the life of the
political community. Such a judgment must always be open to
revision in the light of the facts, but emphasis on the transcendent
dignity of the human person as well as my understanding of the
state make me argue in favor of SCO.

CIVIL DISOBEDIENCE

Paul Ramsey has not only addressed himself to practical questions of international political ethics but also to national or domes-

tic questions. James Childress describes him as the Christian ethicist in the United States who has given the most vigorous attention to issues surrounding the question of civil disobedience.[129] *Christian Ethics and the Sit–In,* which is a comparatively small volume, devotes less than twenty–five pages to the specific question of civil disobedience, but it does develop in some detail the theological and ethical understanding of the state which forms the basis for Ramsey's position on civil disobedience.[130] In addition, the third and last chapter discusses the Christian use of economic pressure to transform race relations. Ramsey in his later writings never returns to a concentrated discussion of this question. Consequently his considerations are limited to the questions that arose in the late 1950's and early 1960's with the one hypothetical example of disobedience if the Supreme Court declares that the "inn keeper's law," which Ramsey assumes most of his readers would accept as the demand of justice, is not the law of the land.

In this context our author develops and applies his insistence on order as a fundamental and independent consideration in questions of the state, especially civil disobedience. In obedience to God's governance and judgment of a sinful world there is a theological ethical justification of legality and order. We must preserve this fallen world while we engage in the struggle for justice within it. Observance of law can be generalized as a Christian principle, although not the only principle. Private individuals have no right to disobey human law *simply* by virtue of an appeal to another standard such as justice or natural law. We cannot go so far as to say that an unjust law is no law at all. No human legal system can tolerate the existence of an independent source of obligation which always prevails over the law of the land.[131]

Especially in a democracy there is a built–in legal way for people to struggle for the cause of right and justice.Democracy incorporates within itself the possibility and the limitation of resistance in somewhat the same way as the Christian teaching on just war in international politics. Democracy in a very real sense is nothing more than a just war by which individuals strive for a greater

129. Childress, *Civil Disobedience and Political Obligation,* p. 87.
130. *Sit-In,* pp. 75–98.
131. *Ibid.,* pp. 76–79.

justice within the existing order, but at the same time limiting their resistance to the form which does not jeopardize the existing order itself.[132] In addition, the law often defines the rights of other human beings in relation to our own. By going against the law we also go against the rights of others.[133] On the basis of these reasons Ramsey thus develops what he calls the conscience of the laws.

The importance of order in the state based on man's sinfulness and God's covenant of preservation is very important in Ramsey's understanding of the state. It seems that Ramsey's approach is basically teleological—one of the purposes of the state is to preserve order as its goal or function.[134] Ramsey also acknowledges justice as a function of the state, although as mentioned he does not always give enough importance to justice. Natural justice or a higher law can never, in itself, justify civil disobedience but is only a criterion.[135] At times, there can be tension between justice and order, but in practice Ramsey appears to stress order.[136]

In the specific, hypothetical, and exceptional case which he considers, Ramsey would allow a person to disobey the law if the Supreme Court rules that the "inn keeper's law" is not the law of the land. However, in this and all other cases such disobedience must be "*conscientious* conscientious objection," which means a respect for the conscience of the law as well as for a higher justice apprehended in one's own conscience. In practice this means that the individual must willingly and voluntarily suffer the consequences of his actions and the sanctions imposed. Socrates remains the great example of such an approach.[137]

In general, my approach to civil disobedience would be more flexible than Ramsey's, although I accept his insistence that one cannot simply appeal to higher justice with no consideration given to order or what he calls the conscience of the laws. However, I give more importance to justice and also see order not only in

132. *Ibid.*, pp. 93, 104.
133. *Ibid.*, pp. 87–90.
134. Childress, *Op. cit.*, p. 96.
135. *Sit-In*, p. 82.
136. *Ibid.*, pp. 51–75.
137. *Ibid.*, pp. 84–86.

terms of sin but in the light of the whole action of God. Likewise by giving significance to the role of justice in the state and not just to the agreement of wills, my position will not be so fearful of the danger of anarchy. Also in Ramsey's approach, disobedience to a particular order or command is too easily interpreted as disrespect for the ordering function of society in general. Despite some reservations about democracy, in terms of its slowness in coming to grips with racial justice in the United States,[138] our author is more optimistic than I about the system of democracy ensuring that justice is furthered in society. In practice I allow for a greater possibility of civil disobedience than does Ramsey.

My theoretical differences also occasion a different understanding of "*conscientious* conscientious objection." I do not think that one must always willingly suffer the penalty for having broken this particular law. One can show general respect for the conscience of the law by his acceptance of the law in so many other areas and by a concern for the society expressed in a number of different ways. One can still conscientiously disobey the law and also try to escape the sanction of the particular law.

Ramsey's discussion of civil disobedience is limited to the type of question which arose in conjunction with the lunchcounter sit–ins. Since that time, many other questions about civil disobedience and the use of force to change our society have arisen. In accord with his principles Ramsey would be quite opposed to most of the types of civil disobedience or the use of force which have been proposed to bring about a greater justice.[139] My own position is more willing to accept some civil disobedience and force, especially non–violent force, than Ramsey's, but I still insist on the need for both justice and an appreciation of law which means that injustice will always be present to some degree in our society. I would caution some advocates of violence and force that their approach often seems to me to be counter-productive and thus disproportionate.

Ramsey's approach to civil disobedience manifests an overall

---

138. *Ibid.*, p. 97.
139. Walter E. Wiest, "Can There be a Christian Ethic of Violence," *Perspective*, X (1969), pp. 127–154.

consistency with his solution to other practical problems and with his general understanding of political ethics and the state. Likewise many of my differences with him on this and other issues stem ultimately from theoretical differences about the meaning and function of the state in Christian ethics.

CHAPTER III

Medical

Ethics

In the last five years, Paul Ramsey has devoted much of his writing and research to questions of medical ethics,[1] a subject area which has received much attention from Roman Catholic theologians and from the hierarchical teaching office in the Roman Catholic church.[2] Until recently, Protestant ethicists, with a few exceptions such as Fletcher and Thielicke, have neglected the area of medical ethics.[3] Today there is much interest in medical ethics on the part of Protestant theologians. Within the Roman Catholic tradition there is a renewed concern with this subject as contemporary ethicists have questioned the traditionally accepted norms proposed by the hierarchical magisterium and by older theologians.[4]

1. Ramsey's two books on the subject are: *The Patient as Person: Explorations in Medical Ethics* (New Haven: Yale University Press, 1970); *Fabricated Man: The Ethics of Genetic Control* (New Haven: Yale University Press, 1970). *The Patient as Person* treats in different chapters the questions of experimentation, death and care for the dying, transplants, and the use of sparse medical resources.

2. Examples of this type of literature in Roman Catholic theology include: Edwin F. Healy, S.J., *Medical Ethics* (Chicago: Loyola University Press, 1956); Gerald Kelly, S.J., *Medico-Moral Problems* (St. Louis: Catholic Hospital Association, 1957); John P. Kenny, O.P., *Principles of Medical Ethics*, 2d ed. (Westminster, Md.: Newman Press, 1962); Charles J. McFadden, O.S.A., *Medical Ethics*, 6th ed. (Philadelphia: F. A. Davis Company, 1967); Thomas J. O'Donnell, S.J., *Morals in Medicine* (Westminster, Md.: Newman Press, 1959).

3. Joseph Fletcher, *Morals and Medicine* (Princeton: Princeton University Press, 1954); Helmut Thielicke, *The Ethics of Sex*, John W. Doberstein, trans. (New York: Harper & Row Publishers, 1964); Helmut Thielicke, "The Doctor as Judge of Who Shall Live and Who Shall Die," in *Who Shall Live?: Medicine, Technology, Ethics,* Kenneth Vaux, ed. (Philadelphia: Fortress Press, 1970), pp. 146–186.

4. E.g., *Absolutes in Moral Theology?*, Charles E. Curran, ed. (Washington: Corpus Books, 1968). Ramsey refers at length to four of the essays in this volume. He

Interest in the area of medical ethics has intensified in the last few years because of the tremendous advances in medical technology and because of the prospects of a biological revolution based on the new genetics. Man in the immediate future might acquire power to determine and guide his own evolutionary future. Paul Ramsey, with his inquiring intellect and his powerfully analytic mind, has been among the first Christian theologians to investigate this field.

Ramsey's medical ethics stands in theological continuity with his general ethical and theological approaches. Basic theological presuppositions which appear throughout his Christian ethics and also in his medical ethics include his understanding of love, of eschatology, and of anthropology. Ramsey's concept of love which is so central in his thinking is the Christian notion of *agape* which is understood in terms of the righteousness of God and his covenant love for man. Jesus Christ reveals to us the love of the Father which is shown above all in his complete giving of self to us sinful men. Christians must act toward their neighbor with this same loving concern which responds only to the needs of the neighbor and is not understood in terms of communion, mutuality or friendship. Christian love for Ramsey is thus understood as faithfulness which in no way depends upon the response of the other.[5]

Intimately tied up with the notion of love as faithfulness is an eschatology which stresses the apocalyptic aspect and the discon-

---

describes the authors as some of the most liberal of contemporary moralists (*PP*, p. 178).

5. *BCE*, pp. 1–190; *PP*, pp. xii, xiii. This is probably the best place for me to briefly indicate my disagreement with Ramsey's understanding of Christian love. I would argue that Ramsey's emphasis on faithfulness is too one-sided, for Christian love has many other aspects besides faithfulness. Ramsey's ethic wants to avoid the concept of love as fulfillment, with its possible teleological and consequentialist understanding, but in theory and in practice he seems to overreact. Theoretically, he takes as his model of love the love of God for his people and of Jesus for the sinner. However, if he took the love of the Trinity or the love of Jesus for his own, there would be more emphasis on communion and other aspects of love. In his *Basic Christian Ethics*, Ramsey describes Christian love but never speaks of the love of the Father, Son, and Spirit or the resurrection and the union of the Christian with the Risen Lord through the power of the Spirit. His theoretical bases and considerations of Christian love narrowly consider only those aspects which would accentuate the notion of faithfulness—the spontaneous and unmotivated love by which God has freely chosen us sinners as his people. Such a concept of love also does not leave enough room for an appreciation of the goodness of the natural. Ramsey's later acceptance of the model of love transforming justice would seem to call for a change in his concept of love.

tinuity between this world and the next. This appeared in the emphasis throughout his political ethics in which the state is seen primarily and sometimes exclusively in terms of an order of preservation against the power of sin until the City of God will spring forth anew at the end of time as God's loving gift to us. In medical ethics, especially in the area of bioethics, Ramsey argues strongly against utopian plans for the future improvement of the human race based on man's scientific knowledge and conquests. He criticizes severely those Christian theologians who would identify such progress with the coming of the kingdom.[6]

Within such a context his anthropology does not see man primarily as sharing in the glory and power of God the Creator and Redeemer. Rather, Ramsey insists that contemporary man because of his scientific capabilities is constantly tempted to *hubris* or pride. Man wants to play God and refuses to accept his own limitations and creatureliness. The quest for the utopian future of man brought about by the biological revolution is man's prideful assertion of himself in his desire to be like God.[7]

Two central concerns of Ramsey's methodology in Christian ethics underlie much of his writings in medical ethics. First, his medical ethics insists on the deontological aspects of Christian ethics. His deontology is closely associated with his concept of love, eschatology, and anthropology with the basic realization that Christian ethics is cut from God and not from man. Morality is derived from the claims of covenant loyalty and not just from the ends in view. This again calls for an independent ethic of means so that means cannot be totally swallowed up by the consequences of the act or by the good that will be accomplished.[8]

Secondly, his medical ethics recognizes the important place of human reason in arriving at ethical knowledge. In these discussions he does not explicitly develop his theological rationale for accepting the place of justice and reason in his methodology, but in practice he does frequently employ such considerations. Again some questions will arise about both the exact understanding of, and the consistent use of, the approach of love transforming justice.

6. *FM*, pp. 22–32.
7. *Ibid.*, pp. 138–160.
8. *PP*, pp. xii–xvi.

Three important themes frequently come to the fore in his discussion of medical ethics: the controlling consideration in his medical ethics is the covenant relationship between the doctor and his patient; the obligations of medical ethics follow from this covenant with the individual patient as person; and canons of loyalty to patients or to joint adventurers in medical research are particular manifestations of canons of loyalty of person to person. Medical ethics explores the meaning of faithfulness of one human being to another in these relationships. Ramsey obviously fears that at times the rights of the individual are too easily trampled upon for some other good to be accomplished.[9]

A second theme concerns the radical equality of all men. The sanctity of human life does not depend on social worth or dignity, but only on the fact that God has called us into existence and given us life. This is the theological basis for the radical equality of all men, so that one can never compare the value or worth of one human life over another as the basis for making choices about who shall live and who shall die.[10]

A third ethical theme is the insistence that man is a sacredness in the biological order. Man is an embodied soul or an ensouled body who within the ambience of the flesh claims our care. The biological aspect of human existence has important ramifications for Ramsey in questions such as the nature of human parenthood and also serves as a limiting factor so that man cannot be understood only in terms of freedom or self-creation.[11]

In light of these and other theological, methodological, and ethical presuppositions and themes, Ramsey considers in a non–systematic way many of the problems in contemporary medical ethics. The following chapter will discuss the newer problems occasioned by the biological revolution and other questions dealing with human reproduction and the future of the species. The present chapter will consider the questions of abortion, experimentation, transplants, scarce medical resources, the definition of death, and care for the dying. My own position in these questions is often quite close to Ramsey's, but most of my differ-

9. *Ibid.*, pp. xii–xiii.
10. Paul Ramsey, "The Morality of Abortion," *Life or Death: Ethics and Options*, Edward Shils, et al., pp. 70–78.
11. *PP*, p. xiii; *FM*, pp. 47–52, 104–138.

ences can be traced to a more nuanced understanding of the three ethical themes of medical ethics based on covenant loyalties, the radical theological equality of man, and the biological nature of man.

ABORTION[12]

Ramsey argues strenuously against an abortifacient mentality which is all too often reflected even in statements issued by churchmen and churches.[13] In the matter of abortion, one is dealing with more than just the rights of the mother. For this reason, he objects to terminology which describes the act as the "interruption" of pregnancy or even the termination of "pregnancy." Too often, the language and the reality of arguments in favor of abortion discuss the entire question without any mention of the fetus. Ramsey prefers as a definition or description of the act of abortion: "killing the fetus to terminate the pregnancy." But he admits that in some cases abortion may be justified.[14]

There are two fundamental moral questions involved in the abortion debate: when does individual human life begin, and how do we solve conflict situations involving the fetus and the mother or other values? Ramsey spends more time on the question of the beginning of human life, for obviously the ethos in an abortifacient society denies that the fetus is a human being. There is some

12. Five articles deal specifically with the question of abortion: Paul Ramsey, "The Morality of Abortion," *Life or Death: Ethics and Options*, Edward Shils et al., pp. 60–93. This book contains the papers presented at a symposium on the "Sanctity of Life" held March 11–12, 1966, at Reed College, Portland, Oregon. This article with some revisions has been reprinted twice: "The Sanctity of Life in the First of It," *The Dublin Review*, CCXLI (1967), pp. 1–21; "The Morality of Abortion," *Moral Problems*, James Rachels, ed. (New York: Harper & Row Publishers, 1971), pp. 3–27. Paul Ramsey, "Reference Points in Deciding about Abortion," *The Morality of Abortion: Legal and Historical Perspectives*, John T. Noonan, Jr., ed. (Cambridge: Harvard University Press, 1970), pp. 60–100. This essay grew out of a paper presented at an international conference on abortion sponsored jointly by the Joseph P. Kennedy, Jr., Foundation and the Harvard Divinity School in Washington in Spetember 1967. Paul Ramsey, "Feticide/Infanticide Upon Request," *Religion in Life*, XXXIX (1970), pp. 170–186. Paul Ramsey, "The Ethics of a Cottage Industry in an Age of Community and Research Medicine," *New England Journal of Medicine*, CCLXXXIV (April 1, 1971), pp. 700–706. This was originally presented as a paper at the Third National Conference on Medical Ethics of the American Medical Association, Chicago, September 19 and 20, 1970. Paul Ramsey, "Abortion: A Review Article," *The Thomist*, XXXVII (1973). This article is not yet published and will be cited from Ramsey's manuscript.
13. "Feticide/Infanticide Upon Request," pp. 170–173.
14. "Ethics of a Cottage Industry," p. 703.

hesitation, development and even vacillation in the specific details of his approaches to both these questions that find at least a partial explanation in the polemical and occasional nature of his discussions about abortion.

The Beginning of Human Life

There are three generic approaches to the question of human life—the genetic approach, the developmental approach, and the social consequences approach.[15] Ramsey definitely opts for the genetic approach, but he does seem willing to accept certain modifications which he adds to the argument from genotype. "According to this view the unique never–to–be repeated individual human being (the 'soul') was drawn forth from his parents at the time of conception."[16] Ramsey adds to his basic argument from gentoype the fact that there is no other point in the development of the fetus at which one can say that human life begins. This argument is germinally present in his first published discussion of the question but receives further development in his later considerations.[17]

Another form of the same basic consideration is Ramsey's argument that it is necessary to propose a justification for abortion which is not at the same time an argument for infanticide. Such an argument is based on the principle of universalizability and is not merely the "camel's nose" argument, which would argue that if you open the door to abortion, this will lead on to infanticide. The principle of universalizability is based on a necessary moral connection between the two acts, and here assumes that there is no relevant moral difference between the fetus and the newly born infant. Ramsey then backs this up by indicating that there is no other time after genotype or segmentation at which one can truly say that human life begins. For Ramsey, neither birth nor viability distinguishes the beginning of human life for they do not tell who or what the fetus is, but just where it is.[18]

Ramsey does realize the problem of calling the fetus a human

15. This division is employed by Daniel Callahan, *Abortion: Law, Choice and Morality* (New York: Macmillan Company, 1970), pp. 349–404.
16. "The Morality of Abortion," p. 62.
17. *Ibid.*, p. 70.
18. "Reference Points in Deciding about Abortion," pp. 79–89; "Feticide/Infanticide Upon Request," pp. 173–177.

person. He objects strenuously to the statement proposed by the Methodist Board of Social Concerns in October 1969, which affirmed that the fetus is not a person but rather tissue with the potentiality of becoming a person.[19] Ramsey prefers to describe the fetus as a human being in the womb who later becomes personal. Ramsey maintains that personhood does not take place until about one year of age when the child begins to speak. Thus, the fetus is a human individual with the sanctity of such a creature of God's, but not yet a fully personal being. To demand that the sanctity of life begins with personhood would mean that a child before one year of age would not enjoy the sanctity and dignity of a human being.[20]

There is, however, some change in Ramsey's judgment about when the individual human being comes into existence. The text of his first article on the question of abortion argues from the time of fertilization on the basis of the strict argument from genotype. Modern genetics seems to have demonstrated what religion never could, and contemporary biological science has resolved an ancient theological dispute. Genetics tells us that the unique, never-to-be-repeated, individual human being comes into existence at the moment of impregnation. In a sense, the genes are formal principles constituting us what we are, so that subsequent development does not involve becoming something we are not but rather the process of becoming what we already are.[21] Consonant with the judgment that an individual human being comes into existence with genotype, he asserts at the end of his first published article on abortion the fact that the intrauterine loop is not only contraceptive but also abortifacient.[22]

In a footnote in the same article he suggests a significant modification of the proof from genotype. In the blastocyst there appears a primitive streak across the hollow cluster of developing cells that signals the separation of the same genotype into identical twins. Before blastocyst, which according to Ramsey occurs about the

19. "Feticide/Infanticide Upon Request," p. 170.
20. "Reference Points in Deciding about Abortion," p. 70; "Feticide/Infanticide Upon Request," p. 174.
21. "The Morality of Abortion," pp. 60–70; *FM*, pp. 11–16.
22. "The Morality of Abortion," p. 87.

seventh or eighth day, the case of twinning indicates that there might not be individual human life. Ramsey says that serious-minded moralists might place the beginning of individual life at this time, so that intrauterine devices and the retroactive pill might not constitute abortion but only contraception or an attack on pre–human organic matter. Although blastocyst occurs about the time of implantation, he carefully distinguishes the two realities.[23] But recall that later in the text of the same article Ramsey described the loop as abortifacient.

In his second article on abortion, published in a symposium edited by John Noonan and which originally grew out of the paper Ramsey gave at an international congress on abortion under the joint sponsorship of the Joseph P. Kennedy, Jr., Foundation and the Harvard Divinity School, in Washington, in 1967, Ramsey admits his doubt on the question of the beginning of human life. "We have then three stages at which it is reasonable to believe that human life begins: conception, when the unique genotype originates; segmentation, or when it is irreversibly settled whether there will be one, two or more individuals; and the early development of the fetus when the 'outline' the cells contained is actualized in all its essential respects, with only growth to come."[24] The difference in his later position is the fact that segmentation is now definitely accepted in the text as a reasonable stage for marking the beginning of human life as well as genotype; but, above all, the third stage of early fetal development is also added and accepted as reasonable.

He does not really add much to the argument for segmentation based on the phenomenon of twinning but he does propose the stage of early fetal development (the first four-eight weeks) as a reasonable criterion for the beginning of individual human life. At the end of six weeks all the internal organs are present in rudimentary formation. At eight weeks there is readable electrical activity coming from the brain. After the end of eight weeks there is growth, but not crucial development yet to take place.[25]

In a later article which primarily argues against the fact that the

23. *Ibid.*, pp. 62–63.
24. "Reference Points in Deciding about Abortion," p. 75.
25. *Ibid.*, pp. 72–73.

fetus is only tissue in the womb of the mother, Ramsey does not refer to genotype or segmentation, but points out the early development state in the fetus to show that the basic human functions of heart and brain are already there. Here, he makes reference to the parallel between criteria marking the beginning of life and criteria for death at the end of life. The question of breathing is being discounted at the moment of death, but it seems to be the only criterion employed by some for noting the beginning of human life. Consistency demands that if the EEG is decisive in determining the moment of death, it should also be decisive about the beginning of life; but the unborn child's brain is active at about eight weeks.[26] In this context one can and perhaps should excuse Ramsey from going into a more precise debate about the beginning of human life. He merely tries to present a very forceful argument against those who hold that the fetus is tissue in the womb of the mother.

In his most recent article Ramsey has developed at greater length the judgment that individual human life begins at segmentation. He now adds to the phenomenon of twinning the fact of recombination. It very occasionally happens, even in humans, that two fertilizations may become one individual. This very rare recombination may happen at some point before or during the time identical twinning may take place. This argues that individuality is not firmly established until this time.[27] He also acknowledges his acceptance of morphological development as a third, arguable, and possibly defendable point at which individual life begins and claims our protection. This is not as decisive a rebuttal of the argument from twinning or from genotype as twinning is a rebuttal of the argument from genotype. However, he still appears willing to accept such a conclusion.[28]

One problem that Ramsey must face is how certain he has to be of a particular opinion before acting upon it. He obviously now acts on the judgment that individual human life begins at segmentation. His acceptance of loops, uterine devices, and retroactive contraceptive pills indicates this, as does his approval of a D and

26. "Feticide/Infanticide Upon Request," pp. 173–177.
27. "Abortion: A Review Article," pp. 25–31.
28. *Ibid.*, pp. 31–39.

C after rape. Even though he at one place indicates that segmentation is a stronger argument than morphological development, he does not appear to exclude the latter. If he proposes it as reasonable and does not exclude it, then such an opinion apparently can stand in practice. However, in his most recent article he insists that when doubt exists if the conceptus is human, respect for life requires us to treat it as if it were human.[29] Would this practically exclude the stage of early morphological development but not segmentation?

The Sanctity of Life

The problem of abortion raises the question of the reasons for the importance, dignity or inviolability of human life. Ramsey, in keeping with his theological position, speaks of this in terms of the sanctity of life because the dignity of human life is not founded on man's utility, worth or accomplishments or on anything intrinsic in man himself, but is this alien dignity conferred by God. The value of human life is ultimately grounded in the value God places upon it. This sacredness does not admit relative degrees of worth.[30] Ramsey strongly criticizes Callahan's so–called developmental approach to the question of the beginning of human life because, in reality, it is worth or dignity and not life which is gradually accumulated.[31]

Ramsey's insistence on this alien dignity, which coheres with his aversion to any forms of utilitarianism or consequentialism which would weigh the value of one individual against other values, leads him to an extreme position in his first article on abortion. After discussing the various theories about when germinating life becomes human and accepting in the text the moment of fertilization (a form of traducianism) Ramsey initiates his discussion of the sanctity of human life by saying that all the distinctions and theories about the beginning of human life from an authentic religious viewpoint do not matter very much. The modern world views the sanctity of life on the basis of something inherent in man, whereas the authentic Christian perspective argues from an alien dignity,

29. *Ibid.*, pp. 51–52.
30. "The Morality of Abortion," pp. 70–78.
31. "Abortion: A Review Article," pp. 14–24.

which is not something in man but an overflow of God's dealing with him. From such a perspective it becomes relatively unimportant to say exactly when we are dealing with an organism which is a human individual.[32]

This clear religious perspective obviously influences Ramsey's choice of fertilization as the beginning of human life. The Lord did not love or choose us because we were anything more than a blob of tissue in the uterus or greater in size than the period at the end of a sentence. In the whole reality of life no one is much more than a fellow fetus.[33] The religious outlook can settle on the moment that man is a unique individual but just a tiny speck because the sanctity of life depends on God's gift and not on man's inherent worth. Ramsey's religious perspective influences him to choose the very first possible moment for the beginning of human life.

I agree with a deep concern expressed by Ramsey—the need to show the radical equality of all human life—a most fundamental consideration for any Christian or, it seems to me, truly human ethics. Ramsey himself, however, does take quite seriously the question of when human life begins. Later he does develop other reasonable stages for marking the beginning of human life on things inherent in man's biological nature with special emphasis on a rudimentary organism with heart and brain functions. It would seem impossible to make any judgment about the beginning of human life without some inherent characteristics in the individual. (Perhaps Ramsey could respond that there is a difference between the judgment about the beginning of human life and the judgment about the reason for the sanctity of human life. However, he clearly does not make that distinction in this case.)

His assertion brings up again the great differences that Ramsey sometimes sees between a Christian perspective and judgment and a human or worldly perspective and judgment. At other times it will be noted that he not only does not stress the difference but emphasizes the fact that the Christian and the human are the same. Here he is clearly employing his neo–Orthodox approach. If followed to its logical and extreme conclusion, this extrinsicist

32. "The Morality of Abortion," pp. 71–72.
33. "Reference Points in Deciding about Abortion," pp. 66–69; "The Morality of Abortion," pp. 71–75.

position would leave no basis for determining the existence of human life on criteria inherent in the individual, as Ramsey himself seems to admit in too easily putting aside the distinctions and theories about the beginning of human life.

Thus I partially disagree with Ramsey's understanding of this alien dignity and also disagree with his dichotomy between Christian and human approaches to the problem. The fundamental reason for this difference probably lies in the traditional difference between Protestant and Catholic morality. Yes, God graciously gives us human life; but God's gift of life becomes effectively present in us, which can then be discerned as being present in man. God's gift of life can only be determined on the basis of criteria inherent in individual human life. There would have to be, consequently, no great difference between the Christian and the human judgment about the beginning of human life.

Conflict Situations Involving the Fetus

The second fundamental question in the abortion discussion centers on the resolution of conflict situations involving the fetus and other values, especially the life and health of the mother. Here again, development and change mark Ramsey's consideration of the question, with his later writings allowing for a greater number of conflict situations. Comparatively speaking, however, he allows very few such situations.

Our author frequently develops his own solution to conflict cases in the light of the traditional Catholic use of the principle of the double effect. It will be helpful to outline briefly and adequately the traditional Catholic approach to questions of abortion. Catholic teaching in its proper ethical discourse never said that all abortions are wrong. The possibility of conflict situations was admitted so that direct abortion was always wrong, but indirect abortion could be permitted for proportionate reasons. Direct was based not merely on the subjective intention of the act but on the objective thrust of the act itself. Indirect abortion is comparatively rare. The two most frequently discussed cases are the cancerous uterus and ectopic pregnancy. In these cases the abortion is indirect because the primary thrust of the action is to remove a pathological organ which happens to contain a fetus.

There is one point which, unfortunately, is often lost sight of in the debate and which does not appear in Ramsey. In situations outside the womb there were two possible types of conflict situation. The concept of indirect killing and the principle of the double effect applied in conflict situations involving innocent lives. Another model, defense against unjust aggression, also had a place. Unjust aggression did not necessarily mean that the aggressor was subjectively or formally guilty. A madman or a drunk could be an unjust aggressor and repulsed in order to save the life or even other equivalent goods of the victim. In this case there is a dispute whether the attacker is killed directly or only indirectly. Some argue that his death is directly intended and directly done as a means to protect one's self. Others maintain that here too the killing is only indirect because the direct intention and action is to incapacitate the attacker and defend one's self. In the case of abortion, however, official Catholic teaching does not allow the use of the unjust aggressor model on the basis that the fetus could not be an aggressor. Thus conflict situations in the womb are reduced to those allowed by the concept of indirect action, and these are comparatively very few.[34]

In his first article Ramsey argues that Protestants should accept the distinction between direct and indirect abortion which is the rule of practice unfolded in Roman Catholicism for the charitable protection of human life. Such an approach proclaims and safeguards the equal right of all to life. The distinction between direct and indirect depends on the primary thrust of the act itself. If the primary thrust of the action is to save the mother's life, then the abortion is indirect and can be permitted.[35] Ramsey has discussed earlier but does not mention here the two most frequent illustrations of indirect abortion which Catholic theology admitted—the cancerous uterus and ectopic pregnancy.[36] Ramsey maintains that Protestant theology too often confuses motive and intention, but the intention of the act is the thrust of the act and not the subjective motive of the person performing the act. Catholic theology

34. Kelly, *Medico-Moral Problems*, pp. 62–83. This paragraph, however, represents my statement of the question.
35. "The Morality of Abortion," pp. 78–80.
36. *WCC*, pp. 52–59, 171–173.

demands that the act of abortion be neither objectively intended nor subjectively wanted.

Ramsey disagrees with the Roman Catholic approach only in the one case in which both the mother and the fetus will die unless one of them is killed. Direct abortion is permissible in this case, but the argument for justifying it cannot be based on the subjective motive of the person or the good consequences that will come from the act. Ramsey comes up with a solution similar to that originally proposed by Thomas Aquinas himself in the case of defense against unjust aggression. The objective intention of the action and its direction is not toward the death of the fetus but the incapacitation of the fetus from what it is doing to bring about the death of the mother.[37]

In this context Ramsey also disagrees with what he interprets to be the Catholic solution to the case of unjust aggression which is based on a concept of natural justice. He accuses Catholic theology in this case of making too much of the non–Christian distinction between guilt and innocence in measuring out sanctity and respect for life. According to Catholic theology a guilty unjust aggressor can be killed if he is formally or subjectively and deliberately guilty. But the fetus is not a subjectively guilty aggressor and cannot be killed. Ramsey objects to such an approach. If our concept of righteousness is based on the righteousness of God who makes his sun shine on the just and the unjust alike, then the determination of right conduct cannot rest on the distinction between the innocent and the guilty. It is not formal aggression but material aggression which justifies the taking of life to stop the aggressive action. Similarly in war, it is not the guilt of the soldier but his combatant role or function as aggressor because of which he can be incapacitated from carrying out this function. Formal guilt or innocence cannot be the controlling concept.[38]

Ramsey does not properly understand the complete Catholic teaching on this point as it existed in Catholic teaching until a few years ago. Catholic theology does not place all the emphasis on formal guilt or innocence. A materially unjust aggressor can also

37. "The Morality of Abortion," pp. 80–84.
38. *Ibid.*, pp. 84–86.

be repulsed and killed, as in the case of a madman or a drunk whom it is necessary to kill in order to save my own life from his attack. Thus, even in Catholic theology of the past, a fundamental consideration was the unjust aggression itself, not merely the subjective guilt or innocence of the aggressor. In abortion, according to the accepted Catholic teaching, the fetus obviously cannot be a formal aggressor for it is incapable. Nor can it even be a material aggressor for it is not doing anything more than what it should be doing, and this cannot be called aggression. (It is precisely on this latter point that I disagree, and it seems to me that Ramsey shares this disagreement.[39])

This is not the first time that Ramsey has developed at length the Catholic teaching on direct and indirect attack. Recall his long discussion of this in his consideration of the principle of discrimination which forbids the direct killing of non-combatants in war. However, there are two important changes in Ramsey's later treatment. A methodological change concerns Ramsey's different justifications in the two discussions of his disagreement with the Catholic solution of the conflict situation between the life of the mother and the life of the fetus. In his earlier discussion he disagreed on the grounds of Christian *agape*. This is a good example of Christian *agape* revising the natural law. Catholic theology stayed only on the level of the natural and did not give enough importance to *agape*. *Agape* will never allow the Christian to stand idly by while one of the companions God has given him dies when he has the power to save one of them.[40] In the article on abortion, Ramsey does not invoke charity but a better understanding of the meaning of direct and indirect attack. Again, it would seem that in practice there is not that great a difference between charity and human reason or between Christian and human morality.

There is also a change in Ramsey's understanding of direct and indirect attack. In the earlier consideration Ramsey gives the following interpretation of the development which took place in Catholic moral theology on this question. Thomas maintained that

39. *Ibid.*
40. *WCC*, pp. 171–191. The same reason of *agape* is invoked in *NMM*, pp. 251–256.

one can never directly intend to kill another even in self-defense. The later tradition (at least the majority of the later moralists) said that one can directly kill an unjust aggressor, but not an innocent person. The difference seems to be that Aquinas understood direct killing primarily in terms of the subjective intention of the person. The modern improvements of the rule of double effect made it clear that direct attack referred not only to the formal object of the intention but also to the immediate material object of the physical act. The good must not only be willed directly but done directly. In the case of self-defense, the killing is directly done as a means of defending self (the good effect). Ramsey sides with the later interpretation.[41]

Now in the question of abortion he realizes there might be another way to interpret Thomas, although he does not explicitly acknowledge this development in his thought. The action which is directly intended and directly done is not the killing of the attacker but the incapacitation of the aggressor. Thus from his own interpretation of the Catholic tradition (and from the proper understanding of both Thomas and the later tradition), Ramsey should conclude that such killing is indirect and therefore permitted in order to save another life. He does in fact justify such killing, but he calls it direct killing.

Ramsey in a revised version of the original article acknowledges the criticism of Richard A. McCormick who pointed out that Ramsey, if he is following Thomas here, should call the killing indirect and not direct.[42] However, Ramsey maintains that he is primarily interested in the moral analysis itself which should be acceptable to both Protestant and Catholic alike and not primarily concerned with the terminology employed by the Catholic tradition. There may still be some point in calling such killing direct.[43]

Thus Ramsey insists on describing the act both as an incapacitation of the fetus and as a direct killing of the fetus. But there seems to be a real inconsistency in holding on to both terms. Why does Ramsey hold on to two descriptions of the human act which are

41. *Ibid.*, pp. 34–59.
42. Richard A. McCormick, S.J., "Past Church Teaching on Abortion," *Proceedings of the Catholic Theological Society of America,* XXIII (1968), pp. 137–140.
43. "The Morality of Abortion," in *Moral Problems,* pp. 22–93.

apparently contradictory? From the context it seems that Ramsey wants to insist that abortion involves the killing of the fetus, a point which is too easily glossed over by those who admit abortion. In the limited conflict situation of life against life in which he admits abortion, Ramsey does not want to forget that the fetus is killed, even though his justification of the killing is the fact that the fetus is incapacitated and its aggression thwarted. There is another reason for his calling it a direct killing. In the consideration of war Ramsey asserts that the killing of combatants is direct. Now in this discussion of the fetus he also says that the combatants are incapacitated, but he does not want to say that combatants are killed only indirectly.

His later writings on the question of the conflict situation help clarify and develop Ramsey's thinking, although some vacillation remains. The vacillation may be partly explained by the different audiences which Ramsey is addressing so that in his more popular articles he cannot be expected to use the precise wording of the theologian. Likewise, Ramsey the polemicist, at times, seems tempted to use the strongest argument he can find, even though it may not dovetail perfectly with what he has mentioned in a different context.

Ramsey insists that all proper descriptions of abortion acknowledge the fact that abortion does involve the fetus and not just the mother. He will not recognize as adequate any definition which avoids "direct reference to a direct act of killing the fetus. It would be better to say killing the fetus to terminate the pregnancy."[44] The point Ramsey is trying to make against the abortionist mentality is quite clear, but somewhat inconsistent with his ethical and theological analysis of the human act. Earlier he had justified such an act as an incapacitation of the fetus.

In his most recent article, Ramsey addresses the conflict situation with greater thoroughness than before. There are three possible approaches: one can remain an equalitarian and stand aside from cases of lives in conflict; one can abandon equalitarianism by comparing the value of different lives; and one can remain an

44. "Ethics of a Cottage Industry," p. 703.

equalitarian and solve conflict situations on the basis of the principle of the double effect. Ramsey chooses the final one.[45]

Ramsey recognizes some befuddlement about his earlier approach and tries to clarify it. In the conflict situation of life on life,
he wants to stress that the abortion is done with observable direct-
ness in the order of physical causality. The abortion is done directly while targeted as a human action upon stopping the fetus'
functional relationship to the mother's death, i.e., stopping its
aggression. However in the same paragraph he does refer to this
act as "willingly causing indirectly" the death of the child. The
target of the action is the child's function related to the life of the
mother and not the life of the child as such.[46] Perhaps this act can
be adequately described as observably or physically direct but
morally indirect.

Thus our author admits two types of conflict situations. The first
are those that are observably indirect such as the cancerous uterus
and the ectopic pregnancy. This type of case is the only type
admitted by traditional Catholic teaching. Ramsey's second type
of case involves the observably direct, but morally indirect, killing
of the fetus in the conflict situation in which the fetus is theatening
the life of the mother.

He enters into dialogue with Germain Grisez, who also argues
against the physicalism in the traditional Catholic approach and
maintains that an agent may initiate an order of physical causation
in which the evil effect comes first and the good effect follows, but
both effects must be morally simultaneous. The test for moral
simultaneity is whether or not any subsequent action is necessary
to bring about the good effect. Ramsey thinks that Grisez's approach is both too restrictive and in another sense too expansive.
Ramsey does not make the intervention of another act to bring
about the good effect decisive. The target in these conflict situations, according to Ramsey, must be the fetus's fatal function. This
can be stopped even though another act is necessary to save the
mother. Ramsey's approach admits the possibility of exceptions in
the cases of primary pulmonary hypertension and radiation

45. "Abortion: A Review Article," pp. 54–55.
46. *Ibid.*, p. 70.

therapy, which also would be admitted by the theory proposed by Grisez. But Ramsey also admits the legitimacy of abortion in cases of misplaced acute appendicitis or the special case of aneurysm of the aorta, even though after the removal of the fatal function of the fetus another act is necessary to save the mother.[47]

In his last article, Ramsey definitely appears as a revisionist of the double-effect principle and allows more exceptions than the traditional Catholic teaching. He goes beyond the position he first held. But he still staunchly supports the basic insight of the principle of the double effect in maintaining the radical equality of all to life. I believe there are two ways of trying to revise the traditional Catholic approach. One approach is to admit in the case of abortion the possibility of defense against aggression, which is admitted outside the womb. Perhaps it is unfortunate that this is called unjust aggression, but the reality referred to is aggression. Those who adopt this approach could then call the killing of the fetus either direct or indirect, depending which position they hold on this question. The other possible approach is to expand somehow the notion of morally indirect to cover this situation.

In 1970, for the first time in print, Ramsey stretched the possibility of abortion beyond the conflict situation involving the life of the mother and the life of the fetus. He now argues that "the mother's psychological health can become overriding, provided the state of the science and the judgments of men are secure. No moralist would value physical life over mental life."[48] This same judgment appears elsewhere.[49] In the 1971 revision of his original article on abortion first published in 1967, Ramsey extends the conflict situation to encompass mental or personal life as well as physical life.[50]

Ramsey adamantly opposes the use of psychological indications to include social, economic, and other non-medical reasons to justify abortions.[51] In contemporary society Ramsey sees a growing

47. *Ibid.*, pp. 53–78. Germain Grisez, *Abortion: the Myths, the Realities, and the Arguments* (New York: Corpus Books, 1970).
48. "Feticide/Infanticide Upon Request," p. 178.
49. "Ethics of a Cottage Industry," p. 702.
50. "The Morality of Abortion," in *Moral Problems*, pp. 17–18.
51. "Feticide/Infanticide Upon Request," p. 178.

away from the "utmost respect for human life from the time of conception which is enshrined in the Hippocratic Oath."[52] Even churches have become acculturated and often pronounce twenty-four hours later what the surrounding culture has said. In this case the churches themselves have often adopted a nethermost respect or no respect at all for nascent life. The medical profession, despite the failure of even the churches, must resist this weakening of respect for nascent life. Very often today non-medical reasons are proposed to justify abortion—a position in keeping with the broad definition of health proposed by the World Health Organization. Such a definition only intensifies the pressures against respect for nascent life. Ramsey argues that abortions should be justified only on medical reasons and not justified on social, economic, or demographic grounds, or on mere individualistic voluntariness.[53] A comment on Ramsey's understanding of medicine will come later.

By accepting psychological life and even psychological health as values that may be proportionate with physical life, Ramsey has raised questions about his consistency. I do not think that his understanding of the sanctity of the human life of the individual as an embodied spirit allows him to compare physical and mental life. I grant that he is not admitting the unequal value of different lives in this situation, but he is making a comparison between physical and psychological life so that other values (psychological health) can be equated with human life in conflict situations. There is only one human life or existence which we know—the life in the flesh. To say that other values might be as important as this means that the sanctity or the incomparability of human life (and human life is one) is not as absolute as his theory indicates. Ramsey must change or at least nuance his understanding of the sanctity of human life if he is going to admit that physical life and mental life are comparable values. Notice that Ramsey speaks not only of psychological life but also of the psychological health of the mother, which seems to be a more accurate term. It would seem to follow from this that Ramsey can not exclude other values that might justify abortion in conflict cases. The fact that he cannot

52. "Ethics of a Cottage Industry," p. 701. Note again some inconsistency because Ramsey himself no longer holds to conception as the beginning of human life.
53. *Ibid.*, pp. 701–704.

draw the line at just medical reasons will be developed in the next chapter.

My own position on abortion closely resembles Ramsey's position, especially as enunciated in his latest writings. I too have developed my opinion in the light of the traditional Catholic teaching and sought to revise that teaching somewhat.[54] On the question of the beginning of human life I choose the time of segmentation.

In this entire question of the beginning of human life, it is helpful to discover why many in our society will not accept such a comparatively early designation. I think one reason the problem exists is "because some people will not accept the biological and genetic criteria establishing the beginning of human life."[55] Theoretically I distinguish between the human judgment and the judgment of any one science so that the human judgment can never be totally identified with the judgment of any one science. This explains why the human at times must say "no" to the possibilities of any one science. Likewise it explains why there are very few political judgments which are not truly human judgments. Too often in the past Catholic theology has made the mistake of identifying the physical or the biological with the human. I do not say this can never happen, but in theory one must always make a distinction between the human and the biological judgment even though a particular human judgment might rely heavily on biological data and indeed be the same as the biological judgment.

In the case of ascertaining the beginning of human life, I do not think the human judgment can ever be settled by just appealing to the biological or genetic data. Other considerations must be brought in to indicate that this is also the truly human judgment. In a somewhat implicit way, Ramsey does bring in two other human arguments to support his contention based on genetics and biology. First, he finds it difficult to find any other time in fetal development when it can be said that human life begins. Second, he brings in the philosophical notion of individuality as a reason

54. Charles E. Curran, *A New Look at Christian Morality* (Notre Dame, Fides Publishers, 1968), pp. 238–243.
55. "The Morality of Abortion," *Moral Problems*, pp. 9–10. Ramsey cites and seems to misunderstand my earlier comment on this question. I will now expand upon it in the text.

for denying the existence of human life before segmentation. I would make these arguments more explicit to indicate that my judgment does rely heavily but not necessarily only on biological data without any other human concerns entering into the picture.

I do not find the argument from early fetal development or the existence of brain waves convincing at this time. EEG at the end of life is a test to see if there is the potentiality of life remaining in the person. It is not necessarily true that the same material test which is used at the end of life should also be used at the beginning.

My solution to conflict cases is somewhat similar to what Ramsey proposes in his latest articles. I think the Catholic tradition was too restrictive in not allowing the aggression situation and also in defining the direct effect solely in terms of the physical structure of the act. In conflict situations the life of the fetus may be taken to save the life of the mother. Even the Catholic tradition in the question of unjust aggression permitted the killing of the aggressor to save chastity or material goods of great value. Thus in conflict situations I would allow abortion to save human life or for other values that are commensurate with human life. This would obviously include grave but real threats to the psychological health of the woman and could also include other values of a socio–economic nature in extreme situations. I want to underline that these cases are comparatively rare and the values must be somewhat commensurate with life itself. Also on the basis of the principle of compromise, I could see the reluctant choice of abortion in situations in which again there must be some value comparable to life.

Before finishing this discussion of abortion, I think I should point out my understanding of what is happening in Roman Catholic ethics on the subject. Even though there is an official or hierarchical teaching (although with varying degrees of authority and weight depending on the interpretation of such words as direct) on this question, there still remains room for legitimate dissent within the church. Anyone familiar with the literature realizes that even now there is a pluralism existing among Roman Catholic theologians on this issue.[56]

56. For an illustration of incipient pluralism on the question of abortion, see *Theological Studies*, XXXI (1970), pp. 3–176.

EXPERIMENTATION

Medical experimentation has made possible almost unbelievable advances in medicine. The future seems to hold out even more alluring possibilities once medicine acquires the needed knowledge through experimentation. However, this situation raises formidable ethical questions which center on a potentially unresolvable conflict between the individual person who is the primary subject and the overall good that might come to humanity in general through medical experimentation.

Ramsey wants to keep crystal clear the distinction between therapy, which is a medical procedure for the good of the individual patient, and experimentation, which involves the individual not for his own good but for the advancement of medical science and the good of future persons or even the human race in general. A crucial ethical consideration involves the consent requirement based on the covenant or canon of loyalty between the man who is patient/subject and the physician/researcher. In both cases consent is required, but there are important differences.[57]

The ultimate reason for the consent requirement rests on the dignity or sanctity of the individual person as such, for only by informed consent can he in the case of therapy or experimentation become truly a joint adventurer. The civilizing task of mankind is to enlarge the consensual community among men. Ramsey is well aware of the fact that certain types of people are more vulnerable than others in this matter: prisoners, the dying, people in clinics, the poor in charity wards. However, their vulnerability should not automatically disqualify them from participating even in experimentation.[58]

In medical treatments or therapy, as opposed to experimentation, consent can be assumed or implied when men are in extreme danger and cannot themselves consent. Medicine exists to help the individual person as patient and thus his consent can be assumed when the procedure is for his own good. Thus, for example, parents can consent to procedures and operations for the benefit of their children who are sick.[59]

57. *PP*, p. 2.
58. *Ibid.*, pp. 6, 42–44; "Ethics of a Cottage Industry," pp. 706–707.
59. *PP*, p. 7.

Ramsey arrives at the conclusion that in experimentation the consent principle is closed to further morally significant alteration or exception. This practical conclusion underscores the temptation of the experimenter not to obtain the necessary consent so that he can more easily obtain his knowledge and research.[60] Ramsey frequently expresses the concern that the general public considers the physician with awe and respect because of the healing function of the profession. However, experimentation has nothing to do with the healing of the individual patient here and now. It is too easy for the researcher to pose in the guise of the physician. Ramsey always requires a truly voluntary and informed consent of the patient in questions of experimentation. Otherwise the individual person is treated as a means and not as a co-adventurer in medical progress.[61]

This general consideration entails some more specific developments. Of primary concern is the question of informed consent. Ramsey does not really develop this aspect, but does add a cautionary note for the ethicist. The competency of the ethicist is to establish and explain this principle of informed consent, but it lies beyond the competency of the ethicist to say what this entails in concrete applications.[62] Rather than develop a systematic treatment of consent, Ramsey concentrates on the prismatic case of experimentation on children or incompetents.

Ramsey allows the consent of parents or guardians in the case of therapy, which is for the good of the child as patient. He insists, however, that children can never be used in medical experimentation, which does not offer benefit to them as individual patients, because they are unable to give the requisite consent. No person may be used as a subject without his will, for otherwise he becomes an object.[63] The parent has a covenantal obligation to the child and cannot submit the child to procedures which are not for the child's benefit.[64]

Ramsey strenuously opposes the proposal of Henry K. Beecher

60. *Ibid.*, pp. 9–10.
61. "Ethics of a Cottage Industry," pp. 703–707. Paul Ramsey, "Shall We 'Reproduce'? II. Rejoinders and Future Forecast," *Journal of the American Medical Association*, CCXX (June 5, 1972), p. 1485.
62. *PP*, pp. 3–5.
63. *Ibid.*, p. 25.
64. *Ibid.*, p. 36.

that parents can consent to experimentation and research upon children when no discernible risk is involved for the child. Ramsey maintains that our moral and legal traditions indicate that consent and not "no harm" is the fundamental consideration. The consent requirement prevents assaults on the human person in terms of any touchings and not just harmful touchings. Children may be offensively touched or used as means without risk of harm. He also mentions the fact that it might be hard to prove there is no discernible risk.[65]

Even if one would allow parents to consent for their children in these situations, one could still argue that children in institutions because they belong to a captive population should never be the object of research and experimentation. Some would argue that prisoners because of the difficulty of giving informed consent and the great danger of abuses should be excluded as a practical rule from being allowed to volunteer for medical experimentation. In the case of prisoners, Ramsey feels these are only cautionary warnings, but imprisonment should not exclude one automatically from the human consensual community. Ramsey would argue for a practical negative rule in the case of institutionalized children or incompetents, if people would not accept his own position that experimentation on children without their consent is wrong, whether they are in an institution or not. Ramsey indicates many of the practical problems that have arisen in the case of children in institutions.[66] In later writings, Ramsey again stresses the fact that parents can submit their genetically defective children to treatment without their consent, but in some cases, such as argininemia, it would seem to be a case not of treatment but of immoral experimentation because the patients themselves cannot be helped by it.[67]

I agree with very much of Ramsey's approach, but I cannot accept the absolute stance forbidding any experimentation on children with the consent of parents. Parents and guardians can

65. *Ibid.*, p. 39.
66. *Ibid.*, pp. 40–58.
67. Paul Ramsey, "Morality and the Practice of Genetic Medicine," *The Vision of a Pilgrim People,* Joseph Papin, ed., Villanova Theology Institute, Vol. IV (Philadelphia: Villanova University Press, 1973). This has not been published so the page reference here (pp. 7–11) and subsequently will be to Ramsey's typed manuscript.

consent for their children when there is no discernible risk. Such a condition is present when the child is exposed to no greater risk than he is normally exposed to by life in this world in the midst of his multiple relationships with other persons and things. This does not involve an unethical touching of the person or a using of the child as a means, nor does it involve a breach of the parents' covenant with their child. All these arguments presuppose an absolutizing of the individual and seem to forget that every individual has a social and a community aspect to his existence because he belongs to the whole family of God and shares creaturehood with many others.

Ramsey seems to resolve the tension between the importance of the individual and the societal and communitarian dimension of human existence in too absolutistic a manner. The required consent of the parents and the criterion of no discernible risk should insure the proper respect for the individual as such and also realize that the individual is more than just an isolated human being. Other safeguards—such as committees with representatives from the whole community to make decisions about such experimentation—would be most helpful safeguards in practice. In general I agree with Ramsey's rule of practice about children in institutions, but I think it would be harder to insure the voluntariness of consent and to protect against abuse in the case of prisoners.

ORGAN TRANSPLANTS

The question of organ transplants involves many concerns which frequently surface in Ramsey's medical ethics—man as an embodied spirit or *sarx*, the consensual nature of human existence, the insistence on the medical covenant with the individual person and the resulting minimal ethic of doing no harm to the individual. Ramsey again does not develop a systematic treatment of the subject and acknowledges that his inquiry into organ transplants is deliberately inconclusive.[68]

The heart of Ramsey's concern is the fact that contemporary

68. *PP*, pp. 165–238.

moralists too easily accept a neo–dualism which does not give enough importance to the reality that man is the body of his soul just as much as he is the soul of his body. The ministry of medicine is to the flesh. He shudders at the thought of what moralists, who forget the fact that man is an embodied individual, will allow in the future. He envisions the time when moralists would propose the following justification of the decision of a forty-two-year-old father to give his heart to his son. The physical aspect of the father's existence is subordinated to the good of his own person. His person exists in terms of relationships with others, especially his family and his relationship with God. His person finds its fulfill-ment in his giving of himself in these relationships. This would be an act of the highest Christian love involving great courage and the ultimate perfection even of the father himself because of his loving gift of himself to his son.[69]

Even Christian moralists will propose such reasoning because they have too easily accepted a contemporary dualism with its Cartesian roots which fails to recognize that man is an embodied spirit who lives and has his being in the flesh. Ramsey thus surfaces his basic conern and fear in the question of transplants. The physi-cal integrity or biological integrity is not an absolute for man, but it does place important limits on what man can and should do even in the service of his neighbor.[70] Insistence on the physical integrity of the person moves Ramsey to prefer transplants from cadavers rather than from living human beings.[71]

Ramsey's discussion of this question takes the form of a dialogue with other moralists on the moral reason justifying organ trans-plants—usually in the case of paired organs. Ramsey especially grapples with newer approaches proposed by Catholic moralists. The principle of totality plays an important role in Catholic moral theology and in the teaching of the hierarchical magisterium, especially in the time of Pope Pius XII. According to this principle a part may be sacrificed for the good of the whole, but the part must have its total being in terms of the whole so that it can be subordinated to the good of the whole—a condition which is,

69. *Ibid.*, pp. 188–192.
70. *Ibid.*
71. *Ibid.*, pp. 198–215.

above all, verified in physical wholes.[72] One can sacrifice one part of the body if this is necessary for the good of the whole body, e.g., one can amputate a member if this is necessary for the good of the whole because the member finds its meaning wholly within the body itself. However, totalitarian governments are wrong in subordinating the individual to the regime or the state because the person has a meaning and a finality apart from the state.

Early papal teaching indicated that organ transplants could not be justified on the basis of the principle of totality because there did not exist here the physical whole to which the individual parts were legitimately subordinated. On this basis, some Catholic theologians denied the morality of organ transplants, but others ultimately found other ways to justify the organ transplants by either invoking charity or expanding totality. In the opinion of one group of Catholic moralists, charity or the needs of the neighbor could justify such transplants. Other theologians expanded totality to include the whole good of the person so that the spiritual good of the person himself demanded that he be allowed to give away one of his organs to his neighbor. Organ transplants thus were justified in terms of the total spiritual good of the donor who is called to a life of charity in relationship with God and man. The same basic approach was employed in the decision of the Supreme Court of Massachusetts, which justified the invasion of the physical integrity of one twin on the basis of the benefits that would come to the donor or the psychological harm which would come to him if he could not give one of his kidneys to his twin brother.[73]

Ramsey dialogues especially with Martin Nolan who has tried to expand the Catholic notion of totality in the above-mentioned way. Ramsey correctly points out, and for him it is a criticism, that Nolan, despite his attempt to liberalize Catholic moral teaching, still maintains the Catholic emphasis on the continuity of nature and grace and the continuity of love and self-fulfillment. Rather than barter totality against love, Nolan expands totality so that totality and love are no longer seen in opposition. Ramsey's criti-

72. Martin Nolan, O.S.A., *The Principle of Totality in the Writings of Pope Pius XII* (Rome: Pontifical Gregorian University, 1960); John J. Shinners, *The Morality of Medical Experimentation on Living Human Subjects in the Light of Recent Papal Teaching* (Washington: Catholic University of America Press, 1958).
73. *PP*, pp. 165–178.

cism is that in so doing Nolan deemphasizes the physical integrity of the individual for the sake of the good of others and of the individual person's total well being. Nolan does admit some limitations, perhaps more than Ramsey recognizes,[74] but he definitely upsets Ramsey by admitting that an individual might maim himself by giving away two of his eyes.[75]

Our author also disagrees with the approach of another contemporary Catholic moralist, Cornelius van der Poel, who describes the complex reality of organ transplants as one single uninterrupted action of taking an organ from one person and implanting it in another. Van der Poel, trying to revise the older Catholic approach, wants to avoid viewing the physical harm done to the donor as an independent act or independent disvalue which is then compared with charity. To safeguard the physical integrity of the person, Ramsey prefers to speak of two termini in this complex curative action.[76]

Some contemporary Catholic theologians are not the only ones who downplay bodily integrity. A Protestant position which sees our bodily existence only as a condition or possibility of covenant, but understands covenants themselves as free actions based on grace would also downplay the aspect of physical integrity. Free and informed consent would be the controlling and maybe the only ethical consideration in this approach. Ramsey does believe there is a biblical view that overcomes the shortcomings of these other approaches by giving importance to the physical integrity of man. However, Ramsey does not develop this biblical notion of man as *sarx* and how precisely it would be applied in this case of organ transplants. Bodily integrity is an operative norm in the question of transplants, even though it may be outweighed. Otherwise, one could argue that my organ belongs to my neighbor as much as it does to me. Making a well person sick or harming him is a unique and novel feature of medical practice which in this case should quickly give way to the use of cadaver organs for organ transplants.[77]

74. Martin Nolan, O.S.A., "The Principle of Totality in Moral Theology," *Absolutes in Moral Theology?* Charles E. Curran, ed. (Washington: Corpus Books, 1968), p. 244.

75. *PP*, pp. 178–181.

76. *Ibid.*, pp. 181–185.

77. *Ibid.*, pp. 185–188.

Perhaps the major difference between Ramsey and the Catholic theologians he criticizes is one of emphasis. The Catholics are trying to overcome the absolutism of physicalism, which in Catholic moral thought made, at times, a perfect identity between the physical aspect of the act and the moral act. This seems to be part of the problem in the official Catholic condemnation of artificial contraception and sterilization. Ramsey, on the other hand, fears that contemporary theologians do not give enough importance to the bodily aspect of human existence and wants to emphasize this aspect. Especially Nolan willingly admits that more than consent is required and that physical integrity does enter into the moral decision. Even Ramsey who insists on bodily integrity realizes that this is not absolute but can be outweighed by other values. In reality, Ramsey must accept an approach which sees bodily integrity as a value to be weighed against other values which he would probably understand in terms of the needs of the neighbor.

I have some difficulties with the fact that Ramsey occasionally refers somewhat pejoratively to Nolan's approach as a "sticky benefits theory."[78] If he refers to the fact that benefits have to be weighed, I think he is vulnerable. Ramsey admits a calculus involved in weighing bodily integrity and other goods.[79] He is probably referring to the problem of weighing the spiritual benefits for the individual donor, which goes back to his criticism of the continuity between love and self-fulfillment in all of Catholic theology. I would tend with some nuances to accept such a continuity. Likewise, I could not absolutely rule out some physical maiming of the donor.

Van der Poel is more open to criticism because he does not refer to the limitations as much as Nolan. He rightly wants to get away from a Catholic approach which denied the morality of transplants because transplantation involved an act of mutilation which could only be justified for the good of the individual. Perhaps the best solution to this problem is one analogous to what Ramsey proposed in his last article on abortion. There are two moral acts involved, but the first act should be described as making an organ available

78. *Ibid.*, pp. 181, 187. Ramsey puts in quotation marks this term which was originally employed in a legal context as a criticism of the ruling of the Massachusetts court.
79. *Ibid.*, p. 195.

for transplant and not as a mutilation. In this way, the first act is viewed in the light of the total human activity of transplantation.

It seems that Ramsey's insistence on an anthropology that gives importance to the embodied nature of man does occasion some overemphasis in his own arguments against the approach of others. Man cannot exist apart from the physical or biological, but not every aspect of human existence demands the physical or biological aspect. There are degrees of physical integrity, and some physical integrity can be sacrificed for porportionate reasons.

There is a very important theological repercussion from Ramsey's discussion of transplants. I have said in general and in theory that some of Ramsey's later positions require him to rethink fundamental notions proposed in his *Basic Christian Ethics*. In this particular case, it seems that the notion of love developed in his first book is not compatible with his present teaching on transplants. Ramsey spoke of *agape* as concern for the neighbor's need. There is no place for a proper love of self except derivatively in terms of the needs of the neighbor.[80] The so–called Protestant argument for transplants in terms of covenant and charity seems congenial to the concept of love proposed by Ramsey, but he rejects it. Now he wants to argue very strongly in terms of obligations to one's self and his own bodily integrity. Ramsey's argumentation in this case calls for an independent and proper love of self in the Christian life.

The discussion on giving or taking cadaver organs for transplants assumes for the most part that Ramsey believes cadavers are a much better source of organs than the living, for here there is no violation of the physical integrity of the person. There are two possible proposals for the future: the routine salvaging of organs in hospitals, or an Anatomical Gift Act which will allow the person to will his organs for this purpose.[81] Ramsey admits that neither of these is inherently wrong, but he favors the giving of organs over the taking of organs. Even here, Ramsey still emphasizes the notion of bodily integrity. The giving of organs is preferable not only because of the nature of a consensual society, but also

80. *BCE*, pp. 92–103.
81. *PP*, pp. 198–215.

because in this way the wish to exercise a more ancient wisdom concerning the integrity of the body ought not to be especially burdened. However, if the buying and selling of human organs from the dead is not proscribed in any possible law, then it would be better to adopt the routine taking of organs, for the consensual aspect of society is not furthered by such buying and selling.[82]

A caveat on heart transplants.[83] Ramsey's caveat on heart transplants stems from a basic understanding of what a heart transplant is. Is it an experiment or therapy? In this connection again there exists a great danger of confusing the role of physician friend and physician investigator. The covenant of the physician with the patient is very different in these two cases, and the requirements necessary for free consent are different in both cases.

Ramsey admits there is some doubt about how heart transplants should be classified at the time of his writing (1970), but he seems to favor the opinion that they are experiments. In such a case, donor and recipients alike must consent to heart transplants as a scientific investigation to benefit medical knowledge and the future but not as a present form of therapy for the recipient.[84] A minority of the medical profession affirms that heart transplants are treatments. Perhaps it is better to say that there is a large gray area between the extremes of pure research and proved treatment. If heart transplants are this combination which can be called investigational therapy, the persons involved must be appraised of the therapeutic worth to the patient. Most of the figures presented in the press about the success of heart transplants were inaccurate, for they did not properly record the length of survival or the cause of death. Figures, such as after one year of heart transplants forty of ninety-nine people who received new hearts were still living, are very misleading. In reality, beside Dr. Philip Blaiberg, only nine of the ninety-nine lived more than three months following heart replacement. One doctor justified the operation as therapy on the ground that the patient lived another six or eight weeks![85]

82. *Ibid.*, pp. 210–215.
83. *Ibid.*, pp. 216–238.
84. *Ibid.*, pp. 221–224.
85. *Ibid.*, pp. 227–235.

In all cases Ramsey strongly objects to the advice that there is no other hope or no other choice, There is another choice–death. Life under the conditions of a few weeks prolongation in a hospital situation after very serious and major surgery must not necessarily be chosen over death. For the Christian and the religious man death is not an end that should always be opposed. Theologians have recognized there is no obligation to use extraordinary means to keep human life in existence. Patients should not be put under the pressure of thinking they have no other choice than the heart transplant operation.[86]

SCARCE MEDICAL RESOURCES

The problem of priorities haunts much of American public life today. In modern medicine there are not enough medical resources for all those who need them. The question most frequently discussed in the medical–ethical literature concerns the use of dialysis or kidney machines in the case of renal failure. Perhaps this problem is not as acute today as it was a few years ago, but this case exemplifies the problem of scarce medical resources. Although the procedure is expensive, bothersome, and calls for a very strict regime, it is the only hope for life for many people in this condition. However, there are many fewer kidney machines than there are people who need them. Who gets the scarce resources? Who determines who will live and who will die? In the future should we spend more money on kidney machines or should we investigate ways of preventing renal failure? Should our nation spend such huge sums in the area of kidney investigation or of sensational heart transplants and operations when infant mortality is rising and many people cannot even have adequate medical care? Then there emerges an even broader horizon: how do medical priorities stand up in comparison with other social priorities? How should we go about deciding the question of national priorities?

A particular case, according to Ramsey, can often be viewed as a prism in which so many different aspects are focused. In many

86. *Ibid.,* pp. 236–238.

ways this particular question is a prismatic case for Ramsey because it brings together many different moral questions of fundamental importance: how is the worth of a human person determined? How does one make judgments involving life and death for the people involved? What should be our attitude toward death? How can justice work in a society in terms of structuring the priorities of the society? Why is utilitarianism an inadequate ethical approach?

Ramsey concentrates on the narrower question of the distribution of scarce life–saving medical techniques when there are not enough to go around. He asserts on two different occasions that the broader question of the establishment of social and medical priorities within our society is almost incorrigible to human reason.[87] This position is consonant with his understanding of the role of justice in society as developed in his political ethics. In the question of priorities within medicine, Ramsey does propose some suggestions for an ordering of medical priorities. Ramsey admits that his proposal is something akin to triage, which in disaster situations says that first priority belongs to the victims who can be more quickly and easily restored to functioning while the more seriously hurt, who require a great deal of time and resources, are put aside.[88]

His hesitant proposals emphasize Ramsey's consistent disagreement with the American way of not dying, which insists that all possible efforts be made to avoid death. The Christian, however, does not always see death as something to be feared, avoided, and pushed back at all costs. "Should medical specialists in last-ditch remedies continue their unspoken and undeliberate 'conspiracy' with the American Way of Not Dying to give these remedies the greater prominence and a powerful claim upon our overall sparse medical and social resources?"[89] Ramsey tentatively argues for greater emphasis on preventive medicine and presymptomatic treatment, rather than sensational attempts to save life at the very end.[90]

87. *Ibid.*, pp. 240, 268.
88. *Ibid.*, p. 258.
89. *Ibid.*, p. 271.
90. *Ibid.*, p. 275.

I agree with Ramsey's comments about the ordering of priorities within medicine itself. Our primary obligations are to make available to all people the things necessary for an adequate care of their health with emphasis on preventive medicine. Heroic measures taken in the face of death should not receive top priority but a very low priority in the distribution of our scarce resources in the area of medicine.

I disagree with Ramsey and see the need to try to establish our national priorities in general and how medical needs fit into this overall picture. I realize the impossibility of any exact hierarchical ordering of all these needs, but men can and should come up with a rather rough idea of the areas that should be emphasized. Many times one can be more certain of negative judgments—areas that should not receive as much emphasis as they do now. Ramsey gives up too easily on the broader question of national priorities and the place of medical priorities within this larger picture. Men will never be able to arrive at perfect agreement on a hierarchical ordering, but we can and must do more than just say that the problem is almost impervious to human reason.

Ramsey outlines three possible solutions to the problem of the distribution of scarce medical resources involving life and death decisions for people: patients should be selected according to their worth and value; randomness should characterize the selection process; and all should die when not all can be saved. Ramsey opts for randomness as best able to realize the ultimate equality of all men in the sight of God.[91]

Generally speaking, our author rejects any comparison of the intrinsic worth of individuals or of their social utility. Implicit in such a rejection is Ramsey's assessment of the sanctity of human life not in terms of anything intrinsic in man or in terms of utility but rather the alien dignity conferred by the gratuitous gift of creation by God. The sanctity of human life in no way depends on social worth or merit. The consciences of men refuse to make judgments of life and death based on social worthiness because of our religious sense of the ultimate "congeneric" covenant among men, and of the incomparable equality among men when they

91. *Ibid.*, pp. 242–275.

face the stark reality of living on only because another man must die.[92] Life is a value incommensurate with all others and so not negotiable by bartering one man's worth against another.[93]

His practical argument against selection on the basis of merit or social worth rests on the fact that man has no way of knowing how to estimate another man's moral worth or his worth to others in the unfocused social situations in which ordinary men and women live their lives. Often it seems that such selection is based on the reality that the bourgeoisie spare the bourgeoisie.[94] How does one compare the worth to society of an artist or composer with the mother of six young children?[95]

Ramsey's argument for randomness is not based on an abdication of a charitable reason in these difficult decisions, but rather it is based on the concern that we should all have for the sanctity of the life of all men which depends ultimately not on social worth but on the equal right of every human being to live. Decisions based on intrinsic worth or social utility offend the equal right of all men to live. Randomness either in the form of a lottery or of a "first come, first served" basis preserves the equal opportunity of all for life.[96]

There can be a describable sort of exception to this rule of guaranteeing by random selection equal possibility of life when not all can be saved. Elsewhere, Ramsey has developed how one sees exceptions to general rules in the form of types of cases which do not come under the general rule.[97] The exception in this case can be made only if a community or its members have been or are reduced to a single focus under some quite extraordinary circumstances. Ramsey gives some illustrations of this. In a military situation in which the objective of maximum fighting power as rapidly as possible is closely defined, the military commander was justified in using scarce penicillin for victims of VD who could quickly

92. *Ibid.*, p. 260.
93. *Ibid.*, p. 256.
94. *Ibid.*, p. 248.
95. *Ibid.*, p. 246.
96. *Ibid.*, p. 256.
97. Paul Ramsey, "The Case of the Curious Exception," *Norm and Context in Christian Ethics*, Gene H. Outka and Paul Ramsey, eds. (New York: Charles Scribner's Sons, 1968), pp. 67–135.

return to the battlefront rather than for severely wounded soldiers who had been wounded on the battlefield and not in the brothel. The morality of triage in disaster situations gives first priorities to victims who can be quickly restored to functioning while victims in need of the most help and resources are left aside. These are cases in which the purposes of a community of men have been very narrowly focused because of the disaster.[98]

The third possible solution rests on the principle that all should die when not all can be saved. This solution was proposed by Professor Cahn in the situation of the overloaded lifeboat from which it was necessary to jettison some passengers if the boat was to stay afloat. Cahn rejects not only the arbitrary choosing of people by the man in charge but also the casting of lots. Cahn argues here, according to Ramsey, that this situation, bringing about the morality of the last days, strips away all human relationships and individuality leaving man a generic creature. Since every person in the boat embodies the entire genus, whoever kills one kills mankind. Where all have become congeners, no one can save himself by killing another, for he has no individuality left to save.[99]

While obviously sympathetic to Cahn for his understanding of the covenant which should exist among men, Ramsey rejects his reasoning. It is the realization of the absolute equality of all men in the situation which Ramsey uses to justify randomness and not to demand that where not all can be saved all must die. Cahn had proposed his solution in the name of an anthropocentric approach, but Ramsey frequently insists in these few pages that Cahn's approach is not an anthropocentric approach. It is rooted in the biblical tradition based on the claim of the righteousness of God. This is the introduction of self-sacrificial love into the decision-making process.[100] But Ramsey argues that such a view of man does not mean that all must die when not all can be saved, but only that each be accorded equal opportunity. Ramsey does not mention it, but obviously Cahn's solution would not work in the situation of scarce kidney machines or other medical resources, for then we would logically have to do nothing in many situations.

98. *PP*, pp. 256–259.
99. *Ibid.*, pp. 261–263. Ramsey has also discussed Cahn's approach in the same way in *NMM*, pp. 245–256.
100. *PP*, pp. 262–266; *NMM*, pp. 245–252.

Perhaps it would have been more proper not to discuss Cahn's position in the context of scarce medical resources because these are not truly situations involving the morality of the last days.

Ramsey presents a formidable case for randomness in selection in life-or-death situations involving the recipient of scarce medical resources. His primary reason is the equal right of all to life, with its ultimate justification for Ramsey in the sanctity of life based on the alien dignity conferred by God. Some objections have already been made about this understanding of the sanctity of life which proposes a radical theological equalitarianism. Such a theological underpining leads Ramsey to a theoretical difficulty in talking about intrinsic criteria for a judgment about the beginning of human life. It also seems to leave him without justification for his willingness to compare psychological life or health with physical life.

My differences with Ramsey on this question are comparably few and of a more theoretical nature. Notice that Ramsey's argument of equality is a deontological argument. However, he also gives important teleological arguments because of the difficulty of knowing social worth in the complex human situation. He does allow the one exception in which the community and its members have been reduced to a single focus, purpose or goal under some quite extraordinary circumstance. Perhaps his theoretical approach could combine better these two approaches. In the particular military situation he describes, I am not so sure that the situation is as narrowly focused as he maintains so that I would have some hesitation in that case. Also it might help to mention that there are situations in which the special moral relations we have with people would place special obligations upon us when only one or a number and not all persons in a similar situation can be saved, as for example, in a burning building.

DEFINITION OF DEATH

In two different places Ramsey has developed basically the same approach to the question of the newer definitions of death which have been proposed in the literature.[101] Ramsey willingly ac-

101. *PP*, pp. 59–112; Paul Ramsey, "On Updating Death," in *Updating Life and Death*, Donald R. Cutler, ed. (Boston; Beacon Press, 1969), pp. 31–54.

knowledges some of the limitations of the theologian and the ethicist in this matter. The question of the moment of death lies beyond his technical competency as such. The determination of death is a medical question, and the theologian and ethicist can "only offer him reflections upon the meaning of respect for life and of care of the dying and issue some warnings of the moral complexities such as are here set down."[102]

The fact that the meaning and criteria of death are being reevaluated today in the light of the need to supply organs for transplant recipients causes concern. The desire for having organs for transplants runs the risk of breaking the covenant between the doctor and his patient, even though the patient may be dying. The danger exists of declaring a person dead before one would ordinarily do so because of the need of another person for a transplanted organ.[103] Medical ethics, appreciating the pressures on doctors and the weakness of man, calls for a separation of powers between the physician or group of physicians who are responsible for the recipient and the physician or group who are responsible for the care of the person who is the prospective donor. If no person's death should be hastened because of the need for organ transplants, so too the definition of death should not be updated for this purpose. Otherwise, the dying patient is used as a means for the prospective recipient and the covenant existing between the physician and his patient is broken.[104]

Ramsey sees the reasons for the updating of the criteria of death in the advance that medical technology has recently made so that today people may be kept alive or hearts kept beating through artificial means when the person is already dead. Ramsey thus accepts the description of these proposals for updating the criteria of death as a set of guidelines on how to use a respirator.[105]

It is necessary to make two important distinctions in this matter —between the concept of death and determining the moment of death and especially between the definition of death, and the methods or criteria employed to see if death has occurred. In the

102. *PP*, p. 104.
103. *Ibid.*, pp. 111–112.
104. *Ibid.*, pp. 102–103.
105. *Ibid.*, pp. 89, 93–94.

context of this latter distinction, Ramsey elaborates three possible positions. The first position defines death in terms of brain death and establishes brain tests, especially the electroencephalograph (EEG), as the criterion of death. This radical position is not held by very many people today despite the popular misconception to the contrary. The second opinion understands death in terms of brain death but requires a number of criteria other than the EEG to determine death. The third opinion retains the more traditional meaning of death as the cessation of heart, brain, and lung activity, but refines and qualifies the tests for these.[106] Ramsey definitely argues against the removal of spontaneous cardiac activity from our criteria for determining death.[107]

In his book Ramsey understands the updating of death to involve three things. First, there is need to distinguish the dead from the dying and the virtually dead. Virtual death and dying are not death, so that one cannot, it seems, take organs from persons described to be in those states. Second, some legal definitions of death which maintain there is life if there is any heart beat or respiration are also rejected. Third, updating death means to dismiss artificially sustained signs of life. Sometimes the heartbeat is present only because the lung-life is being sustained by respirators, but neither breathing nor heartbeat can be truly called spontaneous in these cases. Naturally sustained life in the heart is not being excluded by most discussants from among the signs that a person is still alive. The crucial problem seems to be the need to distinguish between spontaneous and artificially sustained heart activity. In this light Ramsey does not see that these updatings are all that new.[108]

The famous Harvard Report issued in 1968 should be interpreted in this way. The report does accept brain death as a definition of death, but it requires a multiplicity of criteria for determining this. Ramsey argues that the clinical criteria for death proposed by the Harvard Committee cannot be verified in a patient whose heart still beats without immediate or remote artificial support. The problem centers on realizing what is meant by a spontane-

---

106. "On Updating Death," p. 35.
107. *Ibid.*, p. 37.
108. *PP*, pp. 66–68.

ously beating heart. When it is the artificial respirator which continues to allow the heart to beat, then the heart activity cannot be called natural or spontaneous. When there is in the heart no reasonably permanent capacity and the heartbeat is produced by the respirator, then there is no spontaneous or natural heartbeat.[109]

Ramsey at various places proposes reasons for maintaining the importance of spontaneous heartbeat as a sign of life even though he does not attempt a conclusive argument. He also tends toward accepting the older definition of death as the cessation of the functioning of the three vital organs of heart, lungs, and brain. The definition of life in terms of heart and lungs and brain reminds us of the primitive psycho–physiology of the Bible, but this also indicates that the pronouncement of death is a medical question.[110] Ramsey buttresses his position by appealing to human sensitivities by asking who would bury a man whose heart still permanently beats spontaneously?[111]

Why do many still want to maintain that a person can be really dead even in the presence of a spontaneously beating heart? They seem to misunderstand the proper meaning of spontaneous. In addition, Ramsey suspects that some people want to hold on to this terminology so as to open the door to saying that brain damage which is not so deep as to abolish respiration and consequently heart function can be counted as death.[112]

Ramsey's insistence that the definition and determination of death and the question of organ transplants should always be separated in theory and practice is important. However, at times the tone of his presentation seems somewhat one–sided. Even though the questions are distinct, historically the question of transplants has partially occasioned our rethinking of the question of death. I do not think this is bad in itself. If we were too slow in pronouncing the moment of death, this possibility of using the organs of dead persons might help us to better appreciate a more exact meaning of, and criteria for, death. It is interesting how casual some Catholic medical moral books were on the question of determining death. They utilized a distinction between clinical death

109. *Ibid.*, pp. 89–98.
110. *Ibid.*, p. 60.
111. *Ibid.*, p. 76.
112. *Ibid.*, p. 97.

and real death, especially in the context of giving the sacraments to dead persons. The purpose of the distinction was to provide the sacraments for the person even though he was already clinically or apparently dead. Real death might not occur for three or four hours after clinical death.[113]

I agree with Ramsey that the question of organ transplants will put pressure on us to pronounce death earlier than we did in the past. There is need to lean against that pressure, but at the same time perhaps this question of transplants can help us to sharpen our understanding of the criteria of death. Even though Ramsey might have been a bit less negative about the bearing of organ transplants on the theoretical definition of death, I still whole-heartedly agree with the general thrust of his insistence that the pronouncement of death should in the particular situation not be affected by the presence or absence of a prospective organ recipient.

There does seem to be one other somewhat baffling aspect about Ramsey's discussion. He insisted at the beginning of his discussion that the theologian or ethicist cannot and should not talk about the moment of death and the criteria for determining the presence of death but can just raise warnings about the moral complexities involved. This position is consonant with his emphasis on the restricted competency of Christian ethics.

In practice Ramsey seems to go further than just the raising of moral complexities. Even in theory, Ramsey in one place apparently acknowledges a greater role for theology and ethics. Concerning the crucial question in his whole discussion of whether heart function can or should be eliminated from the description of being alive or being dead, Ramsey makes the following remarks. "This seemed to strike at the foundations of not only medical definitions of life and death but as well of a more ancient wisdom concerning the life and acceptable death of all flesh. Only a mechanical notion . . . that man's embodied life consists of an ensemble of 'parts' would not have been shaken. That notion is gaining on us."[114] It seems that Ramsey himself does not stay within the boundaries of the competency of the ethicist as he has defined

113. Healy, *Medical Ethics*, pp. 380–383.
114. *PP*, pp. 62–63.

them. I have a much less restrictive understanding of Christian ethics and do see both teleological calculations and prudential judgments within the scope of Christian ethics.

ON (ONLY) CARING FOR THE DYING

In the discussion of the meaning and criteria of death, Ramsey claims to find a very inconsistent logic on the part of those (including the framers of the Harvard Report) who in speaking about the definition and criteria for determining death recall the teaching of Pope Pius XII that there is no moral obligation to use extraordinary means to preserve life, so that at times death should not be opposed. However, the definition of death and the question of using all possible means to prevent death are two different cases. Do people confuse the two questions because they are not sure about the definition of death they propose? Ramsey also suggests that one possible explanation might be that doctors have some fear that they might be killing the prospective recipient of a heart transplant by removing his own heart in order to make him live again with a new heart.[115] I cannot accept Ramsey's last suggestion, but I agree that the two questions should be kept quite distinct.

Ramsey spends an entire chapter on the question of only caring for the dying; a chapter which well illustrates the methodology and mind-set frequently employed by him.[116] He finds much moral wisdom in the teaching of the past, as has often been indicated in his writings. He tries to reform and build upon this wisdom of the past rather than reject such wisdom or just begin again from the present. In dialogue with the past moral wisdom, especially as it is enshrined in the distinction between ordinary and extraordinary means of preserving life, Ramsey develops a theology of care and only care for the dying. The distinction between the use of ordinary and extraordinary means to preserve life is related to two other important distinctions—the distinction between saving life and prolonging dying, as well as the distinction between direct killing and allowing the patient to die.[117]

115. *Ibid.*, pp. 98–101.
116. *Ibid.*, pp. 113–164.
117. *Ibid.*, p. 118.

The problem becomes acute in the light of scientific and technological developments which allow medicine to prolong life, but
the older theological wisdom set the framework for the discussion
with the wisdom embedded in the distinction between the use of
ordinary and extraordinary means to preserve life. Can the doctor
ever turn off the respirator? Should a baby born with a serious
congenital defect be saved from normal dying by modern incubator technology? Must a terminal cancer patient who contracts
diabetes treat the diabetes?

An ethic of only caring for the dying is opposed to two extremes:
the one that affirms there is never any reason not to use or to stop
using all available means to preserve life, and the other extreme
which justifies positive euthanasia or the direct taking of the life
of the terminal patient. Ramsey vigorously opposes euthanasia,
but he acknowledges that not everything must be done that can
be done to keep the patient alive. In allowing the person to die,
no human agent causes the person's death either directly or indirectly. The person dies his own death from causes it is is no
longer merciful or reasonable to fight with medical interventions.
In fact the difference is not really between positively interfering
to bring about the death of the person and doing nothing. Not
using or withdrawing extraordinary means is not merely doing
nothing but rather can be positively called part of our care for, and
accompanying of, the person in his dying.[118] Since euthanasia
involves an act of positively causing the death of the person, the
Christian tradition has rightly condemned it as murder.[119]

The opposite extreme asserts the necessity of doing everything
possible to keep the patient alive. In two different places, Ramsey
discusses the teaching of Karl Barth on this point. Barth, with his
insistence on the sanctity of life and the alien dignity of man,
which Ramsey enthusiastically adopts in other contexts, at first
defends the need for medicine to do everything possible to keep
in existence the human life which is so valued by God. Barth rules
out any pettifogging distinction between directly killing and allowing to die. However, in a fine print paragraph, Barth later
reverses himself and thinks it is conceivable that a doctor might

118. *Ibid.*, p. 151.
119. *Ibid.*, p. 104.

have to recoil from a prolongation of life which would be the equivalent of human arrogance in the face of approaching death. Ramsey argues that love's casuistry has brought Barth to see that letting life ebb away and euthanasia are not the same thing. The Christian theology of care means that one attend the dying patient and not unnecessarily prolong dying.[120]

On the question of the distinction between ordinary and extraordinary means, Ramsey has studied and generally accepts the representative literature in Catholic theology on the point, especially the doctoral dissertation of Joseph Sullivan and the articles by Gerald Kelly, S.J.[121] The moralist's understanding of ordinary and extraordinary is not always the same as the doctor's. For the doctor the distinction often means what is customary as opposed to what is unusual treatment, whereas the ethicist sees the distinction relative to the condition of the patient. Second, the moralist sees no real difference in the decision to stop using extraordinary means and the decision not to use them originally; whereas the doctor finds greater difficulty in discontinuing a treatment already begun than in not beginning such a treatment. Third, the moralist includes non-medical criteria such as financial conditions and repugnance in determining what constitutes ordinary or extraordinary means.[122]

In general, Ramsey accepts the understanding of ordinary and extraordinary means proposed by Gerald Kelly. Kelly described the ordinary means of preserving life as those medicines, treatments, and operations which offer a reasonable hope of benefit for the patient and which can be obtained and used without excessive pain, expense, or other inconvenience. Extraordinary means are all medicines, operations, and treatments which cannot be obtained or used without excessive expense, pain, or other inconvenience, or which, if used, would not offer a reasonable hope of benefit.[123] Ramsey accepts and amplifies two updatings that Kelly

120. "Reference Points in Deciding about Abortion," pp. 92–94; *PP*, pp. 154–157. Cf. Karl Barth, *Church Dogmatics* (Edinburgh: Clark, 1961), III/4, pp. 423–427.
121. Joseph V. Sullivan, *Catholic Teaching on the Morality of Euthanasia* (Washington: Catholic University of America Press, 1949); Gerald Kelly, S.J., "The Duty of Using Artificial Means of Preserving Life," *Theological Studies*, XI (1950), pp. 203–220; Kelly, "The Duty to Preserve Life," *Theological Studies*, XII (1951), pp. 550–556.
122. *PP*, pp. 118–124.
123. Kelly, *Medico-Moral Problems*, p. 129.

made in the traditional understanding—that there is no duty to use useless means even if they are only natural and not artificial and the fact that the treatment terminates in the person and not in a particular disease, so that insulin for a diabetic with terminal cancer can be an extraordinary means.[124] Ramsey does admit a great relativity in understanding what constitutes an extraordinary means, but such relativity becomes the chief virtue of this distinction which will change with persons and historical and medical developments.[125]

Ramsey finds in this distinction the wisdom which distinguishes the medical moral obligation to the dying from the obligation to the living. The claims of the suffering dying upon the human community are different from the claims of those who are not dying even if they are suffering or even irreversibly ill. Although it may be hard to determine in particular cases, the process of dying begins when one is irreversibly overtaken by his dying. To such people we owe only care and not struggle.[126]

One recent author, Kieran Nolan, argues that the criteria of ordinary and extraordinary means can be reduced to that of usefulness. If something is truly no longer a remedy, it is an extraordinary means. If this is true, then the question of dispensable means becomes in its entirety the question of the irreversibility of the dying process. The distinction between ordinary and extraordinary means becomes the same as the distinction between prolonging life and prolonging death.[127] Ramsey realizes that the distinction between ordinary and extraordinary means involves more than the question of the irreversible dying process, for usefulness is not the only criterion in distinguishing ordinary from extraordinary means. The distinction also applies in situations in which the dying process has not already begun, but a greater part of the distinction does refer to the criterion of usefulness and the dying process.[128]

In the case of the dying process, the medical and the moral duty

---

124. *PP*, pp. 124–132.
125. *Ibid.*, p. 119.
126. *Ibid.*, p. 133.
127. Kieran Nolan, "The Problem of Care for the Dying," in *Absolutes in Moral Theology?*, pp. 249–260.
128. *PP*, p. 133.

are the same—care, but only care for the dying person. Medicine even on strictly medical grounds should do no more than care for the dying person. This care calls for us to accompany the other in his dying. In this connection, Ramsey calls for a systemic change whereby the process of dying would be taken out of the hospital and put back into the home in the midst of family, friends, and neighborhood. Too often today we are not confronted with the reality of dying. Ramsey acknowledges that such confrontation might shatter some families and relatives, but for once they would be shattered by a confrontation with reality. As a result, God might not be as dead as lately he is supposed to be.[129]

The question of extraordinary and ordinary means cannot be completely reduced to the criterion of usefulness and the reality of the dying process. Grounds other than hopelessness can make it morally right to desist or never to begin using medical means even though they may be effective remedies. The older Catholic theology proposed such reasons as leaving home, repugnance, very costly treatments, and amputations, not primarily because of the pain but because of the serious inconvenience of living with a mutilated body. Thus there are broader, non-medical reasons which make certain treatments elective. In these cases, the doctor acts more as a man than as a medical expert. There is a difference between the medical and the moral imperative, but they are not separable in the person or in the vocation of a person who is a physician.[130]

Ramsey, for example, argues that a quadruple amputee has no obligation to choose existence by submitting to any and every means to save his life. Such a theory is also applied to the beginning of human life. Here he rejects both fetal euthanasia and a relentless and unqualified effort to save fetal life. Thus Ramsey believes there is no moral need for parents to allow surgery on a severely malformed infant girl to increase her slender chance of survival. The operation might increase her slim chance of living but would not significantly relieve the exceedingly great deformity of her body.[131]

129. *Ibid.*, pp. 132–136.
130. *Ibid.*, pp. 136–144.
131. "Reference Points in Deciding about Abortion," pp. 97–98.

Ramsey adds a qualification to his ethics of caring and only caring for the dying. Some have proposed that once the dying process has begun, then there no longer exists a significant moral difference between withholding or stopping treatment on the one hand and positively interfering (e.g., by injecting air into the blood stream) to bring about death. Ramsey rejects such an approach. If there is no difference between omission and commission once the dying process has begun, then there is also no difference in the case of the patient who is not dying but is irreversibly ill. Above all, such opinions forget that the distinction is grounded on the principle of caring for the dying. "In caring for the dying we cease doing what was once called for and begin to do what is called for now. To assist the process of dying would be a defection from the faithfulness claim of a fellow human being, for we cannot be released from the claims of Christian charity by a still-living man."[132]

However, Ramsey does propose two exceptions which truly constitute two classes or types of cases that qualify the obligation of care for the dying. If the dying person is already in a state beyond our love and care so that it no longer has any meaning for him, then this is the point where the critical moral distinction between commission and omission vanishes. This might be true in the case of patients in deep and irreversible coma. The second class of exceptions, again based on care for the dying, might occur if there is a kind of prolonged dying in which it is medically impossible to keep severe pain at bay. Again, it is not for the moralist to say if there is such a dying. Ramsey does not believe that these two types of exceptions, based clearly on the concept of care for the dying, would weaken medicine's life–giving mission and open the door to serious abuses.[133]

Once again, I find myself in general agreement with many of the approaches and conclusions reached by Ramsey, but there are significant differences on both substantial and more peripheral matters. It is interesting that in two places Ramsey extensively cites the teaching of Karl Barth on the difference between directly

132. *PP*, p. 160.
133. *Ibid.*, pp. 160–164.

killing and allowing to die. Only with great difficulty and after having first denied the distinction, does Barth tentatively acknowledge such an exception but only in the case of the dying life as such.[134] Notice that the reason for Barth's position is the arrogance in prolonging human life when it seems that God is already encompassing the person with death. However, as Ramsey himself admits, the distinction between ordinary and extraordinary encompasses more than dying life. In fact, later it will be shown that such a distinction when it arose in Catholic theology was probably more concerned with the cases in which the person was not now dying.

Why is Barth reluctant and why does he limit it only to the dying process? I believe that the basis for the Barthian position is the position he takes on the sanctity of life, a position frequently espoused by Ramsey himself. The distinction between ordinary and extraordinary means of preserving life as it originated in the Roman Catholic tradition seems to imply that one can and at times must make judgments about the value of life in comparison with other values (e.g., as Ramsey himself has done in his belief that it is better to die than to live as a quadruple amputee). Such a distinction raises questions about the quality of life and presupposes some way in which one can make the judgment that it is better to die rather than to live in a particular way. It involves a calculus weighing the value of life and existence against such other values as cost, repugnance, physical or mental suffering, deformities and even the locale in which one wants to live his life. Such a calculus seems to be explicitly excluded in a theory of the sanctity of life based solely on the alien dignity conferred by God.

Barth's great reluctance to accept the distinction between direct killing and allowing to die and his apparently narrow restriction on extraordinary means seems to be the logical consequence of his own position on the sanctity of life, for this excludes any judgments comparing human life with other values. Logically, I do not think that Ramsey can so strongly endorse the Barthian teaching on the sanctity of human life and still admit, especially in cases other than in the dying process, the fact that men can choose for

134. *Ibid.*, p. 156.

reasons which center on the quality of life not to use treatments which are medically available and effective in curing disease and prolonging life. This recalls the same apparent difficulty with Ramsey's assertion in the discussion of abortion that no moralist would maintain that physical life is more important than psychological life. Ramsey's theory of the sanctity of life based solely on an alien dignity (excluding now the case of the dying process) seems to provide him no theoretical possibility for the judgment not to use extraordinary means based on "the higher importance of the worth and relations for which his life was lived."[135]

The insistence on the sanctity of individual human life strikes a resonant cord for me and many others contemplating these questions. The dignity of human life cannot rest ultimately on social worth, merit, or what one does. In particular, the state and those who act in an official capacity cannot ordinarily make such comparative judgments about the value of different lives. I share Ramsey's concern that a utilitarian ethic and a technological mentality might not give enough importance to the dignity of individual human life. I disagree with Ramsey's radical theological approach to the sanctity of life as an alien dignity which then does not allow for some of the comparative judgments that I, and even Ramsey, would admit in practice.

Ramsey develops an intriguing theory of care for the dying as distinguished from the arbitrary prolongation of life and the arbitrary shortening of life. There is much merit in such an ethic of care for the dying. I accept many aspects of this, but I do have two difficulties with Ramsey's presentation: the origin of the theory of care for the dying in the distinction between ordinary and extraordinary means, and the exact meaning of care in some cases.

Perhaps the theory of care and only care for the dying, which Ramsey enunciates, is "more creative" than he wants to admit. It may have some roots in the older question about extraordinary means, but that older question was not primarily concerned with the question of care for those who are in the dying process. One must admit that the older question in its origins pertained more to what we call today questions about the quality of life. Ramsey

135. *Ibid.*, p. 137.

rightly points out that it is the criterion of usefulness which reduces the extraordinary means question to the question of the prolongation of the dying process and care for the dying. However, again as Ramsey admits, this criterion of usefulness was only added quite late to the description of an extraordinary means. The older criteria, which at the beginning and for a long time were the only criteria associated with the description of extraordinary means, such as expense, pain, or inconvenience could not be reduced to the question of the prolongation of dying and care for the dying.

The question of extraordinary means appears to have arisen not so much in connection with the prolongation of dying but with the realization that physical life is not an absolute value that had to be kept in existence at all costs. At least in its genesis, the question of extraordinary means was not dealing primarily with the dying process. Obviously, the important concept of care for the dying can stand on its own and does have some relationship to the question of extraordinary means. I do think that Ramsey has somewhat overemphasized the fact that his understanding of care for the dying was always embodied in the wisdom of the question of extraordinary means.[136]

My more important and substantive disagreement with Ramsey concerns the exact meaning of care for the dying. Ramsey understands it as embracing two things: a cessation of attempts to prolong death needlessly, and positive acts of caring for the dying which involve attending and accompanying the dying person, making him as comfortable as possible and expressing in concrete practice his faithfulness claims upon us.

I was one of the theologians mentioned by Ramsey, who suggested that once the dying process has begun the difference between actions of commission and omission ceases to exist. Ramsey argues that if one accepts such a position, it is impossible to admit logically a distinction between commission and omission in the case of the living sick, i.e., those who are seriously ill and irreversi-

136. My interpretation is based on aspects which Ramsey himself admits. For a historical development of the question, see Daniel A. Cronin, *The Moral Law in Regard to the Ordinary and Extraordinary Means of Conserving Life* (Rome: Gregorian University Press, 1958).

bly ill but not dying. However the basis for the distinction remains quite evident—the difference between the person who is living and the person who is dying. Once the dying process encompasses the person, Ramsey himself admits that our relationship to the person and his claims upon us change.

Ramsey also argues that to assist positively the dying process would be a sort of abandonment; "an affirmative abandonment of the dying solely to God's care in separation from ours, a self–contradiction at the heart of Christian charity ceasing, by this act, from its works before released from the claims and needs of a still-living fellowman."[137] Note here some confusion in the fact that Ramsey refers to the person as dying, but later speaks of the claims of the still living. This is the crux of the question—the claims of the person who is dying. Ramsey admits that proper care for the dying can be a shortening of the dying process, or at least not lengthening the dying process. Care for the dying is not just the negative act of doing nothing and accompanying the person in his dying.

The question centers on the dominion which man has over the dying process. I distinguish this from life itself and from other processes. I agree with the traditional argument against euthanasia, that man does not have full dominion over his life and, therefore, cannot positively interfere to take his life. Man does have dominion over his bodily processes so that he can interfere, for example, in the generative process through contraception and sterilization. Man does have some dominion over the dying process because of which he can as a matter of fact shorten the time of his dying by not using or discontinuing even readily available means to prolong life. Some would say that all he does in this case is to accept the shortening of the dying process by doing nothing to ward it off. Is there that great a difference to accept a shortening that one can readily avoid and to positively interfere to shorten the dying process? I do not accept as great a distinction between acts of commission and acts of omission in this case as Ramsey does. Precisely because the dying process has now begun, man's positive intervention is not an arrogant usurping of the role of God but

137. *Ibid.*, p. 160.

rather in keeping with the process of dying which is now encompassing the person. Recall that Ramsey himself does at times admit such positive interference, but in theory I propose the dying process as the time in which the distinction between omission and commission no longer involves a meaningful moral difference.

I have proposed such a solution in the theoretical order, but in the practical order there are a number of difficulties. The first problem concerns the definition of and criteria for the dying process. Can a person in the dying process be distinguished from those who are living even though seriously or irreversibly ill? However, the same problem exists for Ramsey, and he evidently believes that such a distinction can be made in practice. Second, would such a justified positive interference based on the difference created by the claims of the dying person lead to a broader endorsement of euthanasia in the case of others not now in the dying process? In this case the difference is precisely the dying process so there is a strong firebreak that would prevent opening the door to all sorts of euthanasia. As a practical guide I would allow positive interference at the same moment in which treatments and procedures can be discontinued because they are useless. Thus in practice a tentative case can be made for allowing this type of interference in the dying process with the major problem being the criteria for determining and judging the dying process.

There appear to be two other areas of lesser import in which Ramsey's reasoning is difficult to reconcile with other positions he has taken. Ramsey makes the flat judgment that the process of dying should be taken out of the hospital and put back in the home. This is obviously a prudential judgment which elsewhere he put outside the competency of the ethicist or the church as such. Perhaps Ramsey is making the statement only as a man and not as an ethicist, but such does not seem to be the case. I agree with Ramsey's judgment, and in theory I also think that ethicists and the church should make such prudential judgments even though they may at times be wrong.

Another problem arises in the argumentation Ramsey employs in extending to early fetal life the need not to use extraordinary means to preserve life. He argues that if defective people are kept alive at all costs the result will be a steadily increasing number of seriously defective individuals among the population in future generations because these defective genes will be passed on to offspring if these people live and reproduce.[138] Here Ramsey does make a judgment about the individual on the basis of factors affecting the species and other human beings. Also he is making some comparative analysis which his notion of the sanctity of life seems to rule out. I personally would agree with such an analysis, but elsewhere Ramsey has insisted that decisions about the lives of individuals should prescind from the needs of others in society or from the species itself.

The medical ethics of Paul Ramsey constitutes an important contribution to the field. In general, I am in much greater agreement with Ramsey in this area than in the question of political ethics. This greater agreement is rooted both in methodological approaches and in substantive presuppositions such as the dignity of individual human life and equal right of all to life. My disagreements tend to be less and in more minor and peripheral aspects, but here again methodological concerns account for some of these practical differences.

138. "Reference Points in Deciding about Abortion," pp. 99–100.

CHAPTER IV

Genetics

and the

Future of Man

In the last decade a new factor has contributed to a growing interest in medical ethics. Recent developments in molecular biology and genetics provide man with the power now, and especially in the future, to alter himself and to direct the evolution of the human species. Some would call this the most radical of all revolutions in the history of man because it concerns man himself.[1] In the past, medical ethics was concerned with problems raised by treating or caring for a particular patient with a particular disease, but now man can have the power to do much more. Man can interfere not only to eliminate disease and treat the individual person, but he can also positively build in various characteristics in human persons and drastically alter the human species itself. The present possibility of acquiring such knowledge and power raises the fundamental ethical question: Should man do what he can do? Is it ever necessary for man to say "no" to what science makes possible?

Paul Ramsey has discussed these questions of the new biology and genetics more thoroughly than any other Christian ethicist.[2] In general, Ramsey argues in his occasionally eloquent and often

1. Robert T. Francoeur, *Eve's New Rib: Twenty Faces of Sex, Marriage and Family* (New York: Harcourt, Brace, Jovanovich, 1972), pp. 8–11.

2. Three of Ramsey's pioneering essays have been gathered together in *Fabricated Man*. The first essay, "Moral and Religious Implications of Genetic Control," originally appeared in *Genetics and the Future of Man*, John D. Roslansky, ed. (Amsterdam: North–Holland Publishing Company, 1965), pp. 109–169. The second essay, "Shall We Clone a Man?" was originally presented as a paper at a conference on Ethics in Medicine and Technology sponsored by the Institute of.

rhetorical style for an appreciation of man's moral limitations because of which man at times must say "no" to the possibilities of science. In his later writings, Ramsey has tried to distinguish and classify the various types of procedures which are possible now or might be possible in the future.[3] The first generic category consists of non–genetic procedures which may be used to correct a genetic disease or to prevent its transmission. Insulin injections for diabetes, diet for PKU mental disease, and operations for hair lip are all illustrations of corrective non–genetic procedures. Genetic counseling and contraception or sterilization for genetic reasons exemplify preventive non–genetic practices.

Gene therapy or treatment with the metaphor of gene "surgery" describes the treatment whose aim is to change the genes of an existing human individual. A complicating factor arises from the fact that these gene changes in the individual person may be either inheritable or non-inheritable.

A third generic category Ramsey calls "gametic manipulation" and describes with the metaphor of genetic "engineering." These procedures affect the gametes (the sperm and ova and their precursor cells) with the purpose of preventing the transmission of genetic defects or the positive aim of improving the future individual or the species.

A fourth category involves non–genetic procedures such as AID (artificial insemination donor), *in vitro* fertilization and embryo transplants, cloning (asexual reproduction which involves the making of carbon copies of existing individuals from their already existing tissue cells), which have in common the fact that offspring are brought into existence through means other than the sexual union of man and woman. The metaphor of "reproductive engineering" most accurately describes these approaches that find new ways of reproduction either to permit people to have children who otherwise could not have them, to replicate famous

---

Religion at the Texas Medical Center and by Rice University, in Houston on March 25–28, 1968. It was originally published with all the conference papers in *Who Shall Live?*, pp. 78–113. The third essay, "Parenthood and the Future of Man by Artificial Insemination, Etcetera, Etcetera," has not been previously published.
3. I am following the classification proposed by the author in "Morals and the Practice of Genetic Medicine," pp. 1–7. See also Paul Ramsey, "Response," *Philosophy Forum*, XII (1973), pp. 1–4. This and subsequent references are to Ramsey's manuscript, since the issue is not yet published.

people, to improve the human species, or just to save a prospective mother from the burden of childbearing. This chapter will discuss the question in terms of these four categories, but with the third and fourth categories (genetic and reproductive engineering) considered together and receiving a lengthier analysis.

NON–GENETIC PROCEDURES AND GENE THERAPY

Non–genetic procedures do not, in Ramsey's judgment, add any new problems to the accepted understanding of medical ethics and its principles. However, Ramsey does strongly oppose elective abortion, which is increasingly proposed as a solution if the fetus is deformed or defective. If both partners have a recessive gene for a particular defect, there is a one–in–four chance that their offspring will have that defect, while there is a two–in–four chance that the offspring will be a recessive carrier of the defect. If, unfortunately, the fetus is defective, the parents could then decide to abort the fetus and try again to have a normal child. Some refer to such an abortion as a therapeutic abortion, but Ramsey strongly protests the use of such terminology. Such a designation gives to therapy and treatment a meaning which these words have never had and should never have. The primary patient in this case is the fetus, but abortion hardly involves a treatment or remedy for the primary patient. One could justify such procedures only if there are good and sufficient grounds for judging such fetuses to be no part of the human population. The euphemism of thereapeutic abortion in this case constitutes a misuse of language, disguising the fact that we are removing defective lives which are deemed to be of no worth.[4]

The second category of gene therapy or gene treatment, according to Ramsey, introduces no new ethical considerations, since this involves the treatment of an individual patient with the physician, balancing the cure and the risks involved for the individual patient.[5] In general, such procedures try to alter the gene,

4. "Morals and the Practice of Genetic Medicine," pp. 2–4; 20–23; Paul Ramsey, "Genetic Therapy: A Theologian's Response," *The New Genetics and the Future of Man*, Michael P. Hamilton, ed. (Grand Rapids: William B. Eerdmans Publishing Co., 1972), pp. 160–161.
5. *FM*, pp. 44–45; "Morals and the Practice of Genetic Medicine," pp. 5–7.

or genes, responsible for the particular condition of the patient. But there are some aspects of such treatment which do call for special ethical consideration.

An important observation to make about gene therapy is factual. At the present time it is not technically possible or feasible to change a very specific molecule in the complex structure without affecting other molecules. There are problems of specificity, directivity, and efficiency that must be overcome before this becomes a possibility. The fact that most human traits have a polygenic base makes the problem even more difficult.

The two complicating factors entering into the ethical judgment in these cases are the complexity of the procedure and the fact that the untoward changes wrought might be passed on to offspring. The complexity of the procedure of changing genes means that one can run the risk of unpredictable and deleterious results on complex and polygenic traits contributing to behavior and intelligence. Ramsey's specific conclusions on this question changed as he became more conscious of these two different complicating factors, but even his first discussion does recognize the dangers created by the delicacy of the operation and the complexity involved.

The ethical solution first proposed by Ramsey concludes that before doing such a procedure the science of genetics must be fully informed of the facts and have a reasonable and well-examined expectation of doing more good than harm by eliminating the defective gene in question. In the practice of genetic medicine there doubtless will be some errors made in inculpable ignorance, but such injuries, while they would be tragic, would not constitute wrong-doing.[6] Ramsey here is arguing without explicitly enunciating it, that the errors are unintended and justified by the proportionately greater good possible for the individual.

However, Ramsey later becomes more conscious of the danger of slipping a single nucleotide and realizes the need to change the material conclusion that he previously reached. It will be much harder than he first thought for genetic surgery to pass the test of a reasonable and well-examined expectation of doing more good

6. *FM*, p. 45.

than harm.[7] Ramsey, in a later consideration, makes some more specific conclusions. Insulin is likely to remain the treatment of choice for diabetes and diet for PKU mental disease until we can be more sure that disproportionate consequences will not follow from gene therapy. However in severe genetic illnesses, such as argininemia or Tay–Sachs disease, where there are no other remedies, a physician could take the more unsure approach of gene therapy.[8]

The decision to use gene therapy must also cope with another factor—the fact that gene change may be inheritable by offspring. Ramsey brings up this question only in his more recent writings. Obviously, if the good effect is inheritable this is all to the better; but such gene therapy might cause deleterious side–effects in offspring. In this case, gene therapy, because of this hereditary aspect, differs from all other forms of surgery. In these cases Ramsey suggests that we may have to say that an unknown and unforeclosed risk to future generations must outweigh the benefit that could be secured for the individual patient. In a matter of such grave importance "no discernible risk" is not good enough. We need to know that there are no risks—a requirement which inheritable gene therapy is not apt to meet.[9]

Ramsey also forsees some problems in the case in which the gene therapy is non-inheritable. Medicine might be able to replace the defective gene in cystic fibrosis with a normal gene and not affect the person's reproductive cells. In this case we would be keeping people genetically alive who would pass on their bad genes into the human gene pool. Ramsey admits that this brings up the dilemma about the medical needs of the individual person and the effect which his healing may have on the human gene pool.[10]

I disagree with Ramsey's solution in the case of gene therapy which is inheritable. The primary patient in this case is the individual. The therapy is for his benefit. Any other effects, including the unknown risk to future generations, are indirect and unintended. On the basis of proportionality, one could balance the

7. *Ibid.*, pp. 100–101.
8. "Morals and the Practice of Genetic Medicine," pp. 14–15.
9. *Ibid.*, pp. 17–18. "Genetic Therapy: A Theologian's Response," p. 169.
10. "Genetic Therapy: A Theologian's Response," p. 170.

various values involved to see if the good outweighs the bad. The risk to future generations is to be considered in Ramsey's own terminology as collateral damage, which could be proportionate to the good to be attained. Thus Ramsey asks too much in demanding that there be no risk for future offspring, for some risk to future offspring could be justified in terms of the principle of the double-effect. In this case the primary patient is the person and not any possible future offspring. Granted that one has an obligation to possible offspring does not mean that in this case Ramsey cannot logically employ the principle of the double-effect which would not demand the assurance that there be no risk for the future possible offspring.

In addition, after the use of gene therapy it might be possible to determine if there are any inheritable gene changes brought about in the person. If so, there would then be other ways (e.g., not having a child) of ensuring that these were not passed on to offspring. Ramsey in other contexts frequently speaks of the need to use contraception, sterilization, and other means to prevent reproducing genetically defective offspring, for no one has an absolute right to have children.

Perhaps this is the best place to discuss the question of screening which does not fit perfectly into the categories of treatment that Ramsey proposed. Screening is itself not a treatment, but a way of identifying those who have a particular disease or defective genes. Genetic screening is a species of the more general medical screening.

Ramsey proposes the following norms and principles to guide the ethics of screening. The ultimate test of morality cannot be just good results or the net amount of good that is done. Through screening, medicine must strive to identify patients for their own good with the minimum test that medicine can do no harm to the patient. Especially in the case of those who cannot consent, proxy consent can be morally given only if the procedure is for their benefit. Doing no harm to the individual means that a low incidence of risk of damage from the procedure itself cannot meet an acceptable moral standard in the case of individuals incompetent to give consent to screening when it is not for their benefit.[11]

11. Paul Ramsey, "Screening: An Ethicist's View," p. 4. This paper will be cited in the manuscript form in which it was first presented at a conference on "Ethical

On the basis of these principles Ramsey arrives at the following conclusions. First, screening for contagious diseases and screening as an extension of genetic counseling (parents discovering if they are carriers of a genetic defect so that parents can make informed decisions) are clearly justified, if not obligatory. Second, proxy consent to screen for non-contagious diseases in either born or unborn individuals who are incapable of consenting is warranted if the objective is their treatment and only if no harm is done to another life which needs neither help nor the screen. Three, intrauterine screening by amniocentesis is most problematic, if indeed, it is not to be morally censured.[12]

The first two cases are easy to understand, especially in the light of Ramsey's discussion of other topics such as the covenant relationship between physician and patient and the ethics of experimentation. In contagious diseases there is either an actual illness or injury for the individual or the universal risk of infection which justify implying the consent of patients who themselves cannot expressly give consent.[13]

Ramsey devotes most of his article on screening to the case of the unborn or the newly born. In many different places he has reacted negatively to "therapeutic" abortion for eliminating defective fetuses. The process of amniocentesis now affords an opportunity to screen the child in the womb to determine if there are any defective genes present so that elective abortion can follow. Ramsey categorically opposes such abortions as the strangest, most incoherent, and morally outrageous notion of the proper treatment of patients that has ever occurred to the mind of man.[14]

In his long discussion of the screening of the unborn in this particular article, however, he appears to prescind from this argument. It seems as if he wants to give some arguments against such screening followed by abortion if defects are discovered which do

Issues in Genetic Counseling and the Use of Genetic Knowledge," October 10–14, 1971, sponsored by the John E. Fogarty International Center for Advanced Study in the Health Sciences, National Institutes of Health, Bethesda, Maryland. This paper and the proceedings of the conference will be published.

12. *Ibid.*, pp. 4, 5.

13. *Ibid.*, pp. 5–16.

14. *Ibid.*, p. 55; *FM*, pp. 114–115.

not depend on his judgment that the child in the uterus is a human individual. His approach, in my opinion, is not successful.

Ramsey brings up two major difficulties with screening the unborn or the newly born. The first is that the moral norm of the greatest good altogether cannot avoid interchanging non–interchangeable lives. Even proponents of screening admit that some will be falsely identified as positive so that these innocents might be destroyed together with the true positives. Such errors constitute an undefendable catastrophe.[15]

The second difficulty brings up the incomparability of risks. The screening process itself, e.g., amniocentesis, involves some risks. How does one discover the proportion between natural defects and induced damages? Some apparently make the decision only on the basis of the incidence of risks. If there is a two percent incidence of risk in amniocentesis, then there must be a greater incidence of risk that the child is defective to justify the screening process. But this is only a superficial view of the comparison to be made, and one which is easily quantifiable. There are important qualitative aspects that must be a part of the calculus, for one must compare the quality of a natural defect with the quality of the possibly induced defect. This is the quantity of the quality problem stemming from the intrinsically unquantifiable evaluation of incomparable impairments.[16]

I cannot accept the validity of Ramsey's argumentation in these two points. His first reason rightly insists on the non–exchangeability of patients in the procedure. One cannot argue from the greatest net good when this is achieved because of the harm done to certain innocents. However, Ramsey's argument, especially in terms of aborting some who are healthy, is convincing only to those who accept the fact that the fetus is a human individual. If the fetus is not a human individual, then there is no great difficulty in sacrificing some healthy fetuses for the greater good of the human race. His argument stands only on the presupposition that the fetus is a human being, but he appears to prescind from that presupposition.

15. *Ibid.,* pp. 19–26.
16. *Ibid.,* pp. 27–38.

His second argument is also unconvincing. Many human and medical decisions depend on judgments about different aspects which are qualitatively different. The decision not to use extraordinary means involves such a decision for one compares added life against the realities of pain, expense, or inconvenience. Ramsey correctly points out that the incidence of risk is not a sufficient criterion. A qualitative comparison of the different impairments is required, but this is possible. Many human decisions must be made in this way.

In the course of his discussion on the screening of the unborn, two other issues are raised that appear again in his genetic ethics, especially in the consideration of genetic and reproductive engineering. First, he argues against making medical decisions on non–medical grounds for this opens medicine to many possible abuses, especially the doctoring of the wishes or the whims of the patient.[17] Second, he denies that every couple has the right to have a child and a perfectly healthy child.[18]

There is another important problem that troubles Ramsey. In a society that strives to have only normal children, abnormals will be treated as outcasts.[19] There is a real danger here. However, this does not mean that it is wrong to try moral ways to avoid abnormal children. Ramsey himself admits that at times couples should not have a child if it will be abnormal. There will always be a tension between our efforts to have normal children and the realization that this will not always happen. In these cases our care of the abnormal can well be a sign of our own humanity.

Although I do not agree with all the reasons Ramsey offers, I am in general agreement about his position on screening. There is the danger that individuals might be sacrificed to the greatest net good of society. In the particular question of amniocentesis, the procedure must be for the good of the patient involved and proportionate to the risks of the procedure itself. Logically, I could justify aborting the fetus only in the comparatively few cases in which the dying process has already begun. There are also many other subtleties that arise in screening for particular diseases,

17. *Ibid.*, pp. 48–51.
18. *Ibid.*, pp. 40–47.
19. *Ibid.*, pp. 52–57.

especially when the disease is common to a particular race. Another important question is whether or not screening should ever become compulsory. I argue in favor of voluntary programs except in truly emergency situations or in cases of contagious diseases.

GENETIC AND REPRODUCTIVE ENGINEERING

Ramsey himself discusses at much greater length the questions of genetic engineering and reproductive engineering. These procedures have not only the negative goal of preventing the birth of genetically defective lives but especially the positive goal of trying to improve human offspring and the human species itself. Science holds in front of man alluring possibilities about his future. Man can now have greater control over his life and destiny by improving the human species itself. Ramsey, as might be expected, has very serious reservations about the procedures falling under these two categories. His particular ethical difficulties with such approaches include a denial of the very nature of human parenthood; a dangerous dualism that fails to accept that man is an embodied soul; an illegitimate subordination of the individual to the species; and an ethic which thinks only of ends and pays no attention to means.

Theological, Anthropological, and Ethical Presuppositions

Ramsey also finds unacceptable theological presuppositions behind many of these scientific proposals for the betterment of the human species. The worldviews supporting such practices seem opposed to the Christian worldview. In his earliest treatment of the subject, Ramsey contrasts the perspective of the scientist or the geneticist with the worldview of the Christian.[20]

Enthusiastic eugenic proposals are based on the humanism and liberal progressivism which are so prevalent in our society today. Ramsey contracts such a liberal progressivism with Christian eschatology and its understanding of the world. Especially in response to H. J. Muller, the Nobel Prize winner from the University of Indiana, Ramsey brings up the eschatological considerations,

20. *FM*, pp. 11–32.

but he willingly acknowledges that he is not competent to judge Muller's vision. Muller is very pessimistic about the future of the human race because of the mutations and consequent deteriorations in the human gene pool made possible because natural selection no longer effectively weeds out the unfit. Modern medicine now allows people to live and reproduce who formerly would have died and had no offspring. But their defective genes are now passed on to their children. Muller proposes a voluntary program of AID through sperm banks which store the seed of famous men chosen after a waiting period in which their greatness can be properly evaluated. Muller believes that many women and their husbands would willingly accept the opportunity to have a child whose real father would be Einstein or some other outstanding person.[21]

Ramsey refers to Muller's view of the future as a genetic apocalypse which man must avoid through the use of AID and sperm banks. Since the scientist lives in only one city, his hope is based on the need to prevent that apocalypse. The Christian who reads the Bible, which still contains the Revelation of John and other apocalyptic passages, knows that there is going to be an end to this world and his hope is not based on any imperative to prevent such an apocalypse. "Religious people have never denied, indeed they affirm, that God means to kill us all in the end, and in the end He is going to succeed."[22] Whereas genetics teaches that we are genes and unto genes we shall return, Genesis teaches that we are dust and unto dust we shall return. But the Christian puts his hope and trust in God and in his promises. The Christian knows that he does not have to succeed in preventing genetic deterioration any more than he has to succeed in preventing the collision of the planets. God and not the science of genetics will deliver man.[23]

Both Sacred Scripture and sound reason do not promise success to man in human history. Ramsey has only scorn for theologians who have embraced messianic positivism and baptized secular technology especially in the area of genetics and reproduction. Karl Rahner, who emphasizes the role of man as self–creator,

21. *Ibid.*, pp. 22–25.
22. *Ibid.*, p. 27.
23. *Ibid.*, pp. 27–30.

Roman Catholic omega pointers, and Protestant theologians of secular, historical hope give too much importance to the fact that man is here and now building the new heaven and the new earth. They collapse the distinction between being men before God and being God before we have learned to be men. Messianic positivism with its faith and trust in technology, science, and genetics sees a close relationship between the teleological future of man and the absolute future of God. In this connection Karl Rahner can make the statement that there really is nothing possible for man that he ought not to do. For Rahner, man's this–worldly self–creation has a positive relation to his opening of himself to the absolute future of God.[24]

Ramsey cannot accept such an eschatology which sees human, temporal history so positively related to the kingdom of God. Above all he cannot accept what follows from such a close identification; namely, that man should do everything he can do biologically to improve the human species. There always is a great danger in putting the engine of messianic faith behind scientific capabilities. Our absolute future does not depend on our overcoming a genetic apocalypse. For Ramsey, the existence of the two cities seems to mean a great gulf and separation between the two.[25]

Ramsey's eschatology has a number of ethical consequences in the area of genetics. The progress and the coming of the kingdom of God are not at all dependent on scientific progress or on a better human species. Thus Ramsey knows no theological basis for an understanding of moral development in human evolution. In fact, with his insistence on limitation and sinfulness, Ramsey will always be skeptical about any truly human progress or growth. He might not deny some penultimate progress, but he does not positively develop such a possibility. Ramsey does not deny that men and women in their procreation have an obligation to the future of the human race; but man, if he is to remain man and have any basis for a morality, must remember that there may be a number of things that he can do that he ought not to do.

An important ethical difference based on different eschatologies

24. *Ibid.*, pp. 138–145.
25. *Ibid.*, pp. 22–32.

concerns the ethical model itself and the place of an ethic of means. Those who hold to an end or goal which man must attain by his own actions develop a wholly teleological ethic. The geneticist has as a goal to ensure that there will be people like us to come after us or to improve the human species. Ramsey's Christian eschatology knows no such imperative goal. Anyone who expects ultimate success where ultimate success is not to be found is peculiarly driven to adopt whatever means are necessary to achieve that end. Then there is no room in such an ethic for an independent consideration of means. Since Ramsey knows that men have an end other than what the receding future contains, he develops an ethic of means which is not totally dependent upon the goal mistakenly believed to be absolutely required. Ramsey's eschatology supports the deontological aspect of his ethics. In the concrete an ethic which places such absolute importance on the goal to be achieved will tend to see all things as a means to that goal. In this case of genetics, Ramsey frequently points out the danger of reducing the individual person to a means to obtain the goal. Too often proposals for the genetic future of man do not respect the personhood of the individual. There is an alluring temptation to sacrifice the weak, the defective, and the unborn for the absolute goal of genetic progress.[26]

In keeping with his eschatological presuppositions, Ramsey also proposes a Christian anthropology which is at variance with many of the anthropological insights of those who propose progressive schemes for the future evolution of the human race. Ramsey calls attention to the ethical violations on the horizontal plane involved in many eugenic schemes such as coercive breeding or non-breeding, injustice done to individuals or mishaps, the violation of the nature of human parenthood; but these violations point to a fundamental flaw in the vertical dimension; namely, *hubris* or playing God.[27]

In the proposals for the control of the future of man through genetic manipulation and the alteration of human parenthood, as well as in the proposals for the modification of the individual,

26. *Ibid.*, pp. 29ff, 122ff.
27. *Ibid.*, p. 90.

Ramsey perceives an attempt to prove man's limitless dominion over man. The modification or refabrication of man includes such things as spare–parts surgery; the prevention of aging; the making of cyborgs; the cure of all man's ills; the possibility of freezing man now and having him arise in the next century; and genetic and pharmalogical control of man's inner moods and powers. Specifically, Ramsey criticizes the proposals of Professor Gerald Feinberg, who identifies the most serious flaw in man as that we are conscious beings aware of our limitations. This awareness produces the two-fold alienation of distress because we lack the power to do what we want and because we realize that sooner or later death must put an end to all our thinking and doing. Thus Feinberg hopes to see the next century bring about the conquest of aging as well as an increase in intelligence and consciousness. Thus man himself can overcome the limitations of his own finitude.[28] The *hubris* of man, once again moving him to play God and to refuse his own creatureliness, lies at the heart of all the ethical violations conjured up by the messianic positivists.

One of the often forgotten limitations of man concerns his lack of wisdom to guide the evolutionary process. Ramsey refers occasionally to the fact that our genetic policy-planning would be no better than our public policy-making in environmental and political matters. In fact, man's prideful attempts to direct his genetic future and thus gain access to the tree of life could easily cause the genetic death which God once promised and by his mercy withheld so that his creature, despite his sinful attempts to play God, might still live and perform a limited, creaturely service of life.[29]

Not only human sinfulness but also human limitation makes it impossible for man to plan wisely the genetic future of the human race. Things are so complex and multi–faceted that we do not know what effects our tampering hands will produce. If man has lacked the wisdom to plan his environment, how much more will he lack the wisdom to plan his own nature and his future. Ramsey points out the difficulties in determining the qualities and characteristics that men should have. He recalls, as have other commen-

28. *Ibid.*, pp. 151–159. Gerald Feinberg, *The Prometheus Project* (Garden City: Doubleday, 1968), pp. 43–51.
29. *Ibid.*, p. 96.

tators, that H. J. Muller once listed Lenin on his list of famous and important people whose genotypes should be preserved in human life, but he later took Lenin off the list.[30]

Such a lack of wisdom on man's part for shaping his genetic future corresponds somewhat with Ramsey's skepticism about ever knowing and comparing the relative justice of different states and regimes, but Ramsey does not want to assert that man has no wisdom in this area. In response to H. J. Muller's proposals of the importance of, and need for, wisdom, cooperativeness, happiness, harmony of nature, and richness of potentialities, which would leave sufficient variety of specific genotypes, Ramsey concedes some degree of truth in these proposals. Only a thoroughgoing relativist could deny any fundamental competency in man to make moral judgments. However, Ramsey criticizes Muller for proposing the characteristics of a good scientist or community of scientists and not necessarily the characteristics of good human beings as such. In practice Ramsey does admit difficulties in agreeing on the positive goals of a eugenics program. Since it is easier to agree on negative goals, Ramsey, for this reason, leans in favor of negative eugenics (the elimination of certain things) rather than positive eugenics.[31]

Ramsey's later deliberations on the subject appear to be even more negative about man's wisdom in choosing what will be good for the future of the human race. Ramsey asserts that we now realize that we do not and cannot know if an increase in intelligence will be desirable in the community of the remote future. There are too many other factors that must enter into such a judgment. Only God knows enough to hold the future in his hands.[32] Obviously Ramsey's later and more negative remarks are occasioned by his dialogue with the utopian schemes which have been proposed both in the name of science and in the name of theology. In rather rhetorical language, Ramsey insists that man cannot endure if there is no creation beneath him and assumed into his being on which he ought not to lay his indefinitely tampering hands.

30. *Ibid.*, p. 49.
31. *Ibid.*, pp. 53–56.
32. *Ibid.*, p. 130.

Ramsey notices in the anthropological presuppositions behind many of the proposals for remaking man and the human species two apparently contradictory pairs of attitudes—voluntarism and determinism going together on the one hand, and optimism and pessimism joined in the same general proposals. The combination of voluntarism and determinism, which Ramsey often describes as a boundless freedom and boundless determinism, seems to be directly connected with the scientist's or geneticist's perspective on the world and on reality.[33] Many scientists believe that the whole dignity of man consists in thought. Ramsey has constantly argued against those who forget that man is *sarx* (flesh)—the soul of his body as much as the body of his soul. If man is only thought or freedom, then man can be manipulated at will or in accord with the thought of the manipulator who will remake him in accord with his image of what man should be. To rest man's dignity in thought alone parallels the emphasis on man as self–creator, for there are no biological or other limitations that will stand in the way of what man wants to do.

Paradoxically, many genetic proposals reveal that such a boundless freedom is joined with a boundless determinism. Ramsey points out that arbitrary freedom and mechanism frequently go together. Genetics gives man a somewhat mechanistic view of heredity as if all depended on the right genes. Man, the scientist endowed with thought and freedom, is able to use his knowledge about the genetic basis of human behavior to shape the future destiny of man. This linking of freedom and determinism comes not only from a scientific perspective but is also a widespread cultural phenomenon in our day.[34]

Proposals about man's self–reconstruction and control over the evolutionary future of man frequently contain another anthropological paradox—a pessisism and an optimism about man. The obviously utopian plans for the future and the great designs for a better life illustrate the optimism in such a perspective. The biological future of man is held out as the latest and greatest achievement of man come of age. However, this is often linked with a

33. *Ibid.*, pp. 64ff; 92ff, 129ff.
34. *Ibid.*

black despair about the present state of man. Ramsey sees in Feinberg's book, *The Prometheus Project*, a good example of the intellectual's penchant for species suicide. Utopian proposals for the future arise from despair over the present state of man. Feinberg judges it necessary to so change man that he can overcome the existential alienation brought about by man's consciousness of his own limitations. The future of man can only be brought about by the death or extinction of man as we know him today, especially as the Christian tradition sees him as a finite creature of a good God.[35] "In the first genesis, man with expectation high savored knowledge and God–head, death following. In the second genesis men with expectation high savor death to the species of man as he is, God–head following."[36] Such a despairing view of man, according to Ramsey, fails to acknowledge the goodness of God's creation.

Earlier, Ramsey had noticed the same paradoxical combination of optimism and pessimism in the proposals of H. J. Muller. Muller, who is pessimistic because of the increasingly deleterious gene load, writes at times as if he disparages the presently existing human individual. The man of the future will be both a product and a conscious agent (notice again the paradox of freedom and determinism) of man's ability to influence and change for the better the future of man. Thus pessimism and optimism exist side by side in many contemporary proposals for the genetic betterment of man—a pessimism so stark that it despairs of man as he actually is and an optimism so utopian that man will aspire to, and claim for himself, the attributes of God–head.[37] Such a perspective fails to appreciate, as Augustine said of the Manichees, with good and simple faith that for one good and simple reason God created the world—because it is good.[38]

Ramsey has explicitly pointed out that his disagreements about specific proposals for improving the future of man stem from his theological and anthropological presuppositions which differ from the messianic positivism so often present in the plans proposed for

35. *Ibid.*, pp. 153–160.
36. *Ibid.*, p. 160.
37. *Ibid.*, pp. 16–17.
38. *Ibid.*, pp. 17, 160.

the future of man. As mentioned above, these same presuppositions lead to a deontological aspect in Ramsey's ethical theory, although there is still a place for consequences and teleological reasoning. "In fact there is nothing more important in the whole of ethics than the consequences for good or ill of man's actions and abstentions, *except* right relations among men, justice and fidelity with one another."[39] Ramsey insists that some actions based on our obligation to keep convenant with one another can never become right because of the consequences which might flow from them.

Ramsey mentions another telling argument against a totally teleological approach which he describes in terms of his rejection of the category of making, rather than the category of doing to describe the actions of men. H. Richard Niebuhr explicitly developed the teleological model in terms of man the maker and rejected such an ethical model.[40] Ramsey does not explicitly refer to Niebuhr's rejected model of man the maker, but he develops points that are closely akin to Niebuhr's exposition and rejection of this model. Such an ethical model presupposes that man has the power and the ability to make what he wants out of things and to discard whatever does not fit in with the desired goal. This view of man is congenial with the concept of man as self–creator and with the understanding of man primarily or even exclusively in terms of freedom. Man the maker is a congenial model for a technological perspective. There appear to be no limitations on what man the maker can do and should do in plotting his future.[41]

Ramsey argues strenuously against the introduction of the categories of making and manufacturing into our ethical evaluations of human life. We introduce the language and the meaning of manufacturing with great detriment to a truly human and Christian ethics. Ramsey laments that the principles of medical ethics are fast being replaced by the principles, if any, governing biological manufacture.[42]

39. *Ibid.*, p. 122.
40. H. Richard Niebuhr, *The Responsible Self* (New York: Harper & Row, 1963), pp. 48–51.
41. *FM*, pp. 92ff.
42. Paul Ramsey, "Shall We 'Reproduce'? II. Rejoinders and Future Forecast," in *Journal of the American Medical Association*, CCXX (June 12, 1972), pp. 1481–1482.

Our vocabulary reveals that we have adopted the terms and unfortunately the ethics of manufacturing in speaking about medical morality. Ethicists have often condemned the agricultural metaphors of Augustine, especially his references to sexual intercourse in terms of ploughing a field or sowing seeds, but Ramsey asserts that man has no homeland and humanism and morality no future when man is reduced to either agricultural or technological metaphors. Perhaps it all began when we substituted the manufacturing term reproduction for procreation, human parenthood and the transmission of the one flesh of our lives through the generating generations of men. The debates in the current literature indicate how often the categories of manufacturing, of making, and of designing have replaced the language of a personal ethics of doing—biological engineering, the manufacture of chimeras, hybridization of animal and other human life, spare–parts surgery.[43]

All these general theological, anthropological, and ethical considerations have a bearing on two important specific considerations in Ramsey's ethics on genetics and the future of man. The one consideration involves the nature of human parenthood, and the other focuses on the rights of the individual who is to be brought into the world by these newly proposed means.

The Individual-To-Be

In other questions of medical ethics Ramsey constantly stresses the fundamental importance of the dignity, sacredness, and rights of the individual. His discussions on genetics and the future of man repeat some of the same points and develop new ones. Ramsey has previously insisted that the primary patient is the person as such with whom the physician covenants to provide medical care. In the questions of experimentation, transplants, and screening he fears that often the individual person will be unjustly subordinated to the non-patient, the species. The same danger lurks in the proposals of some geneticists and of some Utopian planners of the future of the human race. Scientific messianists who calmly contemplate the removal or suppression of the individual human subject for their own vision of some religious future have destroyed a true humanism with its proper insistence on the dignity of the

43. *FM,* pp. 136–137.

individual. He insists again on the fact that the patient of any medical procedure is the person and his or her probable offspring—not society or the future or distant generations as such.[44] An action cannot be justified in the name of the common good if it does not flow back on all the members of the community.

The sanctity of the individual and the significance of the individual, however weak or in whatever condition of life, stand as the cornerstone of Ramsey's ethic about genetics and the future of man. Revolutionary biological proposals touch the very crucial question of the future of humanism. Francis Crick mistakenly describes the question as involving a dispute between Christians and humanists, who lack the particular Christian prejudice about the sanctity of the individual. Ramsey locates the dispute as one between Christians and humanists on the one hand and messianic positivists on the other. The newer proposals go beyond the voluntary use of AID and sperm banks proposed by H.J. Muller, who remained a true humanist by insisting on the individual's rational and voluntary determination and never subordinating the individual to the good of the species.[45] (However Ramsey should logically qualify his praise of Muller as a true humanist, for he did accuse Muller of violating the nature of human parenthood. Muller is, in Ramsey's perspective, a humanist to the extent that he recognizes the freedom of the individual, but his understanding of the human does not accept the humanness of man's bodily and corporal being.[46])

Some of the projects now being proposed would involve a fundamental violation of man and leave behind any humane form of ethics. Ramsey denies in this case that his controlling principle is derived from *agape* or lies beyond the ken of the human reasoning which is available to all men. In the specific question of his opposition to *in vitro* fertilization our author again insists that his position is not derived from any specific religious or Christian teaching but from a truly humanistic ethics which until now has been incorporated in the accepted principles of medical ethics.[47]

Ramsey's criticisms of teleological ethics and its failure to

44. *Ibid.*, pp. 96ff., 147ff.
45. *Ibid.*, pp. 147–148.
46. *Ibid.*, pp. 16–19.
47. "Shall We 'Reproduce'?," p. 1350.

provide an independent ethic of means also underscores the importance attached to the individual person. The individual human being has claims of loyalty upon us because he is human, and these claims cannot be overridden by the good consequences that might accrue to the future of the human species. Manipulation of the person without his consent constitutes an unethical touching of the individual which becomes even more unethical when there is danger of harm to the individual in such manipulation.

Ramsey argues that genetic engineering and reproductive engineering whether done to prevent the transmission of defective genes (negative eugenics) or to assure the transmission of desired genes (positive eugenics) or to produce a child for an infertile couple constitute a violation of the individual and are ultimately immoral procedures. He insists on the rights of the child–to–be and raises important and even decisive ethical questions which are too easily passed over in much of the literature. Ramsey has consistently referred to the problem of mishaps and even called it the most crucial question in the discussion. This question comes to the fore in considerations of cloning, genetic engineering and *in vitro* fertilization.[48] The formidable moral objection in the case of cloning concerns what to do with the mishaps whether discovered in the course of extracorporal gestation in the laboratory or by uterine monitoring.[49]

Ramsey devotes two recent articles to summarizing and presenting in a more logical form his thesis that "*in vitro* fertilization constitutes unethical medical experimentation on possible future human beings, and therefore it is subject to absolute moral prohibition."[50] Logically such argumentation would apply to genetic engineering and many cases of reproductive engineering, although such an argument would not necessarily apply in the case of AID. Ramsey argues within the context of therapeutic goals

---

48. *FM*, pp. 76ff; 113ff; "Shall We 'Reproduce'?," p. 1347.

49. "Shall We 'Redproduce'?," p. 1347.

50. These two articles are: "Shall We 'Reproduce'? I. The Medical Ethics of In Vitro Fertilization," *Journal of the American Medical Association*, CCXX (June 5, 1972), pp. 1346–1350; "Shall We 'Reproduce'? II. Rejoinders and Future Forecast," *Journal of the American Medical Association*, CCXX (June 12, 1972), pp. 1480–1485. The citation in the text is found on p. 1346.

such as enabling a sterile couple to have a child, but his reasoning would *a fortiori* apply to the more ambitious goals of improving the human species.[51]

In the light of Ramsey's on-going discussion it is now clear from these two recent articles that the question of mishaps and the question of unethical experimentation on possible future human beings form two distinct arguments. Even in *Fabricated Man* there is evidence that the argument based on the unethical experimentation on future human beings is distinct from the question of mishaps.[52] Ramsey now develops the one argument of unethical experimentation on future human beings and prescinds from developing the following arguments against *in vitro* fertilization—one cannot perform this experiment on human beings without having first proved the technique in species closer to man; women volunteers have not given fully understanding consent to what is being done; and the argument from mishaps.[53]

In the process of excluding the argument about mishaps from his present consideration, he refers to the basic reasoning involved. Anyone who believes that individual human life begins with conception or after segmentation or with the morphlogically human fetus or any time before birth must regard *in vitro* fertilization as immoral because the physicians must be willing to discard mishaps that do not measure up to the standards of an acceptable human being any time in that span of time before birth.[54] Thus for Ramsey this is a persuasive argument based on his understanding of when human life begins.

In addition to the argument based on mishaps, Ramsey now wants to develop an argument which does not rest on the belief that human life is present from conception or segmentation or at any point before birth. His argument based on unethical experiments on possible future human beings is intended to convince those who believe that individual human life begins only at birth. The artificial processes involved in *in vitro* fertilization or other forms of genetic or reproductive engineering can cause problems

51. *Ibid.*, pp. 1482–1485.
52. *FM*, pp. 134–135.
53. "Shall We 'Reproduce'?," pp. 1346–1347.
54. *Ibid.*, p. 1347.

and repercussions for the child which will become apparent only after birth.[55]

For *in vitro* fertilization or other instances of genetic or reproductive engineering to be moral in its first attempt, the researcher must exclude the possibility of irreparable damage to the child–to–be. It is not enough that there be no discerned or no discernible risks. Even if experiments had proven totally successful on species less than man, the researcher can never move on to the case of man because he cannot exclude the possibility of irreparable harm which might, for example, come about by the last procedure he employs (the implanting of the zygote in the womb or monitoring by amniocentesis). There are and always will be unforeseeable risks involved in the first human attempt at *in vitro* fertilization, implantation in the womb, and bringing the cases to term and beyond. The risks involved in the first such experiment make it morally impossible for man ever to discover these risks.[56]

One could justify the criterion of no discernible risks or even of some risk that can be overcome by a promised greater good only on the assumption that the child–to–be has a right to exist or is already existing. We certainly have sympathy for the infertile couple who are not able to conceive a child of their own. However, this compassion does not justify the use of any means whatsoever to provide them with a child. In other places, Ramsey frequently argues that there is no absolute right of parents to have a child. There at times are good moral reasons, even of a genetic nature, because of which parents should not have a child. The parents' desire to have a child cannot justify exposing the child to any additional hazard. Only the most blatant pro–natalist position would assert the absolute right of parents to have a child, a position which not even the Roman Catholic church has come close to endorsing. The proper solution in these cases is to have no child. The canons of medical ethics demand that the couple ought not choose for a child whose procreation they are contemplating the injury he may have.[57] The child–to–be is not a volunteer and cannot be a volunteer, and "before his beginning he is in no need

55. *Ibid.*
56. "Shall We 'Reproduce'?," pp. 1347–1348.
57. "Morals and the Practice of Genetic Medicine," p. 13; *FM,* p. 118.

of physicians to learn how not to harm him."[58] In this case the primary patient is the child–to–be, and he cannot be exposed to these risks. The solution for parents in this case must be to have no children, for no goal whatsoever gives them the right to expose the child–to–be to the possibility of any medical damage.

If the child were an already existing person unable to consent, then the parents could consent for him if the operation was for his own benefit, and the induced risks were outweighed by the good to be attained. But this is not the case here, for the child is not yet existing. Minimizing the risks constitutes a sufficient criterion in dealing with an existing patient for his own good, but to manipulate a patient into being requires the far more stringent requirement that every possibility of damage has been foreclosed.[59]

Ramsey takes up possible rejoinders to his argument. "The incidence of . . .'natural' damages is not negligible, and the incidence of possible induced damage can be kept within acceptable bounds, it can be argued, so that the balance of added induced risks and subtracted natural risks can be (by screening, followed by abortion) to the comparative benefit of the possible future human being created by embryo implantation."[60] The argument proposed explicitly is somewhat limited, but it does contain the more general rejoinder which could be posed to Ramsey. There are risks to the future child in the natural process of procreation and childbirth. If the risks involved in *in vitro* fertilization and embryo transplantation or in any other means which Ramsey calls by the prejorative term of "manufacturing" are equal to or less than the risks involved in the natural process, then it seems that such procedures could be justified. Ramsey does recognize this as the crux of the argument to which he must respond. He maintains that anyone who proposes such an argument has already placed artificial fertilization and gestation on a parity with the natural process of human reproduction.[61]

Nature of Human Parenthood

The moral question then revolves around the nature of human parenthood which is the second major cornerstone on which Ram-

58. "Shall We 'Reproduce'?," p. 1348.
59. *Ibid.*, p. 1349.
60. *Ibid.*, p. 1480.
61. *Ibid.*, pp. 1480–1481.

sey builds his opposition to gametic manipulation and reproductive engineering. The nature of human parenthood as involving the conception of the child from the spheres of the one flesh unity of the parents and its subsequent development in the womb of the mother stands as one independent argument agaiut all forms of artificial reproduction and also serves as a supporting reason to the argument based on the rights of the child–to–be. Ramsey has consistently emphasized the nature and meaning of human parenthood in his writings both on sexuality and biomedicine.[62]

His position on the nature of human parenthood coheres with his emphasis on the bodily aspect of human existence so that man is the body of his soul as well as the soul of his body, and with his polemic against substituting the language and meaning of manufacturing for the ethical language and meaning of doing. Ramsey argues that the nature of human parenthood is in keeping with the bodily and fleshly nature of man. Such an assertion does not endorse biologism or physicalism, for the biological dimension of human existence is not just another part of man submissible to the limitless dominion of man the self–creator. These are the true parameters of human parenthood which science must serve and not violate.[63]

In his earlier writings, Ramsey emphasizes that his argument for the nature of human parenthood does not rest on biological or even philosophical considerations but on strictly theological grounds. The nature of human parenthood joins together the union of sexuality, love, and procreation. In Ramsey's Barthian approach, the nature of human parenthood does not depend upon the first article of the Creed, which pertains just to creation, but upon the Second Article of the Creed. The Prologue of John's Gospel (not Genesis) details the Christian story of creation which provides the proper understanding of procreation, just as Ephesians 5 furnishes the moral understanding of the marital covenant of love. Since these two passages point to one and the same Lord —the Lord who presides over procreation as well as the Lord of

---

62. Paul Ramsey, "A Christian Approach to the Question of Sexual Relations Outside of Marriage," *The Journal of Religion,* XLV (1965), 100–118; *FM,* pp. 32–52; 130–138; "Shall We 'Reproduce'?," p. 1482.
63. *FM,* pp. 131–132.

all marital covenants—the two aspects of human sexuality belong together. The reason that procreation and love union belong together does not depend on the fact that they are found together in human and other forms of sexuality. In the reality of human procreation of new beings like ourselves in the midst of our love for one another, there is a reflection of the mystery by which God created us and the world out of his love for us. Thus Christians cannot put asunder these two aspects—procreation and love union which God has joined together. In his discussions of human parenthood Ramsey maintains that creation exists for covenant, but his reasoning does not explicitly use any themes based on creation alone.[64]

There are two further questions or problems about Ramsey's analysis of human parenthood—the methodological question about whence he derives this knowledge of the meaning of human parenthood and the substantive question of the exact meaning of human parenthood in his consideration. On the methodological question, the occasional and polemical nature of his writings prevents a well-balanced and synthetic picture. Especially in his earlier considerations he took pains to establish a definite Protestant basis for his understanding of human parenthood. However, in his later writings on biomedicine he explicitly admits that he cannot improve upon the statement of human procreation and parenthood as it has been proposed by Leon Kass who appeals directly to no religious or Christian wisdom for his postition. The union between sex, love, and procreation describes the human meanings of parenthood.[65] Ramsey thus adopts different methodological approaches to the determination of the meaning of human parenthood which would indicate that neither approach can claim to be the exclusive methodological approach, but some of his earlier statements do seem to exclude the possibility of reasoning on the basis of creation or nature.

I personally have difficulties with arguments based exclusively on considerations of covenant or on Scriptural references. Such approaches cannot give enough importance to the changing, his-

64. "A Christian Approach to the Question of Sexual Relations," p. 109; *FM*, pp. 32–45.
65. "Shall We 'Reproduce'?," p. 1482.

torical characteristics of creation. I do not think that one can legitimately appeal to the Scriptures alone for an understanding of human parenthood which categorically excludes a procedure which has become possible today through modern scientific advances. This is not to say that the Scriptures cannot be of some help in this case, but the Scriptures are limited by the circumstances of their own time and do not necessarily apply in other possible circumstances.

The second question concerns the exact meaning of the nature of human parenthood. The fact that Ramsey develops his thought in response to different challenges, such as arguments for premarital sexuality, for AID, for fertilization in a test tube, indicates that, at times, he will be concentrating on different aspects of human parenthood. Some problems arise from the very terminology itself, for there can be a difference between the terms parenthood and procreation. The general thrust of the meaning is clear: one cannot separate the biological from the personal aspect of both parenthood and procreation. The union of the procreative and unitive aspects of sexuality calls for no radical or in–principle separation between the personally unitive and the procreational aspects of human sexuality.

The official Roman Catholic teaching also insists on the union between the unitive and procreative aspects of marriage and sexuality. This leads to the teaching that every single act of sexual intercourse must be open to procreation. However, Ramsey points out that even official Catholic teaching allows a couple to practice rhythm for a lifetime if the reasons perdure and also allows infertile couples to marry. The error in the Catholic analysis comes from an act analysis of the situation. Every single act of sexual relations must not necessarily join together the unitive and procreative aspects of sexuality. The spheres of personal sexual love and of procreation must be united, but this does not mean that every act must so unite procreation and love.[66]

Contraception and sterilization do separate the act of love from whatever tendency there might be in the act to procreation. "But they [couples using contraception or sterilization] do *not* separate the sphere or realm of their personal love from the sphere or

66. "A Christian Approach to the Question of Sexual Relations," pp. 104ff.

realm of their procreation, nor do they distinguish between *the person* with whom the bond of live is nourished and *the person* with whom procreation may be brought into exercise."[67] Even a couple who practice birth control for a lifetime do not radically separate the spheres of love and procreation. Such people are saying that if they have a child, it will be from their one flesh unity and not apart from it. They do not procreate from beyond their marriage or exercise love's one flesh unity elsewhere. Human parenthood understood in this way is a basic form of humanity, and it is wrong to violate it and dehumanize it for any motive no matter how compassionate it might sound.[68]

Ramsey originally developed this understanding of the nature of human parenthood in responding to the two different questions of premarital sexuality and of AID as proposed by Muller. This understanding of human parenthood furnishes a solid argument in favor of the fact that sexual relations must be within a sphere that is procreative and unitive and with the person with whom one lives in such a union. Thus Ramsey argues for the covenant context of love and procreation for sexual relations. However this is not our main concern. The same understanding of human parenthood forms the decisive argument against AID, whether it is done for the reasons proposed by Muller in advancing the species or if it is done to provide a sterile couple with a child. AID remains a violation of the nature of human parenthood, for here the persons and the spheres of love union and procreation are separated. Procreation with donor sperm comes about outside the love union of husband and wife.[69]

Ramsey does add some qualifications to his condemnation of AID as violating the nature of human parenthood. There are definitely other forms of assault on the nature of human parenthood which would be more wrong than AID. Likewise, the fact that Ramsey judges AID to be morally wrong does not entail the judgment that such a practice should be legally proscribed. In fact, law should not necessarily prohibit this practice which will probably become a minority practice in our society.[70]

67. *FM*, p. 34.
68. *Ibid.*, pp. 32–39.
69. *Ibid.*, pp. 39–40.
70. *Ibid.*, pp. 50–51, 104.

Ramsey would not condemn AIH (artificial insemination with the husband's seed), for here the spheres of procreation and love and the persons involved are not radically put asunder. This practice could also provide germinal insurance for those who undergo vasectomy, which is not reversible.[71]

Our author also proposes one rather weak and unconvincing supporting argument against AID based on possible consequences. The ease and anonymity of therapeutic insemination greatly increase the risk of inbreeding because children of the same father will unknowingly marry one another and reproduce. In the light of this Ramsey asks the rhetorical question of how AID can be a responsible decision, action, or practice any more than marrying someone known to possess the same gravely deleterious recessive gene.[72] Such an argument is far from convincing, unless AID becomes the prevalent practice for procreation in our society.

Ramsey also proposes his understanding of human parenthood on the basis of the biological or fleshy aspect of procreation and parenthood being an essential part of truly human procreation and parenthood. Those who put asunder the bodily transmission of life from bodily love–making substitute manufacturing for procreation. They accept a body–soul dualism which is opposed to the biblical view of man no matter what the techno–theologians will say. Ramsey has mentioned this aspect of human parenthood from his earliest writings, but the theme has become more prominent in his later writings, especially in considering genetic and reproductive engineering.[73]

Once one makes the mistake of radically separating personal love from biological parenthood, then one can disassemble and reassemble parenthood at will. Ramsey takes great pains to show that once you substitute manufacturing the product for the human process of parenthood, you have already opened the door for any type of genetic or reproductive engineering which seeks to perfect the human species. Once this happens we are already on our way to the hatcheries of *Brave New World.*[74]

71. *Ibid.*, pp. 51–52.
72. *Ibid.*, p. 128.
73. The third essay in *Fabricated Man* is entitled: "Parenthood and the Future of Man by Artificial Donor Insemination, Etcetera, Etcetera," pp. 104–160.
74. *FM*, pp. 133–138; "Shall We 'Reproduce'?," pp. 1482ff.

Perhaps it will be helpful to point out that Ramsey's understanding of the nature of human parenthood, coming as it does from two different sources (the union of procreative and unitive aspects of sexuality and substitution of the meaning and language of manufacturing for procreation) and in response to considerations of various forms of genetic and reproductive engineering, does not seem to be entirely consistent. This is somewhat apparent in his reaction to two different specific problems—AIH and *in vitro* fertilization.

His first discussion of human parenthood does not exclude AIH, but his later considerations based on the substitution of manufacturing for procreation might exclude such a procedure. Ramsey himself makes no explicit comment about AIH in this context. Since AIH does involve some human interference in the moral or natural process, it could fall under the ban of manufacturing. This also shows the problem in invoking such a broad concept as manufacturing for it might forbid any kind of intervention in the process. Ramsey does add to this possible confusion by extolling Pope Pius XII as at least a minor prophet because of his condemnation of artificial insemination in 1951 as a step in the transformation of human procreation into manufacturing in laboratories.[75] Ramsey had earlier cited at length from Pope Pius XII's 1951 condemnation of artificial insemination on the grounds that it reduces the conjugal act to a mere organic function for the transmission of the germ of life and thus converts the domestic hearth into nothing more than a biological laboratory.[76]

Pius XII does not explicitly say what type of artificial insemination he is discussing but his main address on artificial insemination was given in 1949. On that occasion he used the same basic argument to condemn AIH as well as AID. AID is wrong because it violates the exclusive and inalienable rights of husband and wife over their bodies, but AIH is wrong not only because of the way in which the semen is procured but also because it violates the nature of the act of marital relations.[77] Even in the text cited by Ramsey there are clear indications that Pius XII is talking about AIH because his argument rests on an analysis of the conjugal act

75. "Shall We 'Reproduce'?," 1483.
76. *Ibid.*, p. 1482.
77. Kelly, *Medico-Moral Problems*, pp. 228–230.

as such.[78] Pius XII definitely uses the manufacturing argument to exclude AIH. Although Ramsey explicitly allows AIH in his one consideration of the nature of human parenthood, his arguments based on manufacturing could be used to condemn AIH. Ramsey praises Pius XII for his manufacturing argument, but the pope did employ it to condemn AIH and not just AID.

In the case of *in vitro* fertilization and embryo transplant, it appears that the notion of procreation and parenthood as opposed to manufacturing asserts more about human parenthood than the notion of procreation and parenthood based on the inseparable union of the procreative and unitive aspects of sexuality. The manufacturing argument would condemn *in vitro* fertilization and embryo implantation. However, the first argument might not necessarily condemn it. If AIH does not separate the two spheres of parenthood, then *in vitro* fertilization and embryo implantation will not necessarily do so if the husband's semen is used to fecundate the ovum of the wife as is proposed in some cases. However, on the basis of manufacture Ramsey wants to condemn this as opposed to human parenthood. There do seem to be some developments and inconsistencies on Ramsey's part in these discussions of human parenthood, but one cannot forget that Ramsey is dealing with new questions that require him to constantly change and adapt his own previous understandings. The newer questions call for a greater emphasis on the manufacturing argument, but this is all the more reason to sharpen that argument so that it does not become too inclusive.

The Principle of Parenthood and Positive Eugenics

Ramsey himself has proposed many general arguments against positive programs for the betterment of the human species. He also recognizes the fact that many people today shy away from any programs of positive eugenics, but there does seem to be a real sympathy for genetic and reproductive engineering in the case of preventive eugenics or especially in the case of providing children for parents who are unable to have a child through the usual means.[79] AID, *in vitro* fertilization, or forms of genetic or repro-

---

78. "Shall We 'Reproduce'?," p. 1482.
79. *FM,* pp. 110–112.

ductive engineering, will probably first be attempted for such reasons, but what begins as an alleviation of the infertility of a couple opens the door to further work on human embryos, cloning, and the creation of chimeras by adding to an embryo the precursor cells for organs from other blastocysts and even from other species.[80] Thus Ramsey wants to alert people to the violations of human parenthood, which if they are once accepted even for a good purpose, will lead to all forms of genetic and reproductive engineering and to the positive eugenics which the majority of people today apparently do not want.

In *Fabricated Man*, Ramsey argues against AID and maintains that once the transmission of life has removed the biological from the personal, then, in essence, one warrants many of these other procedures as well, perhaps even the hatcheries. Ramsey insists that there is no wedge argument. It is not based on the fact that if we allow this, we will then go on to adopt more exquisite procedures; but rather that from a logical perspective once one has assaulted the nature of human parenthood by putting the bodily transmission of life from marriage partners asunder from their bodily lovemaking, then other assaults on human parenthood are warranted.[81]

In his latest public discussion of *in vitro* fertilization, published in 1972, Ramsey does invoke the wedge argument to explain that such a practice will lead to extra-corporeal gestation and the introduction of all types of genetic changes into human germinal material. In *in vitro* fertilization the problem resides in the infertility of the couple, but the clinical defect of infertility is not cured by *in vitro* fertilization. The woman's medical condition might be cured by surgical reconstruction of the oviduct but not by *in vitro* fertilization, which, therefore, cannot be called a truly medical procedure. It is manufacture by biological technology and not medicine. In this case, you are not really giving medical treatment, but rather you are doctoring the desires of the couple. Once medicine accedes to one's desires, is there any reason for doctors to be reluctant to accede to the parents' desires to have a boy

80. "Shall We 'Reproduce'?," pp. 1481–1482.
81. *FM*, pp. 135–136.

rather than a girl, a blonde rather than a brunette, a genius rather than a clout, even a freak to work in the circus? Once medicine begins to respond to the desires of the parents rather than healing or curing specific ills, then all of this will follow. The acceptance of *in vitro* fertilization means that in principle and *in mente* we would have already accepted manufacturing which logically includes all other possible forms of genetic and reproductive engineering.[82]

In other areas of life today we have come to know the need for respecting the natural environment of life. We acknowledge that there are aspects of the cheetah's existence that ought not be violated, but none of man's. There is a renewed sense of the sacredness and inviolability of groves, air, and streams, while scientists are contemplating ways of taking apart and reassembling human parenthood in laboratories throughout the world. *In vitro* fertilization involves the acceptance of a concept of human parenthood which can embrace all these other attempts at reproductive engineering.[83]

Ramsey's own description of the wedge argument in his consideration of *in vitro* fertilization deserves further analysis. The wedge argument or the camel's nose argument is based on what will follow from the action we take. But it is not just extrinsic factors that will lead us to take the next steps. Rather the wedge argument works, that is, we go on to the next step, chiefly but not exclusively because "incipiently and intrinsically the reason behind the justification of a present practice already in principle embraces those other societal practices as well."[84] The reason does not logically compel us to take the next step, but there is some intrinsic connection. We will have to pull our laboring oar against our prèsent reasons if we are not to proceed further along the line already begun.[85]

I interpret Ramsey in this manner. Once you accept *in vitro* fertilization and embryo implantation, you logically accept the concept of manufacturing as replacing procreation and the concept of acceding to the desires of the people involved. All these

82. "Shall We 'Reproduce'?," p. 1481.
83. *Ibid.*, p. 1484.
84. *Ibid.*, p. 1481.
85. *Ibid.*

other attempts at genetic and reproductive engineering also involve manufacturing. One is not forced by logical necessity to accept these means because one could argue against them on other grounds, e.g., we do not have the wisdom to choose what the future of the human race will be. However, there is an intrinsic connection between the first step of *in vitro* fertilization and all the subsequent steps because of which it will be very hard to prevent these further steps from coming into existence.

Ramsey's basic argument is clear. AID, as well as *in vitro* fertilization and embryo implantation, is wrong. Other more positive forms of genetic and reproductive engineering are also wrong. There is also some logical and intrinsic connection between the acceptance of AID or *in vitro* fertilization and the acceptance of all these other procedures. However, there is some confusion in his use of the wedge argument. In *Fabricated Man,* Ramsey reasons that acceptance of AID essentially involves an acceptance of many of these other procedures and affirms that this is no wedge argument. In the June 1972 article, he explicitly affirms and explains the wedge argument as the basis for his assertion that the acceptance of *in vitro* fertilization and embryo implantation leads on some intrinsic grounds to the acceptance of these other reproductive procedures.

Why does Ramsey affirm the wedge argument in the case of *in vitro* fertilization and deny it in the case of AID?[86] I would explain the apparent contradiction on the basis of Ramsey's changing understanding of the wedge argument. His most complete statement of the meaning of the wedge argument appears in *The Hastings Center Report* of December 1971.[87] Ramsey insists that there is more to the wedge argument than just consequences. There is always some principle behind the wedge driving it in. There is

86. One might answer this dilemma on the basis of a difference between AID and *in vitro* fertilization. AID violates the nature of human parenthood understood in terms of the union of the spheres of procreation and love union, and thus logically includes all other violations of the nature of human parenthood. *In vitro* fertilization does not violate the nature of human parenthood understood in this way if the fertilization uses the spern and ovum of husband and wife. However, *in vitro* fertilization as an instance of manufacturing opens the door to all other forms of manufacturing. But I do not believe this is the proper explanation.

87. Paul Ramsey, "The Wedge: Not So Simple," *The Hastings Center Report,* Vol. I, No. 3 (December 1971), pp. 11–12. This article is a response to Sissela Bok, "The Leading Edge of the Wedge," *The Hastings Center Report,* Vol. I No. 3 (December 1971), pp. 9–11.

something intrinsic to the reasoning itself and not just extrinsic forces that push us down the slippery slope. The wrong is in the first step onto the slope and not just in what follows because of social forces and other factors. The same reasoning which accepts the first step can also encompass the second and further steps. It is not merely a case of what consequences might follow from the first step, but the fact that there is some intrinsic connection between the first and the subsequent steps. The reasoning employed in the article on *in vitro* fertilization generally follows the above description of the nature of the wedge argument.

The understanding of the wedge argument in terms of consequences only and not of the wrong in the first step was apparently in Ramsey's mind when he asserted in *Fabricated Man* that the argument that AID would lead to acceptance of many other forms of reproductive engineering was not the wedge argument. In reality it does seem to be the same argument employed in the discussion of *in vitro* fertilization and fits the description of the wedge argument as Ramsey himself proposed it most recently.

The same confusion and same explanation exist in Ramsey's discussion of the relationship between abortion and infanticide. Ramsey earlier insisted that the reasoning that abortion leads to infanticide is not based on the wedge argument but on the principle of universalizability. In this context he describes the wedge argument only in terms of consequences (the good reasons for doing or not doing something are "on account of what may predictably or possibly follow") and not in terms of the wrong involved in the first step.[88] However, in his latest explanation of the wedge argument he does affirm that on the basis of the wedge argument abortion is connected with infanticide—a position he explicitly rejected in his earlier consideration. His wedge argument now is based on consequences alone, but the flawed reasoning involved in abortion also encompasses the case of infanticide. "It is rather that he can see no reason why the justification of the one may not be an equally strong justification for the other practice."[89]

---

88. "Reference Points in Deciding about Abortion," p. 85.
89. "The Wedge: Not So Simple," p. 12. The solution might be for Ramsey to acknowledge two types of wedge argument and to distinguish both types from the principle of universalizability or to identify the one type of wedge argument with the principle of universalizability.

Conclusion

Despite some inconsistencies, Ramsey's general position is clear: genetic engineering and reproductive engineering are wrong. This judgment embraces all those proposals for engineering or making the child–to–be. However, Ramsey himself is not too optimistic about what will happen in the future. He realizes that the theological technocrats, the omega watches and the advocates of self-creation have all abandoned the traditional understanding of human procreation and parenthood.

> Still calculations of effectiveness do not determine the insights to which those who acknowledge our common moral tradition must bear witness. Even a bothersome witness may have some value in the in–between times—amid massive cultural breakdown. They also serve (it seems) who only stand and object to many of the overriding tendencies in the present age—upon good theological warrants. They also serve who only stand and ruminate upon the meaning and essential nature of human parenthood. They also serve who only stand and wait for the renewal of man. And they serve who wait for the emancipation of the transmission of fleshly life from techniques which came to serve and remained to master and to destroy, in the name of an unlimited 'self–modifying' personal freedom. Perhaps God will let loose another Saint Augustine upon this planet, and the wounds men have inflicted upon themselves in the modern period by 'thing–i–fying' the *carnal* life may begin to be healed.[90]

People in the so–called advanced nations, according to Ramsey's pessimistic prognostication, are apt to raise no serious objection to what the manipulators of embryos will do to us and our progeny. Why will we insist on doing to man what we have learned not to do on other natural objects? True, the medical researchers are experts and authority figures, but in other areas of contemporary life we have come to question the experts. In this case, however, the experts are thought to be doctors, members of the healing profession whose concern is the care and good of the patient. But precisely in this role they are not truly doctors practicing medicine but researchers. The origin of the problem lies in the fact that medicine and the profession of medical care have been turned into a technological function. Until medicine restores its own

90. *FM*, pp. 137, 138.

proper self–understanding as serving and caring for man as a natural object, there will be no way to prevent the steady progress of the researchers.[91]

Ramsey has developed a theological ethical position which firmly says "no" to the possibilities of genetic and reproductive engineering, which include such specific procedures as cloning, *in vitro* fertilization and embryo transplantation even without surrogate mothers, AID or any manipulation of the gametes to produce a desired "product." In the contemporary discussion, this places Ramsey at one end of the spectrum, although other thoughtful theological and humanistic ethicists would agree with him.[92]

Critique

Ramsey rightly criticizes many contemporary theological technocrats, and calls to mind aspects of the Christian and ethical perspective which are too often forgotten by others. However, in a somewhat polemical manner he overemphasizes and tends to absolutize some of these considerations, thereby incorporating a lack of balance in his own theological ethical perspective which has its logical ramifications in his practical conclusions. In general, I am often quite sympathetic with his considerations, a point which should not be lost because the following pages will develop the areas of disagreement with his ethics. These areas of disagreement are: theological presuppositions; anthropology; Christian ethical methodology; ethical models; the nature of medicine; and the specific principles on which Ramsey bases his conclusions.

Theological presuppositions. Ramsey's theological presuppositions in the questions of genetics especially center on eschatology which has assumed a central role in much of contemporary theology. Eschatology has become important in this question because it treats the relationship between this world and the kingdom or, in the Augustinian language so often employed by Ramsey, be-

---

91. "Shall We 'Reproduce'?," p. 1485.
92. See especially the writings of Leon R. Kass: "The New Biology: What Price Relieving Man's Estate?," in *Science*, CLXXIII (1971), pp. 779–788; "Making Babies—The New Biology and the 'Old' Morality," in *The Public Interest*, No. 26 (Winter 1972), pp. 18–56; "New Beginnings in Life," in *The New Genetics and the Future of Man*, pp. 15–63.

tween the City of God and the city of man. Ramsey so stresses the discontinuity that he sees little or no positive relationship whatsoever between life in this world and the kingdom, or between true human progress and the reign of God. His eschatology remains one-sided, for he discusses only the apocalyptic aspect of eschatology which highlights the discontinuity between this world and the next. This world is seen primarily as that which must die and pass away so that the fullness of the kingdom may come out of the ashes of the present. A more balanced eschatology would see the teleological and prophetic aspects of eschatology as well as the apocalyptic, so that there would be both continuity and discontinuity between this world and the next. Whereas liberal theology in both its Protestant and now its Catholic contexts forgets the apocalyptic aspects of eschatology with its corresponding call for discontinuity between this world and the kingdom, Ramsey overreacts in the other direction.

There is both a positive and a negative relationship between man's life in this world and the kingdom. Men must strive to cooperate in the work of bringing about the kingdom—but with the realization that their efforts will always be insufficient—for the kingdom remains God's gracious gift to us. Scientific and technological progress can be truly human progress and thus positively related to the kingdom. The theological error of liberal theology especially in its many expressions in the 1960's comes from a very naive understanding of human progress which identified human progress totally with scientific and technological progress. People especially in the developed nations of the world were overly impressed with what appeared to be the great progress made by science and technology. Such technological growth is always progressive, for one development builds on another and thus positive steps forward continually take place. Technological man, lulled into euphoria by his own inventions, thought that human progress was the same as technological progress.

Today one can easily see the difficulties with such an approach. Technological progress and human progress are not the same and never can be precisely because the human and the technological are not the same. Progress in the area of the truly human can never be a continually progressive development as is the case in technology. Even today we appreciate the art, the music, and the drama that was produced centuries ago. Here we are dealing with more human realities—a reminder that truly human progress can never follow the model of technological progress. The ecological and environmental crises have also forced us to question the whole reality of technological progress. What is technological progress might not be human progress. The human vision must control the possibilities of technology and make sure that it serves truly human needs and purposes. If technological development continues on its own in accord with its own internal logic, it will place the truly human in jeopardy.

Ramsey rightly reacts against the naive and Utopian notion of progress often enshrined in liberal theology, but his one-sided eschatology does not give enough importance to the positive relationship between the kingdom and man's life in this world. Ramsey's perspective in this matter appears to be quite consistent, for the same general approach lies behind his political theology.

Anthropology. Ramsey sees behind many genetic proposals the temptation of man to play and become God. Again, Ramsey rightly reacts against those who fail to appreciate the limitations of man coming from the dual source of his finitude and his sinfulness; but Ramsey fails to appreciate, as he has accused some scientists of doing, that God made man and all creation because they are good and that man now shares in the first fruits of the redeeming work of God. The positive aspect of man and his greatness rest firmly on the doctrine of creation and the destination of the whole man—body and soul—for the fulness of the life of the resurrection in which he already participates to some extent, but in this world man will always know the limitations arising from his creatureliness and his sinfulness. In his bioethics, Ramsey does not seem to keep in tension these two aspects of man's human existence.

With a constant guard against the primal sin of pride, Ramsey tends to be too critical and negative toward the reality of man's power and ability to accomplish great things. Here it is interesting to contrast Ramsey's emphasis with that of Harvey Cox, who takes the opposite point of view and sees the primary sin of contemporary man as sloth or the failure to take responsibility for his life in this world.[93] Ramsey too easily dismisses any attempt on man's part to change or better his existence as tainted by pride, whereas Cox is prone to baptize any type of change and identify it with the kingdom of God. A more balanced Christian anthropology sees the place of both capital sins of pride and sloth.

There is a second basis for Ramsey's insistence on the limitations of man. Ramsey frequently inveighs against the concept of man as self-creator. The emphasis on man as self-creator also derives from an anthropology which sees man almost exclusively in terms of thought, spirit, or freedom. I agree with Ramsey that man is more than spirit, and he is also more than a freedom event. Man lives in the flesh with his body, his relationships, his environment and with many other persons. In a sense, all these factors are to some extent limiting in that they do not permit man to do whatever he might want to do. However, we can never forget that the distinctiveness of man lies in his creativity and freedom even though these are limited.[94] Today man has more power, with all its possibilities and pitfalls, than he has ever had. Man is called upon today to make more decisions regarding his own life and his future in this world.

In this connection, Ramsey is rather too harsh in his criticism of Karl Rahner's understanding of man as a self-creator.[95] In the original German, Rahner employs the term self-manipulator, not self-creator.[96] Even in the article cited by Ramsey, Rahner does refer to the limitations of man's human nature and expands on the great limiting situation of death.[97] In other articles in the same English collection, Rahner discusses some human limitations in the light of man's vocation in this world, although his emphasis is

93. Harvey G. Cox, *On Not Leaving It to the Snake* (New York: Macmillan, 1967), pp. ix–xix.

94. Thomas Aquinas in the Prologue to the Second Part of the *Summa Theologiae*, after having considered God in the First Part, now turns his attention to man who is an image of God precisely insofar as he is "endowed with intelligence, free will and a power of actions which is proper to him . . . having a dominion over his own activity."

95. *FM*, pp. 138–142.

96. Karl Rahner, "Experiment Mensch: Theologisches über die Selbstmanipulation des Menschen," *Schriften zur Theologie* (Einsiedeln: Benziger, 1967), VIII, pp. 260–285.

97. Karl Rahner, "Experiment: Man," in *Theology Digest*, XVI (Sesquicentennial issue, 1968), pp. 62, 63, 67, 68.

quite different from Ramsey's.[98] Rahner also has written an article on the precise question of genetic manipulation in which he raises many of the reservations proposed by Ramsey.[99] However, I would argue that Rahner's methodology at times does not give enough importance to the physical, the societal, and the political aspects of reality.

One way in which the question of the human arises in Ramsey is in the relationship between the scientific and the human perspective. I agree with Ramsey that the human perspective must always criticize and guide the scientific perspective. The scientific perspective or horizon will always be narrower and less ultimate than the total human perspective. The scientific remains just one limited aspect within the total human vision. From such an understanding it follows logically that at times the human decision must say "no" to the capabilities and possibilities of scientific technology.[100] Later, I will indicate how this serves as the basis for my criticizing Ramsey's too-great separation between the medical or political aspect and the moral aspect.

The meaning of the human becomes crucial in the debate about man's self–modification through genetic engineering. Some would maintain that the more something is the product of man's rationality the more human it is. Thus procreation in a test tube would logically be more human than the normal way of procreation as we know it today.[101] Ramsey, on the contrary, holds, especially in the area of biomedicine, that the fleshly aspect belongs to the very *humanum* of man. In general I believe that Ramsey rightly points out the importance of the fleshly, the biological, and the physical, especially in the light of the fact that contemporary theorists often overlook this aspect, but at times, Ramsey seems to exaggerate the

98. Karl Rahner, "The Historical Dimension in Theology," and "Christianity and the New Earth," in *Theology Digest*, XVI (Sesquicentennial issue, 1968), pp. 30–42, 70–77.

99. Karl Rahner, "Zum Problem der genetischen Manipulation," *Schriften zur Theologie*, VIII, pp. 286–321.

100. See my *Catholic Moral Theology in Dialogue*, pp. 65–110.

101. Joseph Fletcher, "Ethical Aspects of Genetic Controls: Designed Genetic Changes in Man," *New England Journal of Medicine*, CCLXXXV (September 30, 1971), pp. 780–781; Joseph Fletcher, "New Beginnings in Life: A Theologian's Response," *The New Genetics and the Future of Man*, pp. 86–88.

point and too easily identifies the physical or the biological with the normatively human.

On the ultimate level of human existence, the biological, or the physical, forms an essential part of human existence. There is no human existence without this basic physical or biological component. However, this does not mean that every human doing or human activity has as absolutely essential a biological or physical aspect. The biological constitutes one aspect of the human, but there are many other aspects of the human such as the psychological, the sociological, the political, the hygenic, etc. One can never totally identify the human with any one of these aspects.

Often, the physical or the biological includes many other values such as the psychological. In some cases, the physical and the biological will be the same as the human. However, in other cases, the physical or the biological is one aspect that might be sacrificed in the light of other values and the total human perspective. Catholic theology, in my judgment, in much of its medical ethics and especially in the area of contraception and sterilization has made the biological or the physical the humanly normative.[102] Obviously, Ramsey himself does not always make the biological and the physical normative. Even in the area of life itself, he admits that psychological life may be more important than physical life, so that physical life may be taken in some cases. It seems to me that the role of the biological is more relative in the area of human activity and human doing than Ramsey admits. These considerations set the stage for my later discussion of Ramsey's principle of parenthood, which is the most important area of my disagreement with his emphasis on the physical and the biological.

Christian ethical methodology. This section will consider the fundamental methodological question of the source or origin of ethical wisdom for the Chrstian ethicist. Throughout Ramsey's writings there appears to be, both in theory and in practice, an ambivalence on this question that he has never totally clarified. The question centers on the place of reason and the natural in Christian ethics and its relationship to the specifically Christian

102. See my *Contemporary Problems in Moral Theology,* pp. 97–158.

which for Ramsey is *agape*. The Introduction has already discussed this aspect of the question.[103]

In practice, Ramsey emphasizes different aspects, depending on his particular purposes. He often speaks of a distinctively Christian approach to some problems but in other places accepts a humanistic approach to the same question. At the very least, these differences call for a more systematic discussion of the question on his part and a more consistent application of his basic methodology in this area. Nor can one totally explain the problem in terms of a growth and development in Ramsey's thinking on the question. Obviously there has been such a growth, which is the sign of a true scholar open to be convinced by others and by different reasons, but these apparently different emphases remain side by side even in Ramsey's writings after 1960.

Personally, arguing from within the Roman Catholic tradition, I admit the fact that the Christian shares some ethical wisdom and knowledge with all mankind. In other words, Jesus Christ and revelation are not the only way into the ethical problem for the Christian. My problem with the Catholic natural-law theory, from the theological perspective, comes from its failure to integrate the natural into the whole Christian perspective. In practice, Catholic natural-law thinking too often saw the natural as an area retaining its own validity and unaffected by grace or by sin. This involves the poor relationship that both Catholic theory and Catholic practice previously found between the natural and the supernatural.[104]

---

103. As mentioned I believe that Ramsey's development after *Basic Christian Ethics* in the direction of a greater acceptance of reason and the natural calls for a change in some of the fundamental notions such as *agape* developed in his first book. In this context, I was disappointed with a recent article mentioning some of these aspects. See Paul Ramsey, "The Biblical Notion of Righteousness," *Interpretation*, XXIV (1970), pp. 419–429.

104. *Contemporary Problems in Moral Theology*, pp. 98–104. But I go one step beyond the theological presuppositions of natural law theory. The theological basis for the fact that Christians share much ethical wisdom and knowledge with all mankind is derived not only from the fact of creation which all men share but also is derived from grace, for God's grace is offered to all men. In the light of such an understanding I do not believe there is a distinctively Christian ethics with different content in the area of specific conclusions or even proximate attitudes, dispositions and goals for the ethical life. However, limitation and sin affect both the Christian and the non-Christian alike so that one can never uncritically accept all human activity as coming from the grace of God. See my *Catholic Moral Theology in Dialogue*, pp. 1–64.

Ethical models. Ethical models are often classified into teleological or deontological models. Ramsey apparently prefers to think of agapism as a third and distinctive type of normative theory which is neither teleology (goal seeking) nor deontology (an ethics of duty). If agapism must be reduced to one of the other two types, Ramsey chooses deontology. Christian *agape* is radically non–teleological. *Agape* defines for the Christian what is right, righteous, obligatory to be done; it does not define the good that better be done.[105] Ramsey's ethical model thus coheres with his understanding of morality as cut from God and not from man, with his eschatology, with his emphasis on obedient love and with his central notion of covenant faithfulness.

I have difficulty with such an approach for it appears to give too little importance to the role of man and to historicity. Considerations of anthropology have already indicated that I do not think Ramsey gives enough importance to the creativity and positive aspects of man, even though much of what he says serves as a useful corrective against those who have forgotten human limitations and sinfulness. By its very nature, his approach cannot give enough importance to the changing, historical reality of the human. The failure to give enough importance to changing historical reality has been mentioned both in the context of political ethics (failure to appreciate the great change brought about by nuclear weapons) and of genetics (understanding human parenthood in the light of the Second Article of the Creed).

I do not want to accept a metaphysics of flux or a total existentialism, but there appears to be more discontinuity in human existence than Ramsey's methodology can take into consideration. His approach shares some of the problems of an older Catholic natural-law approach which so emphasized the eternal nature of things that it did not give enough importance to the historical and the contingent. Even revelation itself is historically and culturally limited. Again this indicates a basic theological difference because I tend to see the work of God in man and the world and begin my ethical reflection from this reality and not exclusively from revelation about God.

105. *Deeds and Rules in Christian Ethics,* p. 108.

I agree with some of the reasons proposed by Ramsey for the rejection of the teleological model. Theologically, man does not have that much control over his end nor over the means to attain them. Man is more limited because he is not a self–creator with the power and the freedom to completely fashion his end and use or discard whatever means he wants to in the process. Man must accept many of the limitations of his given creaturely existence. The teleological model does seem to imply a model of man the maker which distorts the true meaning of the human and so easily replaces the human with the model of the technological. Ethically, there is the danger that such a model will subordinate everything including other human persons to a particular goal or end.

It should be remembered that Ramsey does not deny the existence of a teleological aspect in Christian ethics and often argues from proportionality and consequences. However, the general flavor of his ethics, as he points out, is more in keeping with the deontological motif. I do not want to reduce Christian ethics only to teleological concerns, but I cannot accept his understanding of *agape*. Consequently, I opt for a third ethical model or motif— the relationality–responsibility model originally proposed by H. Richard Niebuhr.[106] Such a model is more in keeping with my acceptance of historical consciousness, of a greater emphasis on the subject and his freedom, of a more positive understanding of man and his role in the world.[107] I can now only briefly mention this model of relationality–responsibility and urge that it needs greater development on the part of contemporary Christian ethicists.[108]

The nature of medicine. Ramsey insists on two emphases throughout his writings: first, medicine is concerned with the person who is sick and tries to treat this person who may not be subordinated to any other goal especially to that most famous of non-patients—the human species; second, medicine exists to cure the medical ills of the person but should not be used for non-medical purposes or just for fulfilling the wishes and desires of

106. H. Richard Niebuhr, *The Responsible Self* (New York: Harper & Row, 1963).
107. *Catholic Moral Theology in Dialogue*, pp. 150–179.
108. See Albert R. Jonsen, *Responsibility in Modern Religious Ethics* (Washington: Corpus Books, 1968).

people. Consequently, Ramsey rejects the broader definition of health proposed by the World Health Organization.[109]

In discussing experimentation I have pointed out that Ramsey's insistence on the individual, as important as it is, tends to be too absolutistic. The major concern now is the second insistence which appears to be too narrow a concept of medicine. Medicine, even now, does not always cure a medical ill but can be used because of the desires of the patient. This is the case in cosmetic surgery because there is no medical or biological illness. Ramsey himself argues strenuously against doctors doing abortions for non-medical reasons, but he does admit that mental life may be more important than physical life.

Ramsey's emphasis on the patient as person logically includes a broader understanding of medicine, which is concerned with the whole man. The person is more than his medical or biological aspects, so that the medical and the biological are particular and relative aspects of man. The human as the more universal perspective relativizes the more particular apsects. Thus medicine can be used for truly human purposes which are not necessarily and strictly medical. Ramsey admits sterilization for non-medical reasons. Note some similarities here with a somewhat expanded concept of the principle of totality as involving the whole person, a position with which Ramsey has not totally agreed. This same understanding of medicine and its relation to the human and the person lies behind the distinction of ordinary and extraordinary means for preserving life, although Ramsey proposes a different explanation.[110] In the name of the truly human, one must relativize the function of the purely medical which is to cure ills and realize that at times one should in the name of truly human values say "no" to medical science and technology. The decision to turn off the respirator points to the fact that medicine must always be in the service of the truly human.

109. It might be helpful to distinguish more carefully between definitions of medicine and health, but it is not necessary for the present discussion.
110. It must be pointed out that in the case of not using extraordinary means, Ramsey is consistent with his understanding of medicine. He distinguishes between the medical and the moral imperative. These two imperatives are the same once the dying process has begun and there is no hope of success from treatment. In other cases in which extraordinary means are not used the doctor acts more as a man than as a medical expert. *PP*, pp. 136, 137.

One can sympathize with Ramsey's concern that medicine should not be used to doctor every whim or desire of man, but the solution is not to restrict medicine just to medical ills. We must analyze what are truly human desires and the proportionate reasons that might justify medical intervention on behalf of these needs and desires. Ramsey is concerned especially with the sanctity of the individual and the fear that social, cultural, or economic reasons might erode the rights of the individual person. The better solution is to admit the great importance of the individual in the midst of all these other values.

Ramsey's apprehensions in this area have led him to an understanding of medical ethics and its relationship to human ethics which I find unacceptable. If, according to Ramsey, the broad definition of health is accepted, then medical judgments assume responsibility for the full range of human moral considerations. Medical ethics would have to develop a new moral philosophy because in society today there is no accepted philosophical or social ethics.[111]

The fact that Ramsey is upset with the present state of ethics does not justify his great separation of medical ethics from ethics in general. In my judgment, medical ethics is a species of human ethics and applies the more general ethical considerations to medical questions. However, medical ethics as a human ethic must include all human perspectives in making its judgments about medical procedures, even though it will be heavily concentrating on medical data. Ramsey appears to isolate the area of medical ethics from the fully human in somewhat the same manner as he isolates some aspects of his political ethics from the human and the moral. In practice, this can and does result in too great a confidence in the decisions of politicians and doctors and a failure to realize the critical function of the moral and the human in these areas. It seems that Ramsey shoud have limited his comments to the observation he once made that within the medical community there is an ethos which expresses a great concern for the sacredness of the individual and the fleshly nature of human life; but in the society at large there does not seem to be such an ethos. However, this is a question of ethos and not of ethics.

111. "Ethics of a Cottage Industry," pp. 700–701.

Ramsey's controlling ethical principles and his conclusions.
The first principle regards the individual–to–be and has two distinguishable aspects: the willingness to discard the mishaps of genetic and reproductive engineering; and the morality involved in exposing the individual–to–be to the risks involved in his manufacture. The second principle concerns the nature of human parenthood, and here Ramsey has proposed two different versions of this argument.

The problem of mishaps undoubtedly is an immensely important ethical consideration which others blithely skip over, but I do not think that it results in an absolute condemnation of genetic and reproductive engineering. This is obviously a greater problem for those like Ramsey and myself who hold to an early beginning of human life. It should be pointed out that many mishaps or mistakes cannot be detected until comparatively late in pregnancy so that correction of mistakes by abortion would often occur after ten weeks.

Will it be necessary to be willing to discard or kill any mishaps in the process of developing techniques like *in vitro* fertilization, embryo implantation or more complicated procedures such as cloning? It would certainly be morally wrong to intend to kill such mishaps that are truly human beings. If any procedure demands such an intention, it would be morally wrong. But every procedure does not necessarily involve this intention. One could be willing to accept the responsibility for the mishaps (say in the form of the retarded) who might live. There is also another possibility which Ramsey brings up in another context. Since one does not have to do everything possible to keep human life in existence, it is not necessary to use extraordinary means to keep a fetus alive.[112]

Genetic and reproductive engineering do not necessarily involve the intention of discarding human mishaps. The crucial question then becomes whether one can do these procedures which might result in mishaps. This involves the second aspect of the question: the ethics of experimentation on possible future human beings.

Ramsey insists that because we are dealing with an experiment

112. "Reference Points in Deciding about Abortion," pp. 97–100.

on a not-yet-born human being whose parents have no absolute right to bring him to life, the researchers must exclude the possibility of irreparable damage to the child–to–be. Thus if there are any mishaps or, even stronger, if the possibility of mishaps cannot be excluded, the action is immoral.[113]

In this context, Ramsey's argument rests on his assertion that the parents have no absolute right to have children and consequently no right to expose possible children to these risks. I grant that there are times and circumstances in which parents should have no children. However, there is another aspect of the Christian tradition on marriage and sexuality which Ramsey does not mention in this context although he does develop it at greater length in his considerations of human sexuality; namely, the *bonum prolis*.[114] The child or children constitute one of the essential goods of marriage. Ramsey would willingly admit this, but also quickly add that one does not have a right to have children by any means whatsoever. His independent ethic of means raises the question of means which in this specific case becomes the question of the nature of human parenthood.

Again, one realizes the mishaps and risks that occur in the normal process of procreation and parenthood. The other procedures to be ethical would have to have approximately the same degree of risk as the normal process. But Ramsey says this would be the criterion only if there was no moral difference between laboratory reproduction and the human process of procreation and parenthood. So his argument about unethical experimentation on future human beings with its very strict criterion of excluding the possibility of irreparable damage to the child–to–be does ultimately depend on his argument about the nature of human parenthood and its relationship to artificial forms of procreation.

Ramsey develops the nature of human parenthood in two different ways, but in this particular context of *in vitro* fertilization he contrasts the biological or fleshly aspect of human procreation and parenthood with manufacturing or laboratory reproduction. In examining this argument we will presuppose that the process in-

113. I do have difficulty with Ramsey's terminology about the rights of the child–to–be. Before one comes into existence, it is much better not to speak about rights.
114. "A Christian Approach to the Question of Sexual Relations," pp. 100–113.

volves the fertilization of the wife's ovum by the husband's seed.

The biological or fleshly aspect of procreation and parenthood is not an absolute in every aspect of its existence even for Ramsey. For example, even now it is morally acceptable to take the child from the womb and place it in an incubator before the normal course of pregnancy is over. In the future there will be artificial placentas, which, as Ramsey himself admits, would allow the doctor to take the child quite early from the womb of the mother with the assurance that the child can grow and develop outside the womb.[115] Ramsey readily acknowledges the morality of such procedures when done for the good of an already existing child. All that I want to prove, however, is that the biological or physical, as opposed to the artificial or manufacturing, aspect of the entire process of procreation and pregnancy is not an absolute. For good reasons we may substitute manufacturing or at least artificial procedures for the normal ones.

Ramsey also admits the moral permissibility of AIH, thus, the human process of procreation and parenthood can begin by the artificial insemination of the husband's seed into the uterus of the wife. The "natural" beginnings of the process are not sacrosanct either. In the light of these factors it seems that Ramsey is unable to sustain an argument about the natural process of procreation and parenthood as opposed to laboratory manufacture in the case of in vitro fertilization. *In vitro* fertilization and the implantation of the embryo would obviously involve a somewhat greater degree of artificiality, but one cannot argue that the procedure itself violates the nature of human parenthood if he has already admitted the other possible artificial procedures. Ramsey could argue that *in vitro* fertilization is wrong because it increases the chance of risks, but he seems logically to have difficulty in arguing as he does that it is wrong because it violates the nature of human procreation and parenthood.

I recognize that artificiality and manufacturing are not exactly the same. Ramsey, at times, uses them synonymously, but for him manufacturing does add at times the notion of product design and risk to the child to be. However, the problem at this stage of the

115. "Reference Points in Deciding about Abortion," p. 87.

argument is not the question of risk as such. My later point is if the risks are the same in the natural process as in the artificial or the manufacturing process, then such an artificial process is not necessarily always wrong.

Theoretically I disagree with this principle of parenthood proposed by Ramsey. There are two sources for my disagreement with this principle as enunciated by Ramsey. In his reaction against manufacturing and technology he goes too far. I agree that man must direct technology and at times say a firm "no" to the proposals of technology, but this does not imply that manufacturing or the artificial is always wrong. At the very least Ramsey's position seems to be too broad and unnuanced, as was pointed out earlier. The problem cannot be stated merely in terms of the difference between manufacturing and the natural process.

A second theoretical source of my disagreement with Ramsey's principle of natural parenthood concerns the place of the fleshly and the biological in the process of procreation and parenthood. I strongly agree with Ramsey's anthropology according to which man is flesh and not just spirit, thought, or freedom. But this does not mean as Ramsey himself admits that the fleshly or physical aspect of every human activity is sacrosanct and inviolable. In the question of procreation and parenthood this stress on the fleshly aspect of man too easily becomes a canonization of the natural process. In the context of the question of AID, Ramsey developed his other understanding of human parenthood in terms of the union of the procreative and unitive spheres, but that focused only on the fact that the seed biologically should be the husband's seed so that the child is the fruit of the union of their love and their flesh. In this case, one can easily see the exact meaning of the fleshly or biological aspect of man, but whether or not it is absolute will await later consideration. However, when considering the whole process from fertilization to birth it becomes very difficult to call this natural process an essential aspect of the fleshly nature of man which man can never violate. The fleshly nature of man thus does not seem to extend to the fleshly or biological aspect of the whole process of human procreation and parenthood in the sense that such a process becomes inviolate and may never be interfered with.

There are values involved in the normal process of procreation and parenthood which are not just of the biological order. There are psychological values in the fact that the child grows in the womb of the mother and is so dependent on the mother. This may help to establish a much closer human relationship between the mother and her child which is in keeping with the reality of the family as the closest relationship that exists in this world. But such a value may be sacrificed for the good of the child or the life and health of the mother when the child is removed from the womb after viability but before the baby has come to term.

Does the desire of the sterile couple to have a child justify the fact that fertilization takes place *in vitro* and the embryo is then implanted in the mother's womb? My answer is: yes, but this raises the crucial limiting consideration—such a process cannot expose the individual-to-be to greater risk than the usual process. I am talking about a comparison between the risks involved in the natural process and all the risks involved in the process of *in vitro* fertilization.

My position does not entail any acceptance of the principle that something is more human and desirable the more rational it is. In such a perspective any process designed by man would be more human than the natural process. At times, there are both values and limits or disvalues connected with the natural process. The moral question concerns the weighing of these different values, a process which neither canonizes the normal process nor cavalierly dismisses it as merely biological or physical. All this presupposes that the total risks involved in the artificial process are the same or less than the risks in the natural process. I cannot stress enough that the experimenter must be able to say that the risks involved in the artificial process, whatever they are, are comparable to the risks in the natural process.

In his original consideration, Ramsey developed the principle of parenthood somewhat differently because he was dealing specifically with the problem raised by AID and premarital relations rather than the questions affecting the whole process of procreation and parenthood from fertilization to delivery. Fleshly anthropology in the earlier discussion of parenthood requires that the child should come from the flesh of the husband and the wife; that is, from the union of their sperm and ovum. This principle of parenthood calls for the coincidence of the spheres of procreation and of personal sexual life. Procreation occurs from their one flesh unity and not apart from it. Children are the fruit of the loving gift of husband and wife to one another. This is not just the biological aspect over which man might have dominion, but it is the very *humanum* of human parenthood and the human way of bringing children into the world. AID, cloning, or any other reproductive or genetic engineering which bypasses this process is a violation of the human and cannot be justified no matter what reasons are proposed in its favor.

The crucial moral question concerns the meaning one gives to this understanding of human parenthood. Ramsey sees it as the very nature of human parenthood which can never be violated. I see it as the usual way of human parenthood which incorporates many values and is more than just the biological aspect of life. However, in exceptional cases it may be permissible to circumvent this natural way if there are sufficient reasons to justify it. Ramsey, even if he did not accept that absolute nature of human parenthood as described by him, would still be able to argue that the couple's desire for a child would not be a sufficient reason, for no couple has an absolute right to have a child and often for moral reasons should not have a child of their own. I give more emphasis to the *bonum prolis* as one of the goods of marriage and say that this might allow one to circumvent the normal process provided there is no greater risk of harm for the child. But this will entail a weighing of all the values involved. At the present time, the only possibility that exists is the use of AID, although in the future there may be other means such as cloning.

The major objection against AID has been proposed by Ramsey. AID manifests an overweening and unequal desire to be oneself a biological parent in solitude by technological impregnation and unequally within the community of love and procreation which is marriage.[116] Is not the sterility of one of the partners part of the "worse" which the other partner willingly accepts in the marraige commitment itself? Is it a form of pride or selfishness on the part

116. *FM*, pp. 32–52.

of the wife to have a child even though the husband is unable to do so?

One might mention other aspects of the case. There is the psychological health of the husband which might be greatly affected by this although the very fact that he is sterile would itself be a possible source of psychological problems for him. Ramsey and others mention the apparently contradictory fact that in the midst of an acknowledged population explosion people are still trying to find new ways to have children.

I would not accept an absolute condemnation of AID, but the values involved and the other possibilities would tend to argue against it. Adoption is the much preferred solution in this case. However, if both parties agreed after discussing all the aspects, I could not exclude AID as a possibility. The reasons based on the meaning of convenant and the child as the fruit of their union are not necessarily absolute although they do point to the normal and the desirable situation. However when it is impossible to have a child in this manner, I do not think that all other means are excluded. The argument that this is part of the "worse" involved in the marriage commitment does not constitute the strongest of arguments, for by its nature this is a broad argument that tends to be better as a pastoral solution to help people when there are no other possibilities. Here there might be other possibilities. Likewise, the argument based on overpopulation really does not prove anything because it is so broad. There are some reasons that would seem to discourage AID, but it cannot be absolutely excluded.[117]

Thus, I do not accept Ramsey's absolute condemnation of genetic and reproductive engineering. However, by no means does this imply a ready acceptance of any or all of these means, for as

117. In theory, and from the viewpoint of the principle of parenthood, this conclusion also holds for other possible procedures such as cloning. One might object that cloning constitutes a greater violation of Ramsey's concept of human parenthood than AID. I do not think that cloning is a greater violation of human parenthood than AID; in fact, it might be argued that cloning involves a lesser violation of human parenthood. If the criterion is just artificiality, then cloning would seem to constitute a greater assault on the nature of human parenthood. But I would content that AID constitutes a greater assault on human parenthood because it involves the positive introduction of a germinal element from beyond the loving union of the couple. In cloning, the normal sexual process of reproduction is bypassed, but no element from outside the couple is brought in even though the genes will come from only one of the parents. However, cloning would involve many more risks and be much harder to justify on that account.

mentioned frequently I share many of Ramsey's fears and anxieties. The question of mishaps and the risk to the future child are most important considerations, for they furnish the criteria that any of these procedures is wrong if it involves the direct intention of discarding human mishaps or if it exposes the child–to–be to a greater risk than that which is involved in the ordinary process of procreation and parenthood. These criteria must be strictly adhered to especially as the rivalry among scientists and researchers to become the first one to perform such experiments becomes more intense. It would seem appropriate and even necessary to find some instutionalized way to make sure that such criteria are followed. In practice, such criteria also call for the perfectrion of these techniques on animals closest to man before they are tried on man himself.

Recall that we are talking only about the case in which the sterile couple wants to have a child. For many of the reasons proposed by Ramsey, I am now opposed to any positive eugenic plans. I do not believe than we now have the knowledge or wisdom for such undertakings.

My position allowing *in vitro* fertilization and embryo implantation as well as AID on some occasions must respond to the wedge argument that by admitting some manufacturing (to use the most perjorative term) we have already started down the slippery slope to the acceptance of manufacturing in order to satisfy the mere desires of parents or to improve the human species and society. Obviously there is some risk of this happening, and one can quote scientists who see *in vitro* fertilization and AID as the camel's nose in the tent which will lead to all these other possibilities. To demand that there be no possibility at all of such developments would be to ask too much and for all practical purposes mean that one always enshrines the *status quo*. The rigid acceptance of the wedge argument can have very reactionary effects.

There are important differences between the proposals I have justified in terms of providing sterile couples with a child and the other proposals of a positive eugenics. There is and always will be a great difference between positive eugenics on the one hand, and negative eugenics or the attempt to provide a sterile couple with a child. In the latter case, especially, there is the argument based on the *bonum prolis* as one of the goods of marriage. These differences, together with the fact that positive eugenics raises so many dangers from the viewpoint of genetics itself as well as from the human and Christian perspectives, indicate that the limited acceptance of these proposals will not lead to disastrous consequences for man.

Implicit in all these considerations is the meaning of sexuality and marriage in human life. There has been much recent discussion about the problems of monogamous marriage in our society. However, at the present time I see no substitute for monogamous marriage and think that it should be strengthened as much as possible. In the limited proposals advanced here, I do not see any real threat to marriage.

Thus my conclusions do differ from Ramsey's on these two questions of "the rights" of the individual-to-be and the principle of parenthood. To some extent these two practical differences are rooted in the more theoretical differences I have with Ramsey's approach. However, I do agree with many of the emphases that Ramsey makes both on the level of theory and of practice, but it seems that at times he overreacts and erects into an absoulte what is an important consideration which must always exist alongside other considerations.

EPILOGUE

There are evident similarities in the political and medical ethics of Paul Ramsey. His theological and anthropological presuppositions recall the limitations and even the sinfulness of man which are too often forgotten by many contemporary theologians and ethicists. Thus he argues against the utopian schemes which maintain that politics can exist without force or that genetics can bring about a new human race. An independent ethic of means, which denies that all ethical considerations can be reduced to consequences or the greatest net good for society, forms an important part of his political ethics especially in terms of the principle of discrimination and in medical and bioethics insists on the sanctity of life of the individual and the radical equality of all men in questions touching on life itself.

In general, my critique of Ramsey has been more negative in the area of political ethics. Does this imply that I find some inconsistencies in Ramsey's approach to these different questions?

At first one would be readily inclined to point out some inconsistency, especially on the fundamental question of the value of human life. In medical ethics Ramsey emphasizes the value of one human life, whereas in political ethics this concern seems often overlooked and for the most part, seems not to exert a commanding influence. The rhetoric which he uses so frequently in his medical ethics, such as the sacredness of life and the dignity of the individual as well as the emphasis on the value of human life coming as God's gracious gift to us, never seems to appear in his political ethics and considerations of war. If human life is such an important value, why doesn't Ramsey speak of it consistently throughout his writings? In his writings on political ethics and war, Ramsey justifies quite a bit of direct killing of combatants and indirect killing which he often refers to as collateral damage. The cases of justifiable killing in his medical ethics are comparatively rare.

On the other hand, one could argue that there is no inconsistency in Ramsey's approach to political and medical ethics. Medical ethics stems from the covenant existing between the doctor and the patient. Political ethics stems from the covenant which God made with Noah that the world would always be preserved. Through politics and government God carries out the covenant that is the order of preservation in this world. Direct killing of those who are not bearers of aggression is always wrong. In medical ethics, justifiable killing would occur only if done indirectly or only if the life of another (or something comparable to it) were at stake, since the intended purpose here is the care for the life of the individual patient. In political ethics, the purpose of the state is the preservation of society. In war, only combatants may be killed directly; but, indirectly, comparatively many lives unfortunately may be taken.

I have criticized Ramsey's political ethics for not giving enough importance to the value of individual human life, and I have criticized his medical ethics at times for giving too much importance to the individual. One could conclude then that there is some contradiction in Ramsey. I would prefer to say that there is a consistency in Ramsey's two approaches once you grant him the first premises from which he builds his political and his medical ethics. However, this is where my ultimate problem with his thought lies. The covenant involved in political ethics is based too exclusively on sin and the order of preservation and thus differs too radically from the covenant on which he builds his understanding of medical ethics. In his political ethics he too easily sacrifices other considerations for the sake of order and the state. I am much more in agreement with the covenant between the doctor and the individual which he sees as the cornerstone of medical ethics, but at times he might overstress the rights of the individual as in the case of experimentation on minors where there are no discernible risks.

In this book I have attempted to examine the approach of Christian ethics to questions of politics, medicine, and genetics. My methodology has involved a detailed exposition and criticism of the writings of Paul Ramsey. In the process I have indicated both my agreements and disagreements with Ramsey. Politics, medicine and genetics will continue to be important topic areas in Christian ethics. Any Christian ethicist discussing these questions in the contemporary context must come to grips with the thought of Paul Ramsey. Whether one agrees with him or not, it is not possible just to pass over his thinking. Ramsey himself has written than the highest tribute one can pay to another thinker is to wrestle with his thought.[1] The very fact that no Christian ethicist today can discuss politics, medicine, and genetics without grappling with the thought of Paul Ramsey indicates the importance that Ramsey has for his contemporaries. This book will have achieved its purpose if the reader has entered into the reflective dialogue and the wrestling about these important questions.

1. *NMM*, p. 1; *DRCE*, p. 50.

INDEX

INDEX

BR
115
P7
C83

18,910   CAMROSE LUTHERAN COLLEGE
LIBRARY